Vice Admiral William

BLIGH

FRS

A biography

by

J. Bligh

First published in 2001 by

John Bligh
14 King Edward Road
ROCHESTER
Kent
ME1 1UB
website: www.blighjohn.co.uk
e-mail: johnbligh@jhbligh.freeserve.co.uk

Copyright © John Bligh 2001

The right of John Bligh to be identified as the author of this work has been asserted by him in accordance with the Copyright, Designs and Patents Act 1988

All rights reserved. No part of this publication may be reproduced, stored in a retrieval system, or transmitted, in any form or by any means, without the prior permission in writing of the author nor be otherwise circulated in any form of binding or cover other than that in which it is published and without a similar condition including this condition being imposed on the subsequent purchaser

ISBN 0 9541414 0 7

Designed and produced by

The Short Run Book Company Limited
St Stephen's House
Arthur Road
Windsor
Berkshire SL4 1RY

CONTENTS

Frontispiece	6
Dedication	7
Illustrations and Maps	8-9
Abbreviations and Symbols	10
Acknowledgements	10-11
Appendices	12
Preface	13-15
Chapter 1 Family background, early naval days and romance 9.9.1754 – 20.3.1776	16
Chapter 2 On Captain Cook's third voyage, Bligh's marriage and further naval days 20.3.1776 – 4.6.1783	22
Chapter 3 Merchant marine service and background to the 1st Breadfruit Voyage 4.6.1783 – 6.8.1787	28
Chapter 4 Preparation for the 1st Breadfruit Voyage 6.8.1787 – 23.12.1787	34
Chapter 5 1st Breadfruit Voyage – The Journey to Otaheite (Tahiti) 23.12.1787 – 26.10.1788	39
Chapter 6 1st Breadfruit Voyage – On Otaheite (Tahiti) 26.10.1788 – 4.4.1789	53
Chapter 7 Separation and potential loss of a loving relationship – Fletcher Christian and Mauatua (Isabella)	63
Chapter 8 Preliminaries to the Mutiny in "Bounty" 4.4.1789 – 28.4.1789	66

Chapter 9	The Mutiny in "Bounty" 28.4.1789	73
Chapter 10	The epic open boat voyage to Timor 28.4.1789 – 14.6.1789	82
Chapter 11	The mutineers on Tubuai and Otaheite 28.4.1789 – 29.9.1789	92
Chapter 12	Aftermath of the Epic open boat voyage 14.6.1789 – 15.12.1790	96
Chapter 13	The Pitcairn mutineers 23.9.1789 – 1800	103
Chapter 14	Pursuit and Court Martial of some mutineers and its aftermath 23.9.1789 – 1793	110
Chapter 15	2nd Breadfruit Voyage and its aftermath 29.12.1790 – 1795	119
Chapter 16	The distortion of "faction" especially in films about Wm Bligh	132
Chapter 17	The causes of the Mutiny in "Bounty" 28.4.1789	135
Chapter 18	A preliminary assessment of Wm Bligh following the 2nd Breadfruit Voyage.	150
Chapter 19	Leith, Spithead and the Nore Mutinies and the Naval Victory of Camperdown 1795–1797	157
Chapter 20	The Battle of Copenhagen, surveying, Courts Martial and appointment as Governor of New South Wales 1798 – 29.4.1805	166
Chapter 21	Background to Bligh's Governorship of New South Wales 1787 – Spring 1806	182
Chapter 22	Journey to New South Wales and Governorship 2. 1. 1806 – 26.1.1808	189
Chapter 23	The rebellious Interregnum and Bligh's return 27.1.1808 – 25.10.1810	215

Chapter 24	The Courts Martial of Lt.Col. Johnston and Lt. Kent RN 25.10.1810 – 31.7.1811	231
Chapter 25	The causes of the Rum Rebellion 26.1.1808 – 31.12.1809	245
Chapter 26	Further promotion, retirement and death 31.7.1811 – 7.12.1817	254
Chapter 27	Conclusion	258
Topical Features named after Bligh		263
Bligh's Tomb		270

Appendices:

Appendix 1	Further information on the Family Names	281
Appendix 2	Baptism records of the sons of Vice Admiral Bligh's great grandfather showing the use of the surnames Blight and Bligh	282
Appendix 3	Genealogy of Vice Admiral William Bligh FRS	282/3
Selected Bibliography		284
Alphabetic Index		302

Portrait of William Bligh 1791 by J. Russell
By permission of the British Library 1007628.011

Dedicated to my late wife
Sheila Bligh
"Lovely, loving and dearly loved"
Mother of Andrea and David
Book of Remembrance – Honour Oak, 1990

Also dedicated to my present wife
Gillian Bligh
"Becoming, bounteous and unknowingly benign"
This book would not have been written without their help.

ILLUSTRATIONS AND MAPS

Portrait of William Bligh, 1791, by J Russell	Frontispiece
"Bounty" deck plans with key	32/33
"Bounty" launch plans	83
Route of open boat voyage	84
Sketch of North East coast (Australia) by William Bligh	86
Drawing of Noddy bird by William Bligh	87
Drawing of Flying fish by William Bligh	87
Portrait of William Bligh, 1803, by J Smart	172
Topographical features named after Bligh	**263**
"Bligh County" & "Bligh Parish", New South Wales	264
"Bligh Street", Sydney, New South Wales	264
"Bligh Entrance" to Torres Strait	265
"Bligh Sound", New Zealand	266
"Bligh's Cap", Kergeulen Islands	267
"Bligh Water", Fiji	267
"Bligh Island" and "Bligh Reef", Alaska	268
"Bligh Island", Vancouver	268
"Bligh Road", Gravesend	269
"Bligh Way" and "Bounty Inn", Strood, Kent	269
Captain Bligh's Tomb	**270**
Inscription of William	271
Inscription of Betsy, twin boys and grandchild	272

Colour Illustrations

20th century copy of H.M. armed vessel "Bounty"	273
William Bligh and Tahitian Regent, Tina	274
"Bounty's" Launch away	275
Battle of Camperdown "Director" engaging "Vrijheid"	276
Battle of Camperdown "Director" rakes "Vrijheid"	277
Battle of Camperdown "Director" at the conclusion	278
Portrait of Admiral Bligh FRS	279
Statue of William Bligh in Sydney	280
Blue plaque 100 Lambeth Road, London	280

ABBREVIATIONS AND SYMBOLS

AB	Able Seaman
BM	British Museum
ed	edited by
FRS	Fellow of the Royal Society
HRA	Historical Records of Australia
HR NSW	Historical Records of New South Wales
Ibid	Ibidem – same publication
ML	Mitchell Library State Library of New South Wales
Ms	Manuscript
NSW	New South Wales
PRO	Public Record Office
RN	Royal Navy
Wm	William
( )	Author's brackets – explanatory
- -	Original brackets
[ ]	Author's brackets – exclusion

ACKNOWLEDGEMENTS

I would like to record my appreciation to a number of libraries for enabling me to borrow books, often ones which they in turn had to borrow from other libraries.

West Norwood Library, in the London Borough of Lambeth, kept me supplied with what I required of them. The Naval Historical Library, Ministry of Defence, saw much of me and brought much information to my attention. I have a particular word of thanks to give to Shirley Humphries, Deputy Mitchell Librarian of the State Library of New South Wales for her help in letting me have information about the Bligh Exhibition 1977 at the State Library of New South Wales, also to Lexie Steel, Research Service of the State Library of New South Wales. The Mitchell Library was very helpful in providing access to their rare books, also making transparencies available for a number of illustrations and checking references on my request to use material held by them. I would in particular like to thank Paul Brunton, Curator of manuscripts, State Library of New South Wales. I was able to use the Library of the National Maritime Museum, Greenwich and I much appreciated the Exhibition "Mutiny on the Bounty" 1789-1989 shown there.

The Library of the Law Society provided me with important information.

The British Library was invaluable.

I would also like to thank: English Heritage, Surrey County Record Office, Greater London Record Office and Wapping Historical Association Trust.

The Truro Public Library – Cornish Studies Section – was very useful and the Cornwall Record Office was very helpful.

I would also like to thank the Directorate of Amenity Services, in the London Borough of Lambeth, for facilities to hire film projection equipment.

The word processing service of Kwik Kopy, Herne Hill was much appreciated.

APPENDICES

Appendix 1 Further information on the Family Names   281
Appendix 2 Use of the surnames Blight and Bligh   282
Appendix 3 Genealogy of William Bligh RN FRS
           Key   282
           Genealogy   283

PREFACE

The immediate stimulus to write this biography originated in a challenge by a literary critic more than two decades ago for any member of the Bligh family to respond to attacks on Wm Bligh and to the developing legend of infamy about him.

The critic, I believe, was reviewing a biography of Wm Bligh by Richard Hough.

The task of the biographer in my view is to pursue the truth. There may be consensus on some facts but where there is a conflict of evidence, judicial presentation of the individual pieces of evidence for the prosecution and for the defence is necessary and, I believe, the biographer may reasonably sum up for the reader, who at the end of the day is the jury and final arbiter.

The development of the legend of Bligh's infamy began with evidence prepared by people accused and convicted at a Court Martial of actual mutiny and by a Professor of Law hoping to provide mitigating circumstances for a brother potentially facing a capital charge of mutiny, were he to be apprehended. The legend was further developed by officers and ex-officers of the New South Wales Corps in Australia whose monopoly of liquor was threatened by Governor Bligh.

However, the legend of Bligh's infamy was developed most by fiction in films derived from novels. "Faction" can be described as a dangerous mixture of fact and fiction. Truth may be distorted with facts turned into falsehood and it may be distorted with facts turned into irony or farce.

Biographers have tended to ridicule "faction" but have underestimated the contribution fiction has made to the development of the legend of infamy in this case.

The 1935 MGM film in which Charles Laughton played the part of Captain Bligh was based on the novels by C B Nordhoff and J N Hall, so too was the 1962 MGM film in which Trevor Howard played the part of the Captain. Both films are largely travesties of the truth, as it will be shown and should be regarded as farce.

Although the 1984 film in which Anthony Hopkins takes the part of Wm Bligh purports to follow the biography by Richard Hough, the film script finally departs radically from source material and is badly flawed.

It is very appropriate that, more than two hundred years on from the Mutiny in "Bounty", a member of the Bligh family should take stock.

My father's researches indicated [1] that John Bligh, Mayor of Bodmin in 1588, settled in Exeter and reassumed the name of Blight. My grandfather was a naval engineer, my father was an Army and Royal Flying Corps padre on the Western Front in the first World War. He advised me to revert to the name of Bligh, which I did by Deed Poll in 1946, to avoid the pestilential connotations of the name "Blight". By making such a change, I do not disparage the proud name of Blight. I would like to point with pride in the name of the brothers William and Emmanuel Blight respectively Lieutenant and Midshipman in HMS Britannia, a first rate 100-gun ship of the line at the Battle of Trafalgar [2]. William Blight later became a Rear Admiral [3].

This Biography offers a completely new explanation of the prime cause of the Mutiny in "Bounty" using late 20th century information to solve a late 18th century mystery of the real cause of the Mutiny.

My own background is as follows: I was commissioned as an officer during my National Service at the age of nineteen years. I went on to study Classics and Philosophy at University; then by evening classes, I developed a scientific background. I produced and developed moderators for the nuclear industry before I specialised in the social sciences.

I believe the rigorous application of a proven theory of modern scientific psychology offers a convincing explanation of a two hundred year old mystery.

---

[1] "The Visitations of Cornwall", J L Vivian, Exeter 1887. "The History of the Deanery of Trigg Minor", Sir J Maclean Vol I London 1873-9.

[2] "The Trafalgar Roll", R H MacKenzie 1913.

[3] Navy List 1860.

Preface

The Life of William Bligh has some fascinating components: Extraordinary events leading to the Mutiny in "Bounty", an epic open boat journey of more than 3,600 miles, some rousing naval engagements including the Battle of Copenhagen and Bligh's eventful Governorship of New South Wales in Australia.

I challenge biographers, producers, directors and especially film script-writers to face the truth.

CHAPTER 1

Family background; early naval days and romance.
9.9.1754 – 20.3.1776

An American Secretary of State for Education said[4] that every American child should know what caused the mutiny on the "Bounty". As the cause of the mutiny in "Bounty" requires adult or at least adolescent understanding, I think he should have said that every American adult or adolescent should know the true cause. Certainly it would be much more important for a British or Australian adult or adolescent to read about and know the cause of this mutiny as their countries were the ones involved in what happened.

It is certainly true that no one is going to know the cause of the mutiny in "Bounty" from Hollywood films all of which are based on some fiction or at least a mixture of fiction and some facts, often called faction.

This book aims to get to the truth beginning with the background of William Bligh.

The family name "Bligh" originates from the County of Cornwall and is of Celtic origin. The Celts[5] invaded what is now the United Kingdom and Eire during the second half of the first millennium BC.

Before the first major settlement of the Romans in what is now England and Wales following the invasion by the Emperor Claudius in 43AD, the Celtic language, Brythonic[6], was predominantly spoken and largely continued to be used by the indigenous population during the Roman occupation. Inhabitants

---

[4] "Mr Bligh's bad language" G Dening CUP 1992.
[5] "The Celts" F. Delaney, London 1986.
[6] "The Story of the Cornish Language", P Beresford Ellis, Penguin 1990

Family background

of Ireland, Scotland and the Isle of Man spoke a related Celtic language, Goidelic or Gaelic. The decline of Rome left England vulnerable to Saxon invasion from the 5th Century AD.

From some time after the 6th Century AD the Brythonic languages of Welsh, Cornish and Breton (Brittany) began to go their separate ways.

It was not until the 10th Century AD that the Saxon King of Wessex, Athelston, defeated the last independent King of Cornwall.

What is now called the "Old Cornish" language was spoken and sometimes written up to the 14th Century AD.

It is significant that the word "Bleit", meaning "a wolf", is recorded in the 12th Century AD Cotton Vocabulary [7] of words in the "Old Cornish" language. By the "middle Cornish" language period from the 14th Century AD to the middle of the 17th Century AD, the word "Bleit" was obsolete and the words for "wolf" were "blyth" or "Blaidh" while in the literature [8] "Origo Mundi", mid 15th Century and the Cornish play "Gwryans an Bys" ('The Creation of the World'), early 17th Century AD they were "Bly" or "Blygh'.

The following comparison is convincing and cogent evidence that these words are of Celtic origin as the Brythonic Welsh "Blaidd"[9] means "wolf" and was often used in Medieval Welsh as a "hero", much less frequently in a derogatory sense.

The change[10] from "Blyth" to "Bly" is probably accounted for by the Anglo Norman propensity to drop the "th".

The forms of the family names, e.g. Blight (synonymous with Bleit), Bligh, Blythe and Bly were frequently interchanged from the 16th Century onwards.

There were four Mayors of Bodmin in Cornwall with the name of Bligh or Bleigh between 1505 and 1588, each was Mayor on two occasions.

---

[7] 'Archaeologia Cornu Britannica' W Pryce. Sherborne 1790.
[8] "A New Cornish Dictionary" R Morton Nance Cornwall 1990 (Len Truran).
[9] "A Dictionary of Surnames" P Hanks and F Hodges Oxford 1988 by permission of the Oxford University Press.
[10] A Dictionary of British Surnames" P H Reaney (ed R M Wilson) London 1976.

William Bligh's grandfather, Richard, (genealogy of Elizabeth Bligh, granddaughter of William, dated 1852) first leased in 1709 the Manor of Tinten, St Tudy about six miles from Bodmin. He had seven sons and one daughter. His fifth son Francis was born in 1721 and when thirty two years old married a widow, Jane Pearce (née Bond[10]), then forty one years old who already had a young daughter Catherine. William Bligh was born next year on the 9th of September 1754 as recorded in the family bible of Francis Bligh; so the baby already had a half-sister Catherine.

Francis Bligh was a Customs Officer in Plymouth where he lived and where his yellow wheeled carriage was a familiar sight. His son, William, was baptised in St Andrew's Church, Plymouth on the 4th of October 1754. Francis Bligh was buried at St Andrew's Church and his tombstone there named [11] his father as Richard Bligh of Tinten, St Tudy.

William acknowledged to the Royal Navy (Admiralty records re HMS Hunter) that he was born in Plymouth but he claimed to be a "native of St Tudy" [12]. It would appear that he regarded himself as a Cornishman with his roots in Cornwall, although he was born in Devon and so technically a Devonian. Inhabitants of Cornwall have tended to show a strong local loyalty to their county and a well known jest is that people beyond the county boundary are foreigners. This is hardly surprising as the derivation of the word "Cornwall" is from the Saxon words for "Cornish" and "foreigners". The latter part of this Saxon derivation was also applied to Wales.

At the age of seven years nine months William was entered in the muster-roll [13] of HMS Monmouth on the 1st of July 1762 as Captain's servant to Captain Keith Stewart, a relative of William's mother. This did not mean that William actually went to sea then, but it did count towards his service at sea. John Bond who married his cousin, Catherine, William's half-sister, was then Surgeon on HMS Monmouth.

What is surprising is that the Navy Lists for 1762 show Captain John Storr as Captain of HMS Monmouth. However, the

[10] A Dictionary of British Surnames" P H Reaney (ed R M Wilson) London 1976.
[11] Western Antiquary 1885 Vol iv p 214 Plymouth.
[12] "Biographical sketches in Cornwall" Polywhele vol ii p 19
[13] Log 51/3916 muster 36/6103-4 PRO Admiralty.

Family background

commission for that ship was ended on the 21st February 1763 at Plymouth.

We have very little information about William's childhood, but one story [14] told by Dr A Gatty who knew William much later on is revealing about the standard of living of William's parents. He said that when William Bligh was asked by King George III in what engagement he had received a scar on his cheek, he answered that he received the mark when helping his father catch a horse in their orchard. His father threw a small hatchet to turn the animal and unwittingly struck him.

Francis Godolphin Bond was born to Catherine in Francis and Jane Blighs' House. He was one of five children whose eldest brother was named John Pearce Bond, as recorded in Francis Bligh's bible. Jane Bligh died in 1768 in the year when young William was only 14 years old. Two years later, Francis Bligh married a second time.

We do not know where William had been to school, but he demonstrated later that he had received a good education and developed an enquiring mind. Living in Plymouth at that age, he would undoubtedly have considered whether he really wanted to go into the Navy. He had already had six months "service" as a Captain's servant. A minority of potential Naval Officers went to the small Naval Academy at Portsmouth with only forty places. The majority of potential Naval Officers aimed to become Midshipmen; such a rank required the applicant to have at least two years naval experience and be at least thirteen years old, or eleven years old in the case of sons of Naval Officers. A minority of potential Naval Officers aimed for commissioned rank by way of the lower deck, particularly through the rank of Master's Mate.

It is necessary to look critically at what Sir John Barrow says about Bligh's method of entry as well as Barrow's understanding of Bligh's family background. Sir John as 2nd Secretary to the Admiralty wrote an anonymous book [15] more than ten years after Bligh's death in which he writes: "Seamen will always pay a more ready and cheerful obedience to officers who are gentlemen than to

---

[14] Notes and Queries 1871 4th series vol vii p 432
[15] "The Eventful History of the Mutiny and Piratical Seizure of HMS Bounty: its cause and consequence" London 1831

those who have risen to a Command from among themselves. It is indeed a common observation in the service that officers who have risen before the mast (i.e. from the ranks) are generally the greatest tyrants. It was Bligh's misfortune not to have been educated in the cockpit of a man-of-war among young gentlemen which is to the navy what a public school is to those who move in civil society".

Bligh seems to have become a Midshipman with less than two years experience. He joined HMS Hunter [16] a 10-gun sloop on the 27th of July 1770 as an "Able Seaman" when he was fifteen years old. The log of HMS Hunter under Commander John Henshaw records a flogging of 12 lashes on the 2nd November 1770 for a crew member on the charge of desertion and on the 4th of February 1771 12 lashes on another crew member "for insulting his officer and striking him". Bligh re-entered the same vessel as Midshipman on the 5th of February 1771 about six months later. Midshipmen were called "young gentlemen" and were potential officers in training. He joined a larger vessel 36-gun HMS Crescent [17] as a Midshipman on the 22nd of September 1771 and we know from the Admiralty record that this vessel was based in the West Indies between 1771 and 1774. Richard Humble in his book "Captain Bligh" says that the log of HMS Crescent under the command of John Corner bristles with punishments of 24 lashes. Bligh was present when a British "combined operation" on the 19th November 1772 went in against a Carib force on Grand Sable Island in the West Indies. HMS Crescent became grounded for a while being in great danger, but was refloated. Corner died in the West Indies and was replaced by Charles Thompson, another disciplinarian who records a flogging on his first day in command. Bligh was discharged on the 23rd of August 1774, and joined, as a volunteer Able Seaman, the sloop HMS Ranger [18] under the command of the same John Henshaw on the 2nd September 1774 and re-entered as a Midshipman on the 29th of September 1775. It was during the time HMS Ranger was based in Douglas, Isle of Man, that Bligh met Elizabeth Betham. She was the second daughter of Richard Betham, LLD (Glasgow University), a friend of the philosopher David Hume and of the economist Adam Smith. Richard Betham

---

[16] Log 51/451 muster 36/7868-9 PRO Admiralty
[17] Log 51/204 muster 36/7573-4 PRO Admiralty
[18] Log 51/768 muster 36/7665-6 PRO Admiralty

was the first Receiver General or Collector of Customs as well as Water Bailiff in Douglas, Isle of Man. Elizabeth's grandfather had been Principal of Glasgow University and Chaplain to the King.

Her uncle on her mother's side, Duncan Campbell, was a ship owner, naval contractor, and superintendent of convicts at the hulks (prison ships) in London.

By early 1776, [19] William and Elizabeth had "come to an understanding".

By this time also, Bligh's talents, particularly in the naval skills of cartography and hydrography were becoming known more widely. To be offered the post of Master of "Resolution" by Captain James Cook for his third voyage to the South Seas was a very considerable compliment and he took up this position on the 20th of March 1776.

---

[19] "Captain Bligh and Mr Christian ...." Richard Hough Ch 2 1972

CHAPTER 2

On Captain Cook's third voyage, Bligh's marriage and further naval days.
20.3.1776 – 4.6.1783

James Cook was in the merchant marine service before he entered the Royal Navy. He rose quickly to the rank of Warrant Officer in 1755 but he did not become a commissioned officer until 1768 when he was 40 years old; that was the year in which he began his first voyage to the South Seas. On that voyage he took Joseph Banks as a Botanist and used him also as a trader. In 1778, Banks became President of the Royal Society.

In 1776, James Cook was elected a Fellow of the Royal Society for improvements to health at sea and received a Gold Medal for a paper about that. He gave particular attention to diet, adequate sleep and cleanliness. By introducing a three watch system, he ensured that there was a greater opportunity to obtain adequate sleep between watches. His crew's health record on the three voyages to the South Seas was remarkable. Cook was however a strong disciplinarian and had a seaman flogged for refusing to eat meat.

Cook's fits of rage and bad language particularly on the third voyage, when he was ill, were well known, and a barbaric act in which Cook had a man's ear cut off is recorded [20].

Bligh undoubtedly learned much about health and seamanship from Captain Cook, but Cook did not set a good example with regard to emotional control or use of appropriate language.

After his appointment as Master of Cook's ship, "Resolution", Bligh passed his Lieutenant's certificate on the 1st of May 1776. He

---

[20] "Bligh" Gavin Kennedy Chapter 11 1978

satisfied the formal qualifications [21] of six years service at sea only if his questionable service as Captain's servant on HMS Monmouth is taken into consideration. He was then 21 years old, so he satisfied a further condition of being not less than twenty. He had also to satisfy his examiners.

Cook's third voyage to the South Seas began as "Resolution" and its tender "Discovery" left England on the 14th of July 1776. Evidently, Cook was not dissatisfied with his sailing Master as he called an island [22] "Bligh's Cap" in December 1776 before they reached Adventure Bay, Tasmania, in January 1777. The ships travelled by way of New Zealand to the Friendly Islands in the Pacific where it had been planned to view an eclipse of the sun on the 5th of July 1777. After visiting the Society Islands, Cook later came upon the Sandwich Islands (Hawaii) in January 1778. He travelled to the North West Coast of the American Continent and passed through the Behring Straits; as winter was approaching, Cook finally turned back on the 26th of October 1778 establishing that, as far as he went, there was no North West Passage through to the Atlantic.

It is important to understand what happened to Cook when he returned to the Sandwich Islands as some critics have misrepresented the part which Bligh played in the proceedings.

The Sandwich Islands were sighted again on the 26th of November 1778. By the 16th of January 1779, Cook had decided to use Karakakooa Bay (now Kealakekua Bay) as a place where he could carry out repairs. The crews were first welcomed with Cook identified as a legendary god returning to the Islands, and bearing gifts. On the 4th of February, Cook and his men sailed from the bay, and a few days later met bad weather during which the foremast of "Resolution" was sprung. This damage was considered to be the fault of Deptford yard and its suppliers. Cook decided that they must return to the bay for repairs. Relationships however between the natives and Cook's men began to break down. On the 13th of February 1779, large stones were rolled down towards sailors drawing fresh water. A native was caught stealing from one of the ships and was flogged. A further thief was pursued to the

---

[21] Journal of the Royal United Service Institution vol XL part ii, p 806 & 896.

[22] "A Voyage to the Pacific Ocean"....Captain James Cook Vol 1 p 57 – 9 1784 (third Voyage) – a rock off Kerguelen Islands, Southern Ocean.

shore where a brawl ensued. That night, one of "Discovery's" boats was taken by thieves. Captain Cook ordered Clerke [23] his second-in-command, Captain of "Discovery", to send two armed boats to the southern entrance of the Bay to blockade native canoes within the Bay. Cook planned to send two of his own boats to the northern entrance for the same purpose under the command of Bligh. From the one boat immediately available, Bligh tried to persuade a canoe not to break the blockade, but the canoe persevered and a musket was fired without any casualties. This caused the canoe to make for the southern shore which was reached. At the southern point however Lieutenant Richman, who was in charge of the boat sent by Clerke, fired on and killed [24] a chief.

At 7 o'clock that morning, Cook accompanied by ten marines including Lieutenant Phillips and two non-commissioned officers decided to visit King Terreeoboo to obtain the return of the boat. The King at first was prepared to go with Cook but was prevailed upon by his wife not to do so. It would seem [25] that it was Cook's intention to take the King hostage until the boat was returned. Cook was struck in the face and in defending himself killed a Hawaiian. The marines were ordered to fire and then retreated. Four marines, who were unable to swim away, were killed. Cook himself was overpowered and killed.

Lt James King of "Resolution" was invited to be the official editor to write the third volume of "The Voyage to the Pacific Ocean"; Cook himself had written the first two volumes. King says that Cook's overconfidence was a contributory cause of the tragedy. However, King goes on to say ".... an accident happened which gave a fatal turn to the affair. The boats which had been stationed across the bay, having fired at some canoes that were attempting to get out, unfortunately had killed a Chief of the first rank. The news of the death arrived at the village where Captain Cook was, just as he had left the King and walked slowly towards the shore".

In the Admiralty Library volume [26], Bligh himself added a marginal note "Lt Richman did fire and it was said killed a man; but the Attack was (ov)er and past before that was known". King

---

[23] Clerke's log PRO Admiralty 55/22-3
[24] "Bligh" Gavin Kennedy Chapter 2 1978
[25] "Bligh" Gavin Kennedy Chapter 2 1978
[26] "A Voyage to the Pacific Ocean..." Captain James King Vol III p.44

does not criticise the marines, writing "..... a general attack with stones immediately followed which was answered by a discharge of musquetry from the marines and the people in the boats". To this, Bligh's marginal note reads "The Marines fire(d) and ran which occasioned al(l) that followed, for had the(y) fixed their bayonets and not have run, so frighte(ned) as they were, they migh(t) have drove all before t(hem)".

King describes the events further: "Four of the marines were cut off among rocks in their retreat and fell a sacrifice to the fury of the enemy; three more were dangerously wounded; and the Lieutenant who had received a stab between the shoulders with a pahooa (small spear), having fortunately reserved his fire, shot the man who had wounded him just as he was going to repeat his blow. Our unfortunate Commander, the last time he was seen distinctly, was standing at the waters' edge....". Bligh notes: "A most infamous li(e) for I took down in writing all that happened here before I slept and particularly the Lieutenant's opinion who told me that as soon as the Musquets were discharged they ran to the Boats, having no time to re-load and was stabed in the back when unable to make any resistance". A little later, King writes [27]: "it has been already related that four of the marines who attended Captain Cook were killed by the islanders on the spot. The rest with Mr Phillips, their Lieutenant, threw themselves into the water and escaped under cover of a smart fire from the boats". Bligh notes: "this person, who never was of any real service the whole voyage, or did anything but eat and sleep was a great Croney of C King's...".

King does however recall that Phillips had saved a marine who would otherwise have drowned. Bligh writes however: "The man was close to the Boat and swam nearly as well as the Lieut......".

As Bligh wrote these notes five years after the events occurred, we can realise the anger which Bligh felt towards both King and Phillips, but he does not convincingly establish that King lied although King failed to exonerate Bligh, as he should have done. King's version of these events certainly prejudiced Bligh's immediate chances of promotion in the eyes of Lord Sandwich. Bligh however is intemperate in his abuse of Phillips.

Following the death of Cook on the 14th of February 1779, Lieutenant King asked Clerke for instructions. Bligh was sent with

---

[27] "A Voyage to the Pacific Ocean" Captain James King Vol III p 53

orders to bring everything from the shore base back on board. Bligh and King went ashore. King returned leaving Bligh in charge with instructions to act defensively. Natives attacked the shore post, so the defenders opened fire and killed a native; afterwards a truce was arranged whereby the mast of "Resolution" and the sails were allowed to be taken back to the ships.

"Resolution" and "Discovery" left the Sandwich Islands on the 15th of March 1779 for further exploration under Clerke, who died on the 22nd of August 1779.

From the North East Asiatic coast of Kamschatka, the vessels returned by the East Coast of Japan on the way back to England.

On the title page of "A Voyage to the Pacific Ocean" attributing vol I and II to Cook and Vol III to King, it is stated "Illustrated with MAPS and CHARTS, from the Original Drawings made by Lieutenant HENRY ROBERTS, under the direction of Captain Cook;...." Bligh has written on the bottom of this page on the Admiralty Library office copy "none of the Maps and Charts in this publication are from the original drawings of Lieu' Henry Roberts, he did no more than copy the original ones from Captain Cook who besides myself was the only person that surveyed and laid the coast down, in the Resolution. Every Plan and Chart from the time of C Cook's death are exact copies of my work – signed Wm Bligh".

Bligh said that the following original surveys were his work: The Sandwich Islands, part of the Friendly Islands and on the East Asian seaboard, South of the Behring Straits, Kamschatka, part of the East coast of Japan, Macao and Typa.

"Resolution" and "Discovery" reached England on the 4th of October 1780.

Before he became Master of the frigate "Belle Poule" [28] on the 14th of February 1781, Elizabeth Betham and William Bligh were married on the 4th of February. Francis Bligh, William's father, had died on the 27th of December 1780.

It was while serving in "Belle Poule" that Bligh saw action in the North Sea. Admiral Hyde Parker with seven larger fighting ships of the line, five frigates and seven smaller vessels on the 5th of April 1781 was escorting a convoy of merchant ships from the Baltic

---

[28] PRO Admiralty log 52/2171

to England. Rear Admiral Zoutman with a Dutch fleet of seventeen vessels was also escorting a convoy of merchantmen. Off the Dogger Bank, Admiral Hyde Parker attacked the Dutch vessels; there was considerable loss of life on both sides, and the Dutch lost one 74 gun ship of the line.

Soon after discharge from "Belle Poule" on the 5th of September 1781, Bligh took up his first commissioned post as fifth Lieutenant on a 74-gun ship of the line "HMS Berwick" [29]. It was during the time that Bligh was posted to this ship that Harriet Maria Bligh was born on the 15th November 1781 at Leith. He transferred to a larger vessel, an 80-gun ship of the line "HMS Princess Amelia", [30] as fifth Lieutenant on the 1st of January 1782 and transferred to a first class ship of the line "HMS Cambridge" [31] as sixth Lieutenant on the 20th of March 1782.

It was in this last vessel that Bligh took part in the relief of Gibraltar. On the 11th of September 1782, Admiral Lord Howe led a massive fleet of one hundred and eighty three vessels including thirty four ships of the line from England. Gibraltar was relieved on the 13th of October and the fleet reached England again on the 14th of November.

The prize money arising from the capture of enemy vessels during the relief of Gibraltar amounted for Bligh to the equivalent of sixteen weeks pay.

In 1782, Rodney's victory over the French in the Caribbean had given the British mastery of the Atlantic, but things had gone badly in America for British forces and independence was ceded to the United States in April 1783.

Bligh was "paid off" on the 13th of January 1783 and no comparable job was immediately available.

However Duncan Campbell, Elizabeth Bligh's uncle, on the 4th of June 1783 recommended [32] that Bligh apply to the Admiralty for permission to go into the merchant service. Duncan would be able to offer him a Captaincy of one of his vessels.

---

[29] PRO Admiralty log 51/101
[30] PRO Admiralty log 51/737
[31] PRO Admiralty log 52/2194
[32] D Campbell Letter Book D p 189 ML A3228

CHAPTER 3

Merchant marine service and background to the 1st Breadfruit Voyage

4.6.1783 – 6.8.1787

By the 18th of July 1783, Bligh had received Admiralty clearance and was ready to start a new career in the Merchant Service working for Duncan Campbell.

He was appointed to the command of the vessel "Lynx" on the West Indian run and Duncan Campbell entrusted his son John to be trained under Bligh. On the 21st of November 1783, John Campbell wrote [33] to his father, saying "..... he (Bligh) has behaved to me very kindly and instructed me during my leisure in navigation.... Captain Bligh ... is a stranger to the customs of the mercantile line".

Bligh was Captain of "Lynx" until he took over "Cambrian" for only a short while as he took command of "Britannia", which was a new vessel in 1785.

After the birth of Harriet Maria Bligh in 1781, the Bligh's second daughter Mary was born in Douglas, Isle of Man on the 1st of April 1784, while their third daughter Elizabeth was born at 4 Broad Street, St Georges in the East, London on the 24th March 1786. Their twin girls Frances and Jane were born in 1788 also at 4 Broad Street, while their sixth daughter Ann was born mentally handicapped and epileptic on the 21st February 1791 at 14 Moor Place, Lambeth.

For a period, while being employed by Duncan Campbell, Bligh acted as his agent in the port of Lucea in Jamaica.

---

[33] Private notebooks of D Campbell ML A 3231

At this point, it will be helpful to trace the origins of the 1st Breadfruit Voyage:

The first recorded knowledge of the Breadfruit tree in the West was in 1598 arising from the voyage [34] of Mendana de Neyra. William Dampier wrote about the fruit in 1688: The natives of Guam "bake it in an oven... the inside is soft, tender and white like the crumb of a penny loaf".

Cook and his botanist Joseph Banks became aware of the food value of the Breadfruit at Otaheite (Tahiti) in 1769. It is interesting to know that Cook spoke of the fruit "as disagreeable as that of a pickled olive.... its taste is insipid with a slight sweetness...".

West Indian officials were not slow to lobby [35] Banks to take up their interests on his return from Cook's first voyage to the South Seas. Valentine Morris, Captain General of the West Indies, wrote to Banks on the 17th of April 1772 of food shortages and the need to lessen "the dependence of the Sugar Islands on North America for food.....".

In 1775, the Society of West Indian Merchants [36] had offered to underwrite the expense of importing economic edible plants.

Dr Solander, who was also a Botanist on Cook's first voyage to the South Seas, wrote [35] on the 4th of May 1776 about how the West Indies would benefit from the transportation of the Breadfruit plant from the Pacific.

The Society for the Encouragement of Arts, Manufactures and Commerce offered [37] in 1777 a premium and later a Gold Medal for the first person to deliver to the West Indies ".... six plants of one or both species of Breadfruit tree in a growing state".

In 1784, Hinton East on behalf of West Indian trading interests wrote to Sir Joseph Banks who had been President of the Royal Society since 1778. In 1786, Hinton East was in London, presumably lobbying for the same interests, while Sir Joseph Banks early in 1787 discussed a proposal for a voyage to transport Breadfruit plants from Otaheite to the West Indies.

---

[34] "The Life of Vice Admiral Bligh..." G Mackaness Vol 1 Ch III 1931
[35] "History of the British West Indies" Bryan Edwards Vol 1
[36] "Captain Bligh and Mr Christian" Richard Hough Ch 3 1972
[37] "Life of Vice Admiral Bligh" G Mackaness Vol 1 Ch IV 1931

On the 5th of May 1787, Lord Sydney one of the Principal Secretaries of State wrote [38] on behalf of King George III to the Lords Commissioners of the Admiralty: "....that you do cause a Vessel of proper Class .... to be fitted with proper Conveniences for the preservation of as many of the said trees as from her size can be taken on board....".

Sir Joseph Banks took charge of preparations for the expedition. We know that Duncan Campbell, Bligh's employer, was aware of what was going on because on the 2nd of May 1787 Duncan wrote [39] to a relative "..... I wish him (Bligh) home soon as thereby he may stand a chance of employment in his own line, but of this more by and bye".

Campbell was paying Bligh £500pa[40] which was about seven times as much as Bligh was earning as a Royal Navy Lieutenant (4 shillings per day). Bligh had also received profits [41] on Cook's "A Voyage to the Pacific Ocean" amounting to about £1000, since Sir Joseph Banks, Lord Sandwich and Mr Stephens, an Admiralty official, decided on the apportionment in 1785.

As Captain of "Britannia", Bligh had recommended to him as a Midshipman, Fletcher Christian. Bligh was not able to offer him the post of Master's Mate, but agreed to take him on as an Able Seaman doing duty as Gunner, but "messing" with other Midshipmen. On a second voyage, Bligh took him as a second Mate, again "messing" with the Midshipmen.

On the 8th of June 1787, the Lords Commissioners of the Admiralty informed the Navy Board that "Bethia" was to be listed as "Bounty" and was to have an establishment of forty five men, including twenty five Able Seamen. Before this, "Bethia" had been purchased (£1950) and modification and repair work amounting to more than twice the purchase cost had been put in hand.

Compared to Captain Cook's ship "Resolution", which was 462 tons, "Bounty" at 215 tons was very small indeed. It was even smaller than the consort and tender "Discovery" at 229 tons on Cook's third voyage.

---

[38] "Bligh" Gavin Kennedy Ch 4 1978
[39] ML A 3229
[40] Bligh to Campbell (10.12.1787) ML Safe 1/40
[41] Bligh to Campbell (22.4.1786) ML Safe 1/40

Merchant marine service and background to the 1st Breadfruit Voyage

On the 5th of August 1787, Bligh arrived back in "Britannia". The next day he had the "flattering news" that he was being offered the leadership of the 1st Breadfruit Voyage by Sir Joseph Banks.

He was able to discuss the matter with his wife and make an immediate decision. He replied that same day.

Bligh by Bligh

*"Bounty Deck Plans
Key to small print,
see facing page*

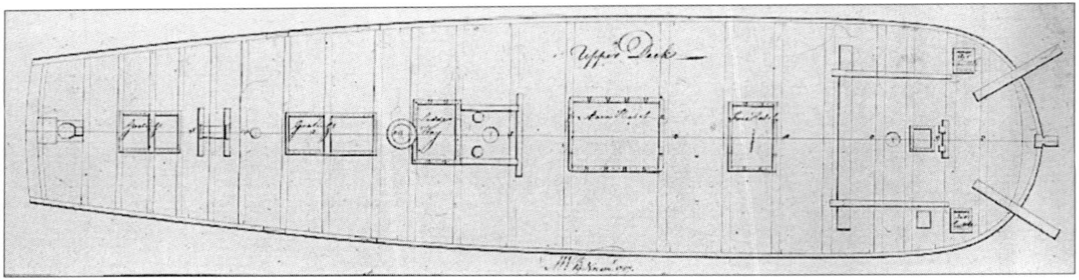

1) Upper Deck

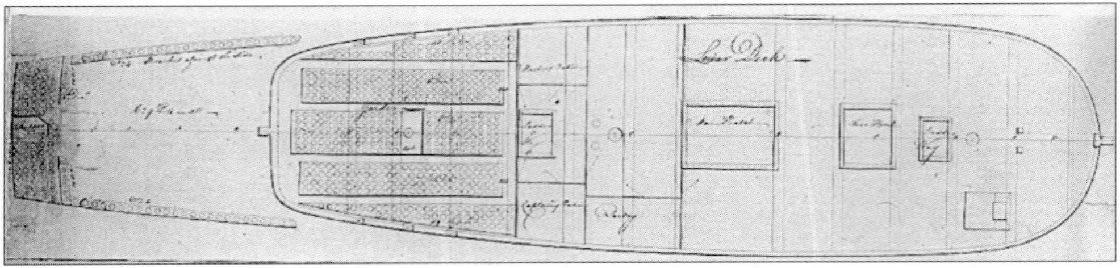

2) Lower Deck

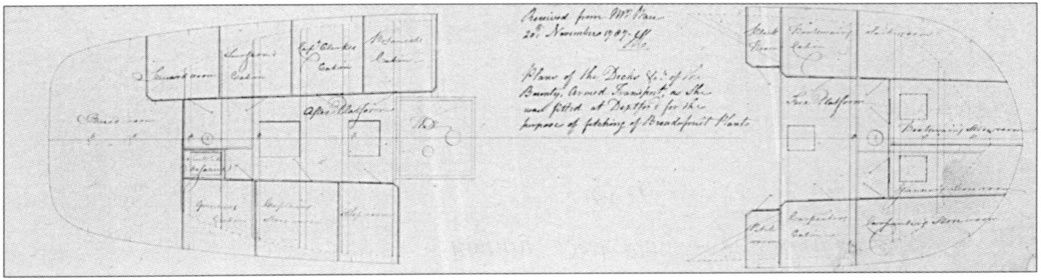

*3) Between decks
additions*

Merchant marine service and background to the 1st Breadfruit Voyage

"Bounty" Deck Plans – Key to small print

1) Upper Deck

Gratings	Gratings	Ladder Way	Main Hatch	Fore Hatch	air cuttle

air cuttle

2) Lower Deck

Master Cabin
(629 Pots) Garden Ladder Way Main Hatchway Fore Latch Ladder Way
Captain's Cabin, Pantry

3) Between Decks additions

Stewards Room	Surgeons Cabin	Clerks Cabin	Botanists Cabin	Received from Mrs. Ware 20th November 1787. Plans of the Decks of the Bounty, Armed Transport, as she was fitted out at Deptford for the purpose of fetching of Breadfruit Plants	Block Room	Boatswain Cabin	Sail Room
Bread Room	After Platform				Fore Platform	Boatswains Store Room	
	Scuttle to Magazine	Slop Room				Gunners Store Room	
Gunners Cabin	Captains Store Room				Pitch Room	Carpenters Cabin	Carpenters Store Room

Permission of the National Maritime Museum, London

CHAPTER 4

Preparation for the 1st Breadfruit Voyage
6.8.1787 – 23.12.1787

Within a few days of Bligh's agreement to lead the voyage, modifications and repairs to "Bounty" were completed and his appointment was confirmed.

He was however aggrieved that no immediate promotion went with the appointment although Lord Howe had promised [42] promotion on his return.

Bligh later wrote to Lord Selkirk, and he in turn wrote [43] to Sir Joseph Banks: "the establishment of Bligh's vessel is that of a cutter.... highly improper for so long a voyage without a Lieutenant or any marines".

"Bounty's" armaments consisted of 4 four-pounder guns and 10 swivel guns; this seems to have been accepted by Bligh without complaint. However, he was dissatisfied with the standard allocation of boats to "Bounty": namely a launch, a cutter and a jolly boat. He was able to obtain a larger launch. Within four days of the confirmation of his own appointment on the 16th of August 1787, he began [44] the appointment of warrant officers, namely the Master, John Fryer, and the Surgeon, Thomas Huggan.

General mobilisation for war began in September 1787 and this clearly added to the recruitment difficulties and meant that Bligh felt the delay to his own promotion more keenly.

Even in October 1787, Bligh was still seeking promotion to make some compensation for the sacrifice he was making in giving up his

---

[42] Duncan Campbell to relative 30.8.1787 ML A 3229
[43] ML A78-4 Series 45.10/cy 3004/36.38.
[44] "Bligh" Gavin Kennedy Ch 4 1978

Preparation for the 1st Breadfruit Voyage

previous salary of £500 pa. He wrote to Banks "... could I not hope that my Lord Howe... might be prevailed on to give me rank as Master and Commander considering that I was going out of the immediate chance of promotion and the great advantage of being in the beginning of a War...".

The crew [45] of "Bounty" was:

Rank	First Name	Surname	
Lieutenant	William	Bligh	
Master	John	Fryer	*[46]
Boatswain	William	Cole	*
Gunner	William	Peckover	*
Carpenter	William	Purcell	*
Surgeon	Thomas	Huggan	*
Surgeon's Mate	Thomas	Ledward	Established as AB
Master's Mate	William	Elphinstone	
"	Fletcher	Christian	
Midshipman	John	Hallet	
"	Peter	Heywood	
" (acting)	Thomas	Hayward	Established as AB
" (acting) [47]	Edward	Young	"
" (acting) [47]	George	Stewart	"
" (boy)	Robert	Tinkler	"
Quartermaster	John	Norton	
"	Peter	Linkletter	
Quartermaster's Mate	George	Simpson	
Boatswain's Mate	James	Morrison	
Gunner's Mate	John	Mills	
Carpenter's Mate	Charles	Norman	
Carpenter's crew	Thomas	McIntosh	
Sailmaker	Lawrence	Lebogue	

---

[45] Based on "A Narrative of the Mutiny" Wm Bligh 1790
[46] *Kings Warrant "Captain Bligh and Mr Christian" R Hough 1972
[47] Acting rank, established as "Able Seaman" "Captain Bligh and Mr Christian" R Hough

35

Armourer	Joseph	Coleman	
Corporal/Master at Arms			
	Charles	Churchill	
Cooper	Henry	Hillbrant	Established as AB
Steward	William	Muspratt	"
Clerk	John	Samuel	
Cook	Thomas	Hall	
Commander's Cook	John	Smith	Established as AB
Butcher	Robert	Lamb	"
Able Seaman (AB)	Richard	Skinner	
"	Alexander	Smith	
"	Thomas	Burkitt	
"	John	Millward	
"	John	Williams	
"	John	Sumner	
"	Matthew	Thompson	
"	James	Valentine	
"	Michael	Byrne	
"	William	McKoy	
"	Matthew	Quintal	
"	Isaac	Martin	
"	Thomas	Ellison	
Botanist	David	Nelson	
Botanist's Assistant	William	Brown	

John Hallet [48] was clearly chosen because his sister was a friend of Mrs Bligh. Richard Betham, Bligh's father-in-law, recommended Peter Heywood [48] who was then not yet fifteen years old. His father was a member of the House of Keys, the Isle of Man Parliament.

Fletcher Christian then in early September aged twenty two years old just before his twenty third birthday was known to Bligh from their sailing together in "Britannia". His family had lived near

---

[48] "The Life of Vice Admiral Bligh" G Mackaness Vol 1 Ch IV 1931

Preparation for the 1st Breadfruit Voyage

Cockermouth (Cumbria) but traced [49] descent to a MacCrysten, a judiciary head in the Isle of Man born in the late 14th century.

Duncan Campbell had recommended Thomas Ellison who was then nineteen years old.

John Adams, an orphan from Hackney, had assumed the name of Alexander Smith and signed on as an AB. Three foreign nationals were among the crew: Henry Hillbrant from Hanover, Michael Byrne from Kilkenny (whom, although nearly blind, Bligh took on as a fiddler to provide music for dancing) and Isaac Martin, an American.

John Fryer, the Master, was brother-in-law to Robert Tinkler, taken on as a Able Seaman but treated among the Midshipmen as a "young gentleman".

Lawrence Lebogue, who sailed with Bligh in "Britannia", appears to have been the oldest person on board being forty years old.

Sixteen seamen deserted during preparations; this compares [50] with sixty men who deserted from Cook's third voyage. Two "pressed" men were sent to "Bounty", but both absconded before the final sailing.

The nature of the provisions which Bligh took is important as it shows that Bligh had learnt from Cook about the importance of a balanced diet including the use of vegetables. His provisions to last 18 months included salt pork and beef, dried peas, sauerkraut, essence of malt, barley, wheat, rum, beer and wine. He also took twelve hens, six sheep and some pigs to supplement the diet.

Particularly important were the metal and glass goods he took for barter.

It must be remembered that the whole of the lower deck from the stern to a point [51] midway between the main mast and the mizzen mast *(the mast between the main mast and the stern)* was sacrificed to the greenhouse. Although space larger than that lost to the greenhouse was added by adapting space in the hold, conditions for all were harsh.

Dr Richard Betham, Bligh's father-in-law, wrote [52]: "I own I have a different idea of it (the Voyage) from what I had conceived

---

[49] "Fragile Paradise", Glynn Christian 1982.
[50] Beaglehole 1974 p 502
[51] "Bounty" restructure plans, NMM.
[52] Betham to Bligh 21.9.1787

before I was acquainted with the circumstances of the vessel and the manner in which it is fitted out. Government I think have gone too frugally to work; both the ship and the Complement of men are too small in my opinion for such a voyage". In the same letter, Richard Betham wrote that Bligh's daughter Elizabeth "little Betsy" had contracted smallpox.

On the 9th of October 1787, "Bounty" left Deptford on the Thames. By the 8th of November, Bligh was ready to leave Spithead, but sailing orders were not received until the 24th of November.

"Bounty" sailed on the 28th of November when weather permitted but Bligh was forced to return to port on the 3rd December due to gales in the Channel. A second attempt was made on the 6th of December, but gales necessitated an almost immediate return to port.

The delay in the receipt of sailing orders had prejudiced his chances of getting past Cape Horn before adverse weather there was predicted to begin and yet his orders required him to go round the Horn. Bligh wrote [53] to Duncan Campbell on the 10th of December: "if there is any punishment that ought to be inflicted on a set of Men for neglect, I am sure it ought on the Admiralty for my 3 weeks detention at this place during a fine fair wind which carried all outward bound ships clear of the channel but me, who wanted it most. This has made my task a very arduous one indeed for to get round Cape Horn at the time I shall be there". On the 17th of December, Bligh wrote [54] to Sir Joseph Banks seeking discretion to go by the Cape of Good Hope, if frustrated at the Horn. He received this discretion by return.

In a letter [55] to Duncan Campbell on the 22nd of December, Bligh revealed that Lord Hood winked at his absence from the ship visiting "my dear little family" just so long as the weather prevented "Bounty" sailing. Bligh wished to keep this a secret, at least from Sir Joseph Banks. On the 23rd of December 1787, the weather allowed "Bounty" to sail.

---

[53] Bligh to Campbell 10.12.1787 ML Safe 1/40
[54] Bligh to Banks 17.12.1787 ML Series 46.18/CY 3004/97.99
[55] Bligh to Campbell 22.12.1787 ML Safe 1/40

CHAPTER 5

1st Breadfruit Voyage – The Journey to Otaheite (Tahiti)
23.12.1787 – 26.10.1788

One of the source documents of this chapter is the personal log of William Bligh. He used this to prepare a shorter log for the Admiralty. Another document [56] concerning this period is the journal of James Morrison, the Boatswain's Mate. This document which was being written [57] in 1792 was not completed until early 1793, about five years after the beginning of this expedition.

Morrison also prepared a "Memorandum and Particulars Respecting the Bounty and her Crew" [58] dated 10 October 1792 with charges against Bligh. The gist of this document must have been used earlier to seek a recommendation for pardon from the Court Martial on the 12th to the 18th September 1792 in which Morrison was charged with mutiny. Morrison's life therefore depended on him being able to bring charges of sufficient seriousness against Bligh, who was out of the country, for members of the Court Martial to feel embarrassed to put such a witness to death. A separate statement on behalf of Morrison at the Court Martial did not attack Bligh, but Morrison although sentenced to death was given a recommendation for pardon because of what the Court said were "various circumstances". The journal was being written after the Royal reprieve was given on the 24th of October 1792, but its author was writing in the light of charges made by him in the Memorandum.

---

[56] ML Safe 1/42
[57] Banks Papers, Brabourne Collection A78-4
[58] ML Safe 1/33

It is probable that Morrison kept a Journal on the 1st Breadfruit Voyage, but that Journal could not have survived the shipwreck in which he was involved and the close confinement to which he was subjected. Even his "Memorandum" under its title has a quotation:

"Say Memory for tis thou alone can tell
What dire mishaps a fated ship befell"

and even the dating [59] of the paper on which the Journal was written corroborates the fact that the Journal was not written at the time these events were happening.

After this necessary discussion of the sources on which this chapter is based, we can return to "Bounty" leaving England.

On the 27th of December 1787, within four days of leaving the country, a gale damaged much of the biscuit (called bread) and washed seven hogsheads of beer overboard.

Bligh's log records on the 3rd of January 1788 that 2109 lbs of "bread" were condemned and one cask of cheese (150 lbs) had been washed to pieces by the previous storm.

When "Bounty" reached Tenerife on the 5th of January 1788, Bligh wrote [60] to Duncan Campbell about his difficulties as purser "... as my pursing depends on much circumspection and being ignorant in it with a worthless clerk, I have some embarrassment, but as I trust nothing to anyone and keep my accounts clear, if I fail in rules of office I do not doubt of getting the better of it...".

It is important to point out Bligh's exaggerated abuse of his clerk as later events disclosed.

On the 11th of January 1788, Bligh's log tells us he introduced a three watch system to encourage more regular sleeping patterns. At the same time, he ordered Fletcher Christian, the Master's Mate, to take charge of one of the three watches.

Fletcher Christian had a brother Charles who had been a surgeon aboard vessels of the East India Company. In his autobiography of 1811, Charles wrote of Fletcher's promotion to acting lieutenant on HMS Eurydice on a run to India before he sailed with Bligh. In this

---

[59] "Bligh" Gavin Kennedy Ch 19 1978
[60] Bligh to Campbell (Tenerife) ML Safe 1/40

capacity Fletcher's companions on that run said he "ruled over them in a superior, pleasant manner".

Due to the earlier loss of biscuit, Bligh found it necessary to reduce the biscuit allowance to two thirds with the crew being compensated in money for the difference at the end of the journey. Bligh claimed that the crew seldom, if ever, consumed more than the new ration. Morrison confirms that Bligh explained this to the crew.

There was however a considerable difference of opinion about another incident, which happened after this, involving cheese. Morrison writes: "the cheese was got up to air, when on opening the casks two cheeses were missed by Mr Bligh who declared that they were stolen. The cooper declared that the cask had been open'd before while the ship was in the river by Mr Samuel's order and cheeses sent to Mr Bligh's house – Mr Bligh without making any further enquiry into the matter, ordered the allowance of cheese to be stopped from officers and men till the deficiency should be made good, and told the cooper (Henry Hillbrant) he would give him a damn'd good flogging" if he pursued the matter further. Morrison continued "These orders were strictly obeyed by Mr Samuel who was both clerk and steward; and on the next banyan (*meatless*) day butter only was issued, this the seamen refused, alledging that their acceptance of the butter without cheese would be tacitly acknowledging the supposed theft and Jno Williams declared that he had carried the cheeses to Mr Bligh's house with a cask of vinegar and some other things which went up in the boat from Long Reach -as they persisted in their denial of the butter, it was also kept for two banyan days and no more notice taken".

Bligh's later answer [61] to this was: "Captain Bligh declares that a cask of store cheese, having signs of getting into a bad state, was brought on deck and there opened was found full and counted out. In the interval of dinner time two of the cheeses were stolen. Captain Bligh considered this an audacious theft and could not be committed without the knowledge of most of the ships company – he therefore in preference to charging the value of the cheese against their wages, ordered it to be stopped from each person untill the whole was repaired".

---

[61] ML – "Remarks on Morrison's Journal" Safe 1/43

It is surprising that Bligh should have accused anybody of theft when supplies were first brought "up to air" or when they were counted before the crew. Bligh's log on the 30th of December 1787 refers to the public opening of pork and beef casks at which 4 out of 160 pieces of pork and 3 out of 86 pieces of beef were counted short. No recriminations were made then because naval suppliers were presumed to have been at fault. Bligh refers to a theft after counting out.

If Bligh had given orders to Mr Samuel to divert provisions to his house, it is surprising that Bligh should have accused others of theft, making an issue out of a matter where he would have been at a disadvantage and prejudicing the goodwill of the crew.

Mr Samuel may have decided on his own initiative to send provisions to Bligh's house, but Bligh would have been acquainted before then by his family with what had been done and it would be surprising if he had mentioned theft by others at or before counting out, because that loss could have been easily written off.

By the time Morrison wrote the Journal, Henry Hillbrant the cooper was dead and John Williams was a mutineer at large.

On the 23rd of January, Bligh records that he now recognised that Thomas Huggan, the Surgeon, was a "drunken sot". He had informed Banks before they left that Huggan was "unfit for the journey" because of indolence and corpulency. Bligh used a seaman's post to take on Thomas Ledward as Surgeon's Assistant.

On the 10th of February, an incident arose about pumpkins, called by Morrison "pumpions", which had been bought at Tenerife. Morrison writes [62]: "As the Ship approached the Equator, the pumpions began to spoil.... they were issued to the ship's company in lieu of bread. The people (the crew) being desirous to know at what rate the exchange was to be, enquired of Mr Samuel, who informed them that they were to have one pound of pumpion in lieu of two pounds of bread, this they refused, and on Mr Bligh being informed of it, he came up in a violent passion, and called all hands, telling Mr Samuel to call the first man of every mess and let him see who would dare to refuse it or anything else that he should order to be served saying 'You dam'd infernal scoundrels, I'll make you eat grass or anything you can catch before I have done with you'".

---

[62] Morrison Journal pp 3-4 ML Safe 1/42

1st Breadfruit Voyage – The Journey to Otaheite (Tahiti)

"This speech enforced his orders, and ev'ry one took the pumpion as call'd, officers not excepted.... and in all probability the grievance would have ended with them, but the private stock (of potatoes held by the seamen) began to decreace and the beef and pork to appear very light, and as there had never yet been any weigh'd when open'd, it was supposed that the casks ran short of their weight, for which reason the people apply'd to the master and begg'd that he would examine the business and procure them redress".

"The master making this known to Mr Bligh, he ordered all hands aft and informed them that ev'ry thing relative to the provisions was transacted by his orders and it was, therefore, needless to make any complaint for they would get no redress, as he was the fittest judge of what was right or wrong. He further added that he would flog the first man severely who should dare attempt to make any complaint in future and dismissed them with severe threats."

"The seamen seeing that no redress could be had before the end of the journey determined to bear it with patience and neither murmur'd or complained afterwards, however, the officers were not so easily satisfied and made frequent murmurings among themselves about the smallness of their allowance and could not reconcile themselves to such unfair proceedings...– when a cask was broached they saw with regret all the prime pieces taken out for the cabbin table while they were forced to take their chance in common with the men of what was remain'd without the satisfaction of knowing whether they had their weight or not...". In "Remarks [63] on Morrison's Journal" – although Kennedy suggests that Bligh was probably working from a similar account in the Memorandum – Bligh replied in the third person: "As in the course of the voyage the ship's company would be at two thirds allowance of bread, he directed 23 pumpkins bought at Teneriffe to be issued to those who liked them, and the amount of what each person took up was to be deducted out of whatever bread might become due to him, at the rate of 2lbs of pumpkin for 1lb of bread."

"Captain Bligh knowing what difficulties he had to encounter off Cape Horn and the length of time he was to be without fresh supplies had directed those pumpkins to be bought and likewise

---

[63] Bligh Bounty Mutineers ML Safe 1/43

two large dripstones to get his people pure water – These were certainly acts of kindness and not oppression."

"(re) the beef and pork now began to appear light etc etc. He would give no redress etc etc – he would flog the first man who complained again – this was the cause of no complaint ever after -"

"It is a well known thing that an officer attends the opening of all casks of beef and pork and sees the whole weighed and divided according to Navy Rules of 4 lbs to a piece of beef and 2lbs to a piece of pork – it is done publickly before the ships company... – As to choosing particular pieces of meat I deny it – it stands on record in my general orders that such a thing is forbidden on any pretence whatever... so happily did every person with him feel themselves that letters from the people and warrant officers from the Cape of Good Hope were particular in remarking how happy they were under Captain Bligh's command...'.

Bligh attempts to deal with complaints about the pumpkins and allegations of short measure in respect of beef and pork. The allegation that he attempted to deny opportunities for complaint is serious and he attempts to counter that argument by pointing to unsolicited statements of satisfaction by the crew.

In a letter to Duncan Campbell dated the 17th of February 1788 which was given to a British whaler on route to England, Bligh wrote [64]: "...My men (are) all active good fellows and what has given me much pleasure is that I have not yet been obliged to punish anyone... My men are not badly off either as they share in all but the poultry...".

On the 2nd of March 1788, Bligh's log states "I gave to Mr Fletcher Christian... a written order to act as lieutenant ...". Prior to this, the Master would have been seen as Bligh's deputy, but this action designated Christian as Bligh's deputy and this Mr Fryer, the Master, clearly resented, but Fryer would have been only too well aware that ships' masters at this period were not eligible for promotion to acting commissioned rank during the time of the present voyage.

A reaction to that decision was soon evident. Of the events on the 10th of March, Bligh wrote [65]: "Upon a complaint made to me

---

[64] Bligh to Campbell 17.2.1788 ML Safe 1/40
[65] "A Voyage to the South Sea" Wm Bligh 1792

1st Breadfruit Voyage – The Journey to Otaheite (Tahiti)

by the master, I found it necessary to punish Matthew Quintal... with two dozen lashes for insolence and mutinous behaviour. Before this, I had not had occasion to punish any person on board".

In his log on that date, he wrote "Untill this Afternoon I had hopes I could have performed the Voyage without punishment to any One, but I found it necessary to punish Matthew Quintal...".

A complaint by a warrant officer for "insolence and contempt" which was an offence [66] under Articles XXII and XXIII of the Articles of War was not one which could be ignored without damaging discipline.

On the 23rd of March 1788, the day South America was first sighted, Bligh's log states "In the morning, I killed a sheep and served it to the ship's company, who gave them a pleasant meal".

Of the same event, Morrison wrote: "One of the sheep dying this morning Lieutenant Bligh order'd it to be issued in lieu of the day's allowance of pork and pease, declaring it would make a delicious meal and that it weighed upwards of fifty pounds, it was divided and most part of it thrown overboard and some dried shark supply'd its place for a Sunday dinner, for it was no other than skin and bone". Of a similar event later on the 18th of April 1788, Morrison wrote "A hog was killed which tho' scarce anything else but skin and bone was greedily devoured".

Bligh replied again in the third person [67]: "It is a general rule on board ship not to suffer anything that died to be used by the seamen because they would always find means to kill any animal if they knew this rule was not observed – By Captain Bligh's log, it appears however that both the sheep and hogs were killed and on those days the people considered their allowance as a feast to them, 'greedily devoured' seem to apply the same thing."

"But Captain Bligh declares on his honor, he never did or could permit his people to eat anything that was improper – If Captain Bligh thought proper to shorten any allowance, he lived on the same himself and it is known to the lowest seaman in the King's service, that if he has not his full allowance, he is paid for it by Government in money and the Captain can draw bills to pay such

---

[66] MacArthur 1813 Vol 1 Appendix 1 p 325-336
[67] "Remarks on Morrison's Journal" ML Safe 1/43

account when he is employed abroad: If on his return, such payment due to the ship's company has not been made, the Captain is obliged to press an account for the same, and every man and officer will be paid all short allowance money that is due for the voyage at the time they receive their wages – for this reason, it would be extremely vicious in a Captain to put his men at less than full allowance unless from a prospect of being in want of supplies – the men who came home with Captain Bligh received their short allowance money".

Within a day of sighting the coast of Terra del Fuego at Cape Horn, storms began and, for almost a month, Bligh tried to make progress. On the 17th of April 1788, he seemed to have given up the struggle but turned for one last attempt. On the 22nd of April, he could ask no more of his crew and made for the Cape of Good Hope. On that day, he records in his log "The Sails and Ropes were worked with much difficulty and the few Men who were obliged to be aloft felt the Snow Squalls so severe as to render them almost incapable of getting below and some of them sometimes for a While lost their Speech; but I took care to Nurse them when off duty with every comfort in my power...".

Bligh records that two people were affected by rheumatism, four people had colds, the Surgeon had dislocated a shoulder and Thomas Hall, the crew's cook, had fallen and broken a rib.

Morrison attributes this last casualty to complaints about the quality of food; speaking of boiled wheat and barley, he writes: "The quantity was so small, that it was no uncommon thing for four men in a mess to draw for the breakfast, and to divide their bread by the well known method of 'who shall have this' nor was the officers a hair behind the men at it... the quantity of wheat boild was one gallon for 46 men, of which they all partook and of barley two pounds for the like number – the division of this scanty allowance caused frequent broils in the gally and in the present bad weather was often like to be attended with bad consequences and in one of these disputes the cook, Thos Hall, got two of his ribbs broke and at another time Churchill got his hand scalded and it became at last necessary to have the M^{rs} (Masters) Mate of the watch to superintend the division of it".

In the storms at Cape Horn, Bligh gave up his own cabin "to be appropriated at nights for use of those poor fellows who had wet berths".

1st Breadfruit Voyage – The Journey to Otaheite (Tahiti)

The obituary of Peter Heywood, written anonymously in 1831, referred to Bligh keeping the fifteen year old youth aloft at Cape Horn during a snow storm. There is no reference elsewhere to Heywood being treated differently to other Midshipmen then. If Heywood had been subjected to "mast heading", a traditional punishment for offending seamen, there is no doubt that Morrison would have recorded this.

Bligh was not ungrateful to his officers and men for perseverance in appalling conditions; Morrison wrote: "As the people began to fall sick the duty became heavyer on the Well, but was still carried on with alacrity and spirit, and the behaviour of the seamen in this trying situation was such as Merited the entire approbation of the officers and Mr Bligh's thanks in a Publick speech".

Cape Horn's aftermath resulted in a quarter of the ship's company being on the sick list with an increase in rheumatic complaints.

The Journey to the Cape of Good Hope took a month. Bligh records on the 25th of May 1788 that he ordered six lashes for John Williams for endangering the ship by "neglect of duty in heaving the lead". In his log on the same day, Bligh set out his approach to health management: "... a strict adherence to the first grand point, cleanliness in their persons and bedding, keeping them in dry Cloathes and by constant cleaning and drying the Ship with Fires.... but Scurvy is realy a disgrace to a ship where it is at all common, provided they have it in their power to be supplied with Dryed Malt, Sour Krout and Portable Soup... Cheerfullness with exercise and a sufficiency of rest are powerful preventitives to this dreadfull disease... to assist in the first two particulars every opportunity I directed that the Evenings should be spent in dancing and that I might be secure in my last I kept my few Men constantly at three Watches".

Bligh wrote [68] to Duncan Campbell from the Cape and pointed to the contrast in health management in ships from Holland: "... a Dutch Ship came in today having buried 30 Men and many are sent to the Hospital, although they have only been out since the last of January".

Bligh visited the Governor van de Graaff and arranged for daily supplies of meat and green vegetables to be supplied to "Bounty".

---

[68] Bligh to Campbell – ML Safe 1/40

From the Cape of Good Hope, Thomas Ledward, Assistant Surgeon, wrote [69] a letter about what happened at Cape Horn including: "The Captain was obliged to bear away and I have no doubt will gain much credit by his resolution and perseverance and by the extreme care he took with the Ship's company".

It is interesting to note Bligh's views on the treatment of slaves at the Cape of Good Hope:

"Slaves are a property here as well as in the West Indies, and the number imported by the French – to whom that Trade has been confined – from Madagascar, Musambique, Sumatra and Mallaca have been considerable, but it appears there is in some degree a Stop put to this trade, for the seller has now only permission to part with as many as can pay for the supplies he absolutely is in need of. To this if the Police could oblige the owners of these Poor Wretches consigned to constant drudgery, to cloath and feed them properly it would be much to their honour and humanity, for it is distressing to see some of them carrying Weighty burdens naked, or what is worse in such rags that one would imagine could not fail to reproach the owners of a want of decency and compassion in not relieving such a degree of wretchedness of which they were the cause, and had every call on their humanity to remove. Some of these poor wretches I have seen pick up the most offensive offals and claim them for food".

The recaulking treatment of the hull involved a stay of just over five weeks at the Cape of Good Hope. "Bounty" left on the 1st of July 1788 for a seven week sailing of 6000 miles to Tasmania.

"Bounty" reached Adventure Bay, Tasmania on the 21st of August. While there, Bligh wrote, on seeing approximately twenty Tasmanian aboriginals about twenty yards away: "One of them was distinguished by his body being coloured with red oker... but all the others had laid an additional coat of black over their faces and shoulders and it was laid on so thick that it totally prevented me at this distance to say anything exact of their features...".

At Adventure Bay, Bligh recorded the following incident in his log: "My Carpenter (Wm Purcell) on my expressing my disapprobation of his Conduct with respect to orders he had received from me concerning the Mode of working with the

---

[69] Notes and queries (1903) 9th Series Vol xii p 501

1st Breadfruit Voyage – The Journey to Otaheite (Tahiti)

Bligh had seen cases of Scurvy, most recently among Dutch Seamen at the Cape of Good Hope. He records in his log on the 24th of October "... few invalids recovering fast... having no eruptions or swellings convinces me that their complaint is not scorbutic. Their Gums also are sound as any can be expected after such a length of Salt Diet and their breath is not offensive neither is their teeth the least loose".

That same day, Bligh ordered Huggan's liquid store to be removed. Perhaps it is not surprising Huggan then re-diagnosed Thomas McIntosh and John Millward as having Scurvy.

We know from other expeditions how devastating Scurvy could actually be. During Anson's expedition [72] in 1741 two thirds of the crew of the 50-gun ship "Gloucester" died of this disease. Lind's critical experiments [73] with lemon and orange took place in 1747, but his remedies were not officially prescribed in the Navy until 1795. Bligh did however have with him three of Lind's books: "An Essay on the most effective means of preserving the Health of Seamen", "An Essay on diseases incidental to Europeans in Hot Climates" and "A Treatise on the Scurvy".

Before reaching Otaheite (Tahiti), Bligh wrote "I therefore ordered every person should be examined by the surgeon and had the satisfaction to learn from his report that they were all perfectly free from any venereal complaint". Owing to the poor relations between Bligh and Huggan, there will be some doubt as to whether this was the true state of affairs.

The muster lists of the Bounty kept by the surgeon showed that Huggan treated eight people and Ledward twelve people for venereal disease, of whom two people were treated by both Huggan and Ledward. Both Fletcher Christian and Peter Heywood were among the names of those treated.

The official log shows that five unnamed people were treated for venereal disease by the surgeons during the stay at Otaheite.

"The pox" [74] as venereal disease was generally called and from which the small pox was distinguished was, as is well known,

---

[72] "The Royal Navy – a History" Laird Clowes vol iii 1714-1793 Ch xxix London 1898
[73] "Medicine and the Navy" C Lloyd, JLS Coulter vol iii 1714-1815 p 300
[74] Ibid p 357/8

extremely prevalent in the 18th century. Mercury treatment was still the usual method of cure. But since supplies were limited and since the Admiralty regarded such complaints as the responsibility of the individual alone, all sailors so affected were stopped 2 weeks pay as a fine to be paid to the surgeon.

A surgeon, called Trotter, considered the venereal fines to be iniquitous, because the men delayed reporting the discovery until it was too late for a mercury cure. Trotter was in a position to stop the practice in 1795.

On the 16th of October 1788, "Bounty" reached Matavai Bay, Otaheite.

CHAPTER 6

1st Breadfruit Voyage – On Otaheite (Tahiti)
26.10.1788 – 4.4.1789

An excerpt of a well known poem by Rupert Brooke best gives the atmosphere of a special kind of heaven to which Bligh and his crew were coming. This is entitled "Tiare Tahiti":

"... the calling of the moon,
And the whispering scents that stray
About the idle warm lagoon.
      Hasten, hand in human hand
Down the dark, the flowered way,

...

And in the waters soft caress
Wash the mind of foolishness

...

Spend the glittering moonlight there
Pursuing down the soundless deep
Limbs that gleam and shadowy hair
Or floating lazy, half asleep.
Dive and double and follow after,
Snare in flowers, and kiss and call
With lips that fade and human laughter
And faces individual
Well this side of Paradise".

Bligh had, of course, been here before with Captain Cook and he formulated "rules of conduct" to ensure that he could achieve the object of the expedition. One of these rules was to forbid mention of the death of Captain Cook.

"Bounty" was greeted in exceptionally friendly fashion, as Bligh, Peckover and Nelson were already known to some of the islanders.

A potentially critical situation arose when Bligh was told that they already knew of the death of Cook, but fortunately not the nature of that death. David Nelson was sufficiently alarmed to say that Bligh was "the son of Cook" and everybody else had to accommodate to that falsehood.

The Regent arrived the next day and told Bligh his name was now "Tinah" [75]. He was about thirty five years old, a very tall man of at least 6ft 4ins and somewhat stout. As a younger man he had been a member of the Arreoys, a warrior association committed to infanticide. His first born child was killed at birth, but he left the Arreoys before his second child was born. The custom was that the eldest living son should succeed his father at birth, so Tinah became Regent on the birth of his second son.

His wife, called Iddeah or Itia, was about twenty four years old.

Within four days of landing, Bligh decided that action was required to reduce the pilfering that was taking place. "He ordered every Man except the Cheif's Attendants out of the ship".

The Matavai Regency had enemies which had been active recently. Tinah was anxious that Bligh should stay with him and be his ally, particularly as Bligh possessed weapons. The development of Bligh's diplomatic moves is interesting. He wrote about events on the 1st of November 1788:– "Tinah, understanding from my conversation that I intended visiting some of the other islands in the neighbourhood, very earnestly desired I would not think of leaving Matavai. 'Here' said he 'you shall be supplied plentifully with everything you want. All here are your friends and friends of King George; if you go to the other islands, you will have everything stolen from you'. I replied that on account of their goodwill and from a desire to serve him and his country, King George had sent out those valuable presents to him 'and will you not, Tinah, send something to King George in return'? 'Yes' he

---

[75] Morrison calls him "Matte", others "Tynah" or "Teina".

said 'I will send him anything I have'; and then began to enumerate the different articles in his power, among which he mentioned the breadfruit. This was the exact point in which I wished to bring the conversation, and seizing an opportunity which had every appearance of being undesigned and accidental, I told him the breadfruit trees were what King George would like; upon which he promised me a great many should be put on board, and seemed much delighted to find it so easily in his power to send anything, that would be well received by King George".

On the 2nd of November, Bligh set up a shore camp on what was called Point Venus and he put Fletcher Christian in charge of the party of seven of the crew, the Botanist and Botanist's Assistant.

Pilfering was still a major problem and one which could threaten the viability of the whole expedition. Bligh decided to make an example before the Chiefs of the seaman who lost a piece of equipment to pilferers. A boatkeeper, named [76] by Bligh as Alexander Smith, lost the gudgeon pin of the cutter's rudder and was given a dozen lashes. The theft of some of an officer's sheets went unpunished, probably because it was unclear who was responsible for allowing this. Matthew Thompson was however given a dozen lashes for "insolence and disobedience of orders" on the 5th of December.

Bligh had to spend considerable time with the Regent to ensure that diplomatic relations were kept as friendly as possible. He was invited by Tinah to a "heiva" or dance involving four men and two girls and he comments "this lasted half an hour and consisted of wanton gestures and motions...".

The Carpenter, William Purcell, was still causing Bligh trouble. He refused to cut grinding stones which Bligh wanted to give to the natives to sharpen their hatchets, because Purcell said it would damage his chisel. Bligh had him confined for a day.

On the two nights following the 5th of December, there were gales at Matavai. There was no damage to the ship or shore camp, but Bligh was warned that further gales could be expected at that time of year. He decided that a move to Oparre three miles from Point Venus was required to reduce risk of damage to "Bounty".

---

[76] Admiralty Ships Logs, Supplementary 2nd Series, No 151, PRO

On the 9th of December Thomas Huggan, the Surgeon, died in an alcoholic coma. Although Bligh had confiscated his alcohol store, he had clearly found means to continue his drinking.

The move to Oparre took place on Christmas Day and involved taking the breadfruit plants in more than 700 pots of which 302 had had to be replaced. The launch was leading "Bounty" into Oparre when an officer in charge of the launch, unnamed in the official log, and John Fryer, the Master, allowed "Bounty" to come between the launch and the wind. This becalmed the launch and left "Bounty" undirected before it ran aground. Bligh would not have been amused with either Fryer or Christian, the officer in charge of the launch. "Bounty" was safely floated off into deeper water, after a further incident in which anchor cables became entangled.

On the 27th of December, William Muspratt received twelve lashed for "neglect of duty" soon after arrival at Oparre. On the 29th of December, Robert Lamb, the Butcher, received twelve lashes for loss of his cleaver. Tinah managed to recover the cleaver and agreed that islanders should receive the same punishment which Bligh gave to his crew.

James Morrison wrote of troubles, as he saw it, in the market for hogs in December: "The market for hogs beginning now to slacken Mr Bligh seized on all that came to the ship, big and small, dead or alive, taking them as his property, and seizing them as the ship's allowance at one pound per man per day. He also seized on those belonging to the master, and killed them for the Ship's use,... and when the master spoke to him, telling him the hogs were his property, he told him that 'He Mr Bligh would convince him that evry thing was his, as soon as it was on board, and that he would take ninetenths of any man's property and let him see who dared say anything to the contrary', those of the seamen were seized without ceremony, and it became a favour for a man to get a pound extra of his own hog."

"The natives observing that the hogs were seized as soon as they came on board, and not knowing but that they would be seized from them, as well as the people (the crew), became very shy of bringing a hog in sight of Lieut. Bligh, either on board or on shore, and watched all opportunities when on shore to bring provisions to their friends, but as Mr Bligh observed this and saw that his

1st Breadfruit Voyage – On Otaheite (Tahiti)

diligence was like to be evaded he ordered a book to be kept in the bittacle wherein the mate of the watch was to insert the numbers of hogs or pigs with the weight of each that came into the ship to remedy this, the natives took another method which was cutting the pigs up and wrapping them in leaves and covering the meat with breadfruit in the baskets and sometimes with peel'd cocoanuts, by which means, as the bread was never seized, they were a match for all his industry and never suspected their artifice". Bligh replied [77]: "The curing of pork and everything respecting it is particularly explained to the Admiralty in Captain Bligh's Log Books and it is particularly mentioned to their lordships that the ship's companies under his command were supplied with everything to the amount allowed them, except liquor, by his influence with the natives of Otaheite during the ship's stay there... Besides all this every man's friend was bringing him roasted hogs every day and when they bought live ones as I could not permit them to run about the ship, the person who they were brought to always went to the Gunner (who purchased for the whole) and of him they received the market price which at that time was considered no less a favor than an indulgence to them."

"To prevent the people getting the hogs a book was kept in the binnacle for the officer of the watch to enter every hog that was brought on board and, no one could consider this against the ships comp^y (company), by this means every person knew the number received – Captain Bligh declares it was for no other motive but curiosity to ascertain the number of hogs received to show the supply the country gave them".

On the 5th of January 1789, Charles Churchill, Master at Arms, William Muspratt, Steward, and John Millward, Able Seaman, went missing [78]. Morrison gets his dates wrong here, by putting this event on the 24th of January.

The three deserters stole an arms chest and then the small cutter.

Desertion at this time [79] was a capital offence spelt out as "Death or such other punishment as the circumstances of the offence shall deserve".

---

[77] "Remarks on Morrison's Journal" ML Safe 1/43.
[78] Admiralty Ships Logs, Supplementary 2nd Series No 151, p 143 PRO
[79] MacArthur 1813, Vol i p 330 Article XVI.

The Mate of the Watch when this happened was Thomas Hayward, Midshipman. Bligh writes: "Had the Mate of the Watch been awake no trouble of this kind would have happened – I therefore disrated and turned him before the Mast. Such neglectful and worthless petty officers I believe never was in a ship as are in this. No orders for a few hours together are Obeyed by them and their conduct in general is so bad that no confidence or trust can be reposed in them – in short, they have drove me to everything but Corporal punishment and that must follow if they do not improve".

Bligh had to handle sometimes difficult relationships with the local inhabitants. The incident involving the taboo associated with the Tutuee tree is a good example. An unnamed officer at the shore camp had taken a branch of the tree to the tent and also fastened it to a post, presumably to keep out intruders. The islanders to whom the tree was taboo were insulted by this usage and stopped trading with the crew of "Bounty". Bligh negotiated with Tinah to remove the taboo and resume trade.

On the 16th of January 1789, a native accomplice of the three deserters visited "Bounty" when Bligh was on shore. Fryer, the Master, was unable to detain him and the man jumped overboard to escape.

The next day, Bligh writes [80]: "This morning, the sail room being cleared to take the sails on shore to air. The new fore top sail and fore sail, main topm^t (top mast) stay sail and main stay sail were found very much mildewed and rotten in many places... If I had any officers to supercede the Master and Boatswain or was capable of doing without them, considering them as common seaman, they should no longer occupy their respective stations. Scarce any neglect of duty can equal the criminality of this, for it appears that alth' the sails have been taken out twice since I have been in the Island, which I thought fully sufficient, and I had trusted to their reports, yet these new sails never were brought out or it is certain whether they have been out since we left England, yet notwithstanding as often as the sails were taken to air by my orders, they were reported to me to be in good order".

I profoundly disagree with Hough [81] in his understanding of senior management and delegation, when he writes "a basic tenet

---

[80] Admiralty Ships Logs Supplementary Series No 151 p 160 PRO
[81] "Captain Bligh and Mr Christian" R Hough Ch 5 p 128 (1972)

1st Breadfruit Voyage – On Otaheite (Tahiti)

of leadership which Bligh never learned is that you never delegate responsibility".

In this case, Bligh had reasonably delegated responsibility for these tasks to the correct level. The fact that the warrant officers failed to discharge this responsibility does not invalidate Bligh's original decision. Of course, Bligh was still "accountable" for the Voyage and for the ship. His anger is quite understandable.

"Bounty's" log on the 23rd of January 1789 records the arrest of the three deserters. Bligh received intelligence about the deserters from the Chiefs. The deserters left the island on which they were hiding, but were then secured by natives. The deserters however broke their word and escaped. Bligh left "Bounty" and went after them. He tracked them down and finally arrested them. Bligh decided on summary punishment rather than taking them back to England for Court Martial.

Hayward was publicly rebuked on the 23rd of January, but the log the next day records "it is an unpleasant thing to remark that no feelings of honour or sense of shame is to be Observed in such an Offender".

We know from Morrison [82] that Hayward had a native friend or "tyo" called Wyetooa, who was in fact Tinah's younger brother. If Hayward had been flogged as well as the three deserters, Wyetooa, who was armed with a club among those watching the punishment, had planned to kill Bligh. It is significant therefore that Bligh had no marines for his protection. Hayward was put in irons but not flogged.

On the 26th of January, the three deserters wrote to Bligh thanking him for his decision of summary punishment rather than confining them for a Court Martial "the fatal consequences of which are obvious". By their letter, they hoped that Bligh would remit the rest of the punishment, a second flogging, due on the 14th of February.

Soon after the first flogging of the deserters, Isaac Martin, the American Able Seaman, was involved in a fight with a native whom he suspected of stealing. For this breach of the "rules of conduct", Bligh was proposing twenty four lashes but reduced this to nineteen on the intercession of the Chiefs, including Tinah.

---

[82] Morrison Journal p 101a ML Safe 1/42

The three deserters did not have the rest of their punishment remitted and were reflogged on the 14th of February. Thomas Hayward remained still in irons, presumably because he showed no remorse.

Morrison tells [83] us that Hayward's "tyo" Wyetooa, had "the Bounty's" cable cut or rather two or three strands of it" because he was angry at Hayward's confinement in irons. He was prepared to have the ship wrecked "to get his friend out of Mr Bligh's power". Bligh was unaware of the perpetrator of this act at the time and did not suspect that the person with this animosity towards him was so close to Tinah.

On the 27th of February 1789, the log indicates that David Nelson, the Botanist, forecast that the breadfruit plants would be ready for transportation in a month's time, that is, at the end of the rainy season; it was also when trade winds would be favourable for the return.

Further thefts were noted in the log on the 2nd of March, namely an empty water cask, part of an azimuth compass and the bedding of Mr Peckover's hammock. These were stolen from the shore camp. The cask and relevant part of a compass were recovered by the Chiefs, who demanded that Bligh take the life of the thief. Bligh refused that demand but negotiated a severe flogging of a hundred lashes and agreement to keep the offender as a hostage.

During the Watch in which George Stewart, Midshipman, was Mate of the Watch on the 7th of March, the hostage broke out of his irons and escaped although Stewart did go in pursuit. Bligh wrote: "I have given Written orders that the Mate of the Watch was to be answerable for the Prisoners and to visit and see that they were safe in his Watch, but I have such a neglectful set about me that I believe nothing but condign punishment can alter their conduct. Verbal orders in the course of a Month were so forgot that they would impudently assert no such (orders) or directions were given and I have been at last under the necessity to trouble myself with writing what by decent Young Officers would be complied with as the Common Rules of the Service – Mr Stewart was the mate of the watch".

---

[83] Ibid

1st Breadfruit Voyage – On Otaheite (Tahiti)

Kennedy appears to me to exaggerate when he writes [84]: "The necessity for written orders to the midshipmen is the surest sign there could be of Bligh's collapsed authority and of the dangerous slackness and indifference that was everywhere in the ship". Bligh's authority certainly hadn't collapsed and he was challenging any slackness or indifference as soon as it manifested itself in a situation hardly conducive to efficiency and naval discipline.

On the 23rd of March 1789, Mr Hayward was released from irons and re-rated Midshipman which must have been much to the satisfaction of his "tyo".

Two days later, Bligh managed to obtain the restoration of a mat and a piece of cloth which the Master, John Fryer, had taken from the native woman staying with him. This dispute had resulted in the relatives of the woman assaulting William Peckover in the course of his commercial dealings and putting "Bounty's" trading at risk.

In exactly a month from the date of Nelson's prediction, breadfruit plants began to be moved from the shore camp to "Bounty". The crew were at the same time told to restrict their acquisitions to the contents of each person's sea chest. On the same day, the 27th of March, Tinah gave Bligh two "parais" or mourning dresses for King George, while Bligh gave Tinah two muskets and one thousand rounds of ammunition as a present. The loading of the 1015 breadfruit was complete on the 1st of April; however, the weather was not suitable for leaving. On the 3rd of April, Tinah and Iddeah dined on board; Bligh writes: "In the evening there was no dancing or mirth on the beach such as we had been accustomed to, but all was silent".

It is important [85] to understand, as Lawrence Lebogue, the Sailmaker, later testified at the Guildhall, London, that Fletcher Christian "had a girl who was always with him". Joseph Coleman, the Armourer, testified: "...I remember Christian having a girl, and of her going with him to the island Tobooy and lived with him...". John Smith, the Commander's Cook, also testified "...I never told Mr Edward Christian that his brother never kept a girl, for I remember he had a girl, and she was called 'Tittriano's girl' which was the name Christian went by...".

---

[84] "Bligh" Gavin Kennedy Ch 11 1978.
[85] "An Answer to Certain Assertions..." Wm Bligh No XI, XII and XIII 1794.

Her name was "Mauatua" [86], or "Mauatea", a chief's daughter, whom Christian called "Isabella". She was tall and was later given a nickname "Mainmast" or "Mi'mitti". About a month before she died in 1841 she told George Gardner [87] of HMS Curaçao that she remembered Captain Cook at Tahiti and had then been a mother. It is likely that she was referring to Cook's last visit to Otaheite in 1777, so she would have been older than Fletcher Christian but probably less than 30 years old. There is neither reference to the father of her child nor to the child in other sources. She was however able to give her time to Fletcher Christian.

Christian was then twenty four years old, about 5ft 9ins in height and had been tattooed [88] in native fashion with a star on his left breast and another tattoo on his backside. This blackening of the entire buttocks was a sign of an initiated Polynesian male. "Bounty" had been at Otaheite for just over five months.

On the 4th of April 1789, the weather permitted "Bounty" to leave Otaheite.

---

[86] "Fragile Paradise" Glynn Christian (1982).
[87] Journal of George Gardner quoted by Glynn Christian in "Fragile Paradise".
[88] Bounty Mutineers ML Safe 1/43 p 1.

CHAPTER 7

Separation and potential loss of a loving relationship – Fletcher Christian and Mauatua

The last chapter showed that Fletcher Christian and Mauatua, daughter of a Chief, were always together and, in those blissful conditions, were likely to have developed a potentially long-term relationship.

If they did develop such a relationship we need to examine what the separation and potential loss of that relationship would have meant to Fletcher Christian. 20th century psychology, readily understandable in this instance by the general reader, enables us to use a sound scientific theory to predict at least some of the behaviour expected. I would like to distinguish theories using scientific method from those which do not, because this will have a bearing on what level of credibility the reader may give to the evidence.

A sound scientific theory is one where a hypothesis has been tested and refined against sufficient data current at that time and found to be sound. Some psychological theories do not use scientific methods. Such an unscientific theory is one where a hypothesis is supported only by some past or speculative data.

The biographer M Darby [89] followed such psychology of the latter type in believing that Fletcher Christian suffered from "paranoid delusions". She wrote: "Freud said this type of delusion could be detected from the fact that 'the person who is now hated and feared for being a persecutor was at one time loved and honoured'... Freud describes the stages by which paranoid delusions are reached: 'I love him. No, that is shameful. I don't love him; I hate him. No, that is sinful. It is he who hates me. And thus my hatred of him is justified'".

---

[89] "Who Caused the Mutiny on the Bounty" M Darby Ch 10 1965.

Before I examine a relevant sound scientific theory, I would like to draw attention to the unspecified psychological theory used [90] by Gavin Kennedy in considering Fletcher Christian's position: He writes: "The question is whether this was a hell created in Christian's mind by himself or by Bligh. I am in favour of the first view and there are various pressures we can point to which could have upset an unstable young man. One is his forced parting from his Tahitian woman 'Isabella'... And we have to think of what he had come back to; a thickening atmosphere of distrust, arguments and breakdown of authority and a changed Bligh who had lost faith in the promising young officer he had promoted... It is this book's hypothesis that the mutiny is best explained by the coincidence of the collapse in the authority of the commander and an emotional storm in an immature and possibly mentally unstable young man".

The following theory does not require us to assume that Fletcher Christian is either immature or of a mentally unstable make-up, nor does it require an assumption that there was a collapse in the authority of the commander prior to the mutiny. Nor does it require us to assume that Bligh is a persecutor. A sound scientific theory [91] of a four phase reaction to loss or potential loss has been developed by Bowlby and independently by Parkes. This reaction presumes the existence of a potentially long term relationship, the loss of which is feared. The first phase reaction to such loss is one of numbing, lasting up to a week. The second phase is one of yearning, pining and searching for the loved one. Each phase may oscillate with a phase next to it. The third phase is one of depression, disorganisation and despair and the last phase only emerging after somewhile is one of reorganisation or recovery.

The potential loss of a loved one arouses very intense emotion and distress and can impair one's capacity to function normally. Any frustration of searching for the loved one will result in anger, accusations and aggression against the person frustrating the search. There will be ambivalence or an oscillation between love and hate for any person held in regard but who also frustrates the searching.

---

[90] "Bligh" Gavin Kennedy Ch 13 1978.
[91] "Loss" John Bowlby Penguin Education 1981 vol iii p 85 and p 92.
"Bereavement" Colin Murray Parkes Pelican 1975 p 21.

We can therefore make predictions about Fletcher Christian, as a result of his potential loss: during the first phase we can expect disbelief and inactivity; during the second phase, we can expect searching, expressions of strong emotion, distress, anger, accusation and aggression against his Captain; during the third phase, which may oscillate with the second, we can expect extreme discomfort, hopelessness and despair to be expressed by Christian. We have no need to explore predictions of the fourth phase, because the loved one was recovered and was no longer lost.

Christian thought that Matthew Quintal was the only one of the seamen who had formed a serious attachment [92] at Otaheite by the time of the Mutiny.

The term "grieving" may be used to describe the first three phases of the reaction to loss or potential loss.

Whereas non-scientific psychological theories are sometimes ridiculed as "psycho-babble", such ridicule cannot be levelled at sound scientific psychological theories.

In the next chapters, we will need to see how the predictions of modern scientific psychological theory match up to what actually happened.

---

[92] "Narrative of a Voyage to the Pacific" Captain F W Beechey 1831.

CHAPTER 8

Preliminaries to the Mutiny in "Bounty"
4.4.1789 – 28.4.1789.

After leaving Otaheite on the 4th of April 1789, "Bounty" sailed close to the island of Huaheine and took part in some minor trading. On the 11th of April, they discovered a new island Whytootachee now called Aitutaki in the Cook Islands.

The next day, John Sumner was found to be in "neglect of duty" and the log records that he received 12 lashes. Between that date and the 22nd of April, there was little to report; Morrison speaks generally of "high spirits".

On the 23rd of April [93] 1790, "Bounty" reached Annamooka, (also called Nomuka), in the Friendly Islands. The log reported: "The Bower Buoy was seen to be sinking, and for want of a little exertion in Mr Elphinston, the mate, in getting into a boat to get hold of it, it went down".

Bligh's log book records what happened to two parties sent out to collect wood and water: "Those a-watering under the command of Mr Christian and consisting of 11 men and the wooders under the direction of Mr Elphinston, mate of the ship, consisting of four men... To these people I not only gave my orders, but my advice; that they were to keep themselves unconnected with the natives; they however had not been an hour on shore before one man had lost his ax and the other an adz. The cause of this was that the officer (Fletcher Christian), contrary to my direct orders, suffered the Indians to croud around them and amuse them and by that

---

[93] Discrepancies between sources of 1 day arise from use of the standard clock beginning midnight and the maritime clock beginning midday cf "Narrative ..." W Bligh p11 1790.

means the theft was committed... As to the officers I have no resource, or do I ever feel myself safe in the few instances I trust to them..."

Morrison's account of the same incident is that the natives were "so troublesome that Mr Christian, who had command of the watering party, found it difficult to carry on his duty; he informed Lieut Bligh of this, who damn'd him for a cowardly rascal, asking him if he was afraid of a set of naked Savages while he had arms; to which Mr Christian answer'd 'the arms are no use while your orders prevent them from being used'."

Bligh was sufficiently relaxed to observe and write in his log about the sailing canoes at Annamooka. He said that on the largest canoe ninety people had been counted.

On the 26th of April, Mr Fryer had been sent by Bligh to help Christian in his supervision of the watering party, but further thefts took place with Mr Fryer, the Master, losing a grapnel from a boat and Mr Nelson a spade. The latter article was returned later. Bligh wrote: "I secretly determined to confine two after I got under way until the grapnel should be returned".

Morrison [94] continues after the confinement: "At this the chiefs seemed much displeased and were ordered down to the messroom where Mr Bligh followed them and set them to peel coco-nuts for his dinner. He then came up and dismissed all the men but two that were under arms – but not till he had passed the compliment on officers and men to tell them that they were a parcel of lubberly rascals and that he would be one of five who [would] with good sticks would disarm the whole of them and presenting a pistol at Wm McCoy threaten'd to shoot him for not paying attention –".

Bligh's later response [95] to this account is not to deny the confinement, but to deny the treatment during confinement, especially cruelty; he wrote: "To the charge – he made three chiefs peel coconuts, he replies: The folly and viciousness of this design to impute cruelty is evident – it would have been impolitic. The chiefs did no such thing, but parted with Captain Bligh very affectionately, loaded with presents".

---

[94] Morrison Journal ML p38 Safe 1/42
[95] "Remarks on Morrison's Journal" ML Safe 1/43

Bligh by Bligh

Morrison gave the initial impression that Bligh's abuse is directed at all the officers and men but he went on to put in Bligh's mouth the words "one of five who with good sticks would disarm the whole of them". This must refer to the four remaining warrant officers and himself, pointedly omitting reference to Fletcher Christian and ignoring the Midshipmen. As there were more than four Midshipmen, he could not refer to them.

Gavin Kennedy, the biographer, writes [96] of this incident: "If this is anything near true, it shows that Bligh lost his head. His position was compromised.."

The evidence does not suggest to me that Bligh lost his head or had his position compromised. He called the crew together to deliver a dressing down which was well deserved in the light of the poor implementation of orders. Bligh has to prepare his crew for the exact seamanship required to pass safely through Endeavour Straits. Some tightening up on discipline was in order.

On the 27th of April 1789, "Bounty" left Annamooka and sailed westward.

That same day, there was an incident about some coconuts. Morrison writes [97]: "In the afternoon of 27th a Number of Cocoa Nuts were missed by Mr Bligh from the Quarter Deck upon which all the officers were called and on their declaring they had not seen any person take them, he told them they were all thieves alike" footnote: "He particularly called Christian a Thief and Villain and challenged him with the Theft of the Nuts". Later Morrison wrote [98] "...'I hope you don't think me so mean as to be guilty of Stealing yours' Mr Christian answered. Mr Bligh replied 'Yes, you dam'd Hound I do ...'"

Fletcher Christian's brother, Edward, who was a Professor of Jurisprudence campaigning in 1794 to prepare mitigating circumstances in case Christian was arrested and to limit damage to his family name, wrote [99]: "The Captain ordered the officer of the

---

[96] "Bligh" Gavin Kennedy Chapter 12 1978.
[97] Morrison Memorandum ML Safe 1/33 p32/3 (1792)
This is copy of the original. There is therefore no evidence whether the footnote (see later) was added after.
[98] Morrison Journal p40/1 ML Safe 1/42
[99] Appendix p63/4 to Minutes of the Proceedings of Court Martial 12.8.1792. Stephen Barney 1794.

morning watch, Mr Christian, to be called; when he came, the Captain accosted him thus 'Damn your blood, you have stolen my cocoa nuts'. Christian answered 'I was dry and I thought it of no consequence, I took one only, and I am sure no one touched another'. Bligh then replied 'You lie, you scoundrel, you have stolen one half'".

Fryer's Journal which was written well after these events as it has reference to Bligh's narrative of 1790, but before Morrison wrote his Memorandum, says [100] that Bligh threatened to reduce the allowance of "1½ lbs of yams (sweet potatoes) to ¾ lb, if he did not find out who took the nuts". Fryer does not mention Christian here at all.

Bligh replied [101] later "When the ship sailed from Annamooka and every part of the ship was filled wth (with) yams – see the evidence in the Court Martial when all declare the boats were full and obliged to be cleared before they could be hoisted out -. A heap of cocoa nuts were between the guns under the charge of the officers of the watch with orders for no one to touch them untill the ship was clear of the land, when they could be issued equally and considered highly refreshing, without which caution some would have and waste half and others would have none."

"In one night -the first- the officers permitted the whole within a score to be taken away. As this was evidently done through design, Captain Bligh ordered all the cocoa nuts to be replaced – the officers of the watch declared they were taken away by stelth – here was a publick theft, a contumacy, and direct disobedience of orders – the particular offenders could not be found out, any more than had been effected in private thefts which has been frequently committed; could therefore either the epithet thief or villain, had it been used, have justified their taking the ship next day".

Richard Hough suggests [102] that the evidence mounts that Bligh was seized by a form of paranoia which manifested itself in violent outbreaks against his officers in general and Fletcher Christian in particular and that Bligh's madness infected first Christian and in a diminished degree his other officers.

---

[100] (Ed) Owen Rutter 1934, including Fryer's Journal.
[101] "Remarks on Morrison's Journal" Bligh Bounty Mutineers ML Safe 1/43
[102] "Captain Bligh and Mr Christian" R Hough Ch 7 1972

Bligh was certainly easily provoked by inefficiency and particularly by theft of goods for which he was responsible. His language was, under such circumstances, highly abusive, but I do not find evidence to justify the term "paranoia". Hough in the same chapter does draw attention to important evidence that Fletcher Christian started giving away mementos which he had bought at Annamooka.

Edward Christian, Fletcher's brother, gives us some important evidence [103] about later that day. He obtained this evidence in 1793 from William Purcell, "Bounty's" Carpenter, who had been reprimanded at his Court Martial in 1790 on charges laid by Bligh. Purcell said that there was another row between Fletcher Christian and Bligh at 4pm that afternoon and, following that, Christian had "tears running fast from his eyes in big drops". Purcell is said by Edward Christian to have had the following conversation the day before the mutiny with Fletcher who said: "You have something to protect you and can speak again; but if I should speak to him as you do, he would probably break me, turn me before the mast and perhaps flog me; and if he did it would be the death of us both, for I am sure I should take him in my arms and jump overboard with him".

Edward Christian also quotes other unnamed witnesses as saying that Fletcher Christian exclaimed "I would rather die ten thousand deaths than bear this treatment" and "That flesh and blood cannot bear this treatment".

In the early evening, Bligh thought first to send an invitation to Christian to join him for supper as normal. Christian declined, saying that he was unwell.

Morrison gives [104] us some interesting details of his account of what happened later that evening: "finding himself much hurt by the treatment he (Fletcher Christian) had received from Mr Bligh, he had determined to quit the ship the preceeding evening, and informed the boatswain, carpenter, Mr Stuart (Stewart) and Mr Hayward of his resolution, who supplied him with some nails, beads and part of a roasted pig with some other articles, which he

---

[103] Appendix p64/5 to Minutes of the Proceedings of Court Martial 12.8.1792. Stephen Barney 1794

[104] Morrison Journal ML Safe 1/42

put into a bag which he got from Mr Hayward. The bag was put into the clue of Rob't Tinkler's hammock, where he found it at night; but the matter was then smothered and pass'd off – he also made fast some staves to a stout plank which lay on the larboard gangway, with which he intended to make his escape; but finding he could not effect it in the first and middle watches, as the people were all a-stirring, he went to sleep about half past three in the morning."

Morrison adds when writing about events the next day: "I then recollected seeing him make the staves fast to the plank the night before and hearing the boatswain say to the carpenter 'It won't do tonight' and afterwards seeing Mr Stuart and Mr Christian several times up and down the fore cockpit where the boatswain and carpenters cabbins were and where Mr C seldom or ever went".

Edward Christian confirms [105] that Fletcher asked Purcell, the Carpenter, for some planks, rope and nails to make a raft; he also confirms [106] that Fletcher told Stewart of this plan.

As James Morrison was trying to discredit the evidence of Thomas Hayward, Midshipman, and to protect the interests of Peter Heywood who was also on trial for his life at the time Morrison was preparing his Memorandum, we need to look critically as to whether Thomas Hayward had been told of Christian's plan and whether he contributed towards Christian's plan for desertion.

Fryer's Journal confirms [107] that Robert Tinkler, Fryer's brother-in-law, found the piece of roast pork.

Christian's plan was also confirmed by Captain Beechey in his account [108] signed by Alexander Smith in 1825: "His plan... was to set himself adrift upon a raft and make his way to the island (Tofoa) then in sight..."

It is difficult to conceive the danger which this plan would have involved for Christian. These were shark infested waters and even

---

[105] Appendix p65 to Minutes of the Proceedings of Court Martial 12.8.1792. Stephen Barney 1794
[106] ibid Appendix p71
[107] (Ed) Owen Rutter 1934
[108] "Narrative of Voyage to the Pacific" F W Beechey 1831

if he reached the island of Tofoa on a plank, he could not be sure of survival, if the natives were hostile. Bligh himself wrongly considered [109] the story as ridiculous.

It will be helpful to make a preliminary summary of those aspects of Christian's behaviour which are relevant to the theory considered in the last chapter.

There is so far no evidence relevant either to support or contest the first phase, lasting up to a week in which the person suffering a loss or potential loss of an established loving relationship feels "numb". There is evidence that Christian was later not fully on top of his job and that Bligh sent John Fryer, the Master, to help in supervision.

There is much evidence of the second phase of "yearning and searching". Christian made a plan to return to his loved one by planning to leave the ship on a mere plank of wood, using staves as paddles in a shark infested sea, aiming to reach an island about thirty miles away where, as we shall see later, the natives were basically hostile.

His expressions of emotion, "I would rather die ten thousand deaths than bear this treatment" quoted by Edward Christian, are more extreme than could be accounted for by Bligh's occasional abuse. There is also some evidence of Fletcher Christian showing some signs of despair – a component of phase three: He gave away mementos which he had obtained at Annamooka island, while the plan to return to his loved one was a desperate one under such conditions.

In the next chapter on the Mutiny, we will notice further evidence supporting the theory and confirming that Fletcher Christian was believing that he was losing his established relationship with Mauatua, his "Isabella".

---

[109] "Remarks on Morrison's Journal" Bligh/Bounty Mutineers ML – Safe 1/43 p51.

CHAPTER 9

The Mutiny in "Bounty"
28.4.1789.

The Articles of War were read out to the ship's company at least every week by the Captain of the vessel, in this case Lieutenant Bligh. The following two articles are relevant [110]:

Article XIX: "If any person in or belonging to the fleet shall make, or endeavour to make, any mutinous assembly, upon any pretence whatsoever, every person offending herein, and being convicted thereof by the sentence of the court martial, shall suffer death." Article XX: "If any person in the fleet shall conceal any traitorous or mutinous practice, or design, being convicted thereof by the sentence of the court martial, he shall suffer death, or such punishment as a court martial shall think fit".

The knowledge that mutiny or concealment of mutinous design was a capital offence would have been well known therefore to "Bounty's" crew.

In the last chapter, we left Fletcher Christian going to sleep at 3.30am, but his watch was due to begin at 4am. Morrison tells [111] us: "When Mr Stuart call'd him to relieve the Watch he had not Slept long, and was much out of order, and Stuart beg'd him not to attempt swimming away, saying 'the people are ripe for anything', this made a forceable impression on his mind and finding that Mr Hayward, the mate of his watch – with whom he refused to discourse – soon went to sleep on the arm chest which stood between the guns and Mr Hallet not making his appearance, he at once resolved to seize the ship and disclosing his intention to Quintrell (Quintal) and Martin...".

---

[110] MacArthur 1813 Vol 1 Appendix 1 p332.
[111] Morrisons Journal p46. ML Safe 1/42

Christian later told Peter Heywood and George Stewart that when Stewart came to relieve the watch on the morning of the mutiny "his brain seemed to be on fire".

Certainly his mental state was complex; the agony of the threatened loss of his loved one, the ambivalence of his relationship to Bligh, the exhilaration of mutinous action and tiredness from too little sleep.

At some stage, [112] Christian planned to do away with himself, if the Mutiny was unsuccessful; he deliberately concealed a lead weight beneath his clothing to cause drowning if he jumped overboard.

From a later source [113], but one signed by Alexander Smith, we learn that Christian spoke first to Quintal whom he thought was the only one of the seamen who had formed a serious attachment at Otaheite, about the idea. Quintal thought the action too dangerous and refused to take part. Christian accused him of cowardice but Quintal denied it. Christian then put the idea to Isaac Martin, the American, who replied "I am for it, it is the very thing". Christian was then in a position to approach others. Other sources say that Martin refused to take part, while it was Quintal who cooperated with Christian.

Morrison continues [114] the story: "they call'd up Churchill and Thompson, who put the business in practice and with Smith, William(s) and McCoy he went to Coleman and demanded the keys of the arms chest – which Coleman, the Armourer, always kept- saying he wanted a musquet to shoot a shark which happened to come alongside; and finding Mr Hallet asleep on the arm chest he roused him and sent him on deck, the keys were instantly procured and his party arm'd...". Christian then accompanied by his armed followers, went to arrest the Midshipmen, Hayward and Hallet, and to secure the arms chest on deck. Hayward had been sleeping on this arms chest, as Morrison noted, but Norman had woken him to look at a shark.

---

[112] "Who caused the mutiny on 'the Bounty'?" M Darby Ch 11 1965
[113] "Narrative of a Voyage to the Pacific" Captain F W Beechey 1831
[114] Morrison Journal ML Safe 1/42

Bligh wrote: "Just before sunrise, Mr Christian and the master at arms (Charles Churchill) and several others – (a marginal note in his log states: Fletcher Christian, Chas Churchill, Thos Burkitt, Jno Mills, Alexander Smith, Jno Sumner, Matthew Quintal assisted under arms on the outside) came into my Cabbin while I was fast a Sleep and seizing me tyed my hands with a Cord and threatened instant death if I made the least noise. I however called sufficiently loud to alarm the officers, who found themselves equally secured by Centinels at their Doors – there were now three men at my cabbin door and four inside. Mr Christian had a cutlass and the others were armed with Musquets and Bayonets. I was now carried on Deck in my Shirt, in torture with a severe bandage round my wrists behind my back...". He adds: "The master's (Fryer's) cabbin was opposite to mine – he saw them in my cabbin for our eyes met each other through his door window, and he had a pair of ship's pistols loaded with ammunition in his cabbin. A firm resolution might have made good use of them.... After he (Fryer) had sent twice or thrice to Christian to be allowed to come on deck, he was at last permitted and his question to Christian then was 'will you let me remain in the ship?'. (Christian's answer:) 'No. Have you any objections, Cap't Bligh?'"

"I whispered to him (Fryer), 'knock him (Christian) down. Martin is good', for this was just before Martin was removed from me.... as to the pistols he (Fryer) was so flurried and surprised that he did not recollect he had them...".

Thomas Ellison left the wheel and took up a cutlass, which action was to cost him his life at the Court Martial of some of the mutineers.

In a letter to his wife, Bligh writes [115] later: "Besides this villain (Christian) see young Heywood, one of the ring leaders, and besides him see Stewart joined with him...".

Edward Christian writes [116] that Stewart was dancing and clapping in Tahitian fashion.

Christian's original plan was to set just four people – Bligh, Samuel, Hayward and Hallet – adrift in the jolly boat, but he

---

[115] Bligh – William to Betsy 19.8.1789 ML Safe 1/45

[116] Minutes of Court Martial 12.8.1792 S Barney Appendix p 72 London 1794

altered his plan and decided on ridding himself of other crew members likely to be hostile.

The log reads: "the boatswain was now ordered to hoist the small cutter out but on representation that this boat was very leaky, he was directed to hoist the launch out".

Morrison writes [117] : "Seeing Mr Bligh in his shirt with his hands tied behind him and Mr Christian standing by him with a drawn bayonet in his hand... the Lieutenant then began to reason, but Mr Christian replied 'Mamoo (silence), Sir, not a word, or death's your portion'... the boatswain and carpenter came aft – the master and gunner being confined below – and begg'd for the launch which with much hesitation was granted....".

The log records how supplies were put in the launch: "the boatswain and seamen who were to go in the boat set to work and collected canvas, twine, lines, sails and cordage and an eight and twenty gallon cask of water with four empty beakers and the carpenter got his tool chest – Mr Samuels got about 150 lbs of bread with a small quantity of rum and wine and was allowed to take a quadrant and compass into the boat, but forbad on pain of death of touching any map whatever, Ephemerise, book of astronomical observations, sextants or timekeeper, or any of my drawings or surveys".

Morrison writes [118] : "The boat was got out, when evry one ran to get what he could into her and get in themselves as fast as possible, the officers were hurry'd in as fast as possible and when Mr Bligh found he must go, he begg'd of Mr Christian to desist, saying 'I'll pawn my honor, I'll give my bond, Mr Christian, never to think of this if you'll desist' and urged his wife and family to which Mr Christian reply'd 'No, Captain Bligh, if you had any honor, things had not come to this; and if you had any regard for your wife and family, you should have thought on them before, and not behaved so much like a villain'. Lt Bligh attempted again to speak, but was ordered to be silent; the boatswain (William Cole) also try'd to pacify him to which he replied 'tis too late, I have been in hell for this fortnight passed and am determined to bear it no longer, and

---

[117] Morrison Journal ML Safe 1/42
[118] Morrison Journal ML Safe 1/42, pp 42-43

you know Mr Cole that I have been used like a dog all the voyage'. The Master beg'd to be permitted to stay, but was ordered into the boat and Mr Christian gave Churchill orders to see that no arms went into the boat. In getting things into the boat, a dispute happened between Churchill and the carpenter about the latter's tool chest, which Churchill wanted to keep in the ship, but by Mr Christian's orders it was suffered to go into the boat, but he told Churchill to keep the carpenter's mates on board and the armourer – the mast and sails were got in and all the new light canvas with nails, saws, trade and the Lieutenant's and masters cloaths, two gang casks of water, four empty breeves, 3 bags of bread and Mr Bligh's case, some bottles of wine and several other things, insomuch that she almost sunk alongside. The Lieutenant then beggd that some of the people would stay and asked Mr Christian to let the master stay with them, but he answered 'the men may stay, but the master must go with you'. Mr Bligh then said 'Never fear my lads you can't all go with me, but I'll do you justice, if ever I reach England'."

Bligh records his view of a surprising event: "Isaac Martin (the American), one of the guard, I saw I had brought to a sense of his duty, and as he fed me with a shaddock [119] – my lips being so parched in endeavouring to bring about a change in my situation – we explained to each other by our eyes reciprocally our wishes. This was however observed and Martin was instantly removed from me whose inclination then was to leave the ship, but for a threat of instant death if he did not return out of the boat..." and adds "... to the latter (Samuel) who got leave to quite his cabbin, I am indebted for securing my journals, my Commission and some material ships papers, also my uniforms and some Cloaths – with the former I had nothing to certify what I had done and my honor and character would have been in the power of calumny without a proper document to have defended it – All this was done with great resolution".

Bligh records in his log the names of the eighteen other people who went in the launch:

---

[119] Fruit like a grapefruit.

John Fryer Master
Thos Ledward Surgeon
David Nelson Botanist
Wm Peckover Gunner
Wm Cole Boatswain
Wm Purcell Carpenter
Wm Elphinston Master's Mate
Thos Hayward Midshipman
Jn° Hallet Midshipman

Jn° Norton Qu^{r}master
Peter Linkletter Qu^{r}master
Lawrence Lebogue Sailmaker
Jn° Smith AB
Thos Hall AB
Geo Simpson Qu^{r}master's Mate
Robt Tinkler AB
Robt Lamb AB
Mr Samuel Clerk

The following were kept "contrary to their inclinations": Jos^h Coleman, Armourer; Thos McIntosh, Carpenters crew and Chas Norman Carpenter's Mate. Bligh listed "Mich Byrn A.B. Fidler" among those who remained on board as pirates and under arms, but later agreed that he was kept contrary to his inclination.

Bligh was the last to leave. He records [120] the following comments and interchange of words with Christian: "Not withstanding the roughness with which I was treated the remembrance of past kindnesses produced some signs of remorse in Christian. When they were forcing me out of the ship I asked him if this treatment was a proper return for the many instances he had received of my friendship? He appeared disturbed at my question and answered with much emotion 'That Captain Bligh, that is the thing; I am in hell – I am in hell'."

Morrison adds [121] a further detail "After Mr Bligh was in the boat he begg'd for his Commission and sextant; the Commission was instantly given him with his pocket book and private journal by Mr Christian's order and he took his own sextant... and handed it into the boat... saying 'there, Captain Bligh, this is sufficient for every purpose and you know the sextant to be a good one.'"

Bligh records the bitter humour arising from his request for arms and ammunition. The mutineers said he was well acquainted with where he was going and therefore did not want them.

Four cutlasses were however dropped into the launch.

---

[120] "A Voyage to the South Sea" Wm Bligh p 161 1792
[121] Morrison Journal ML Safe 1/42

"Bounty" at first sailed WNW away from Otaheite but this was seemingly at odds with the cry of "Huzza for Otaheite" which was shouted by some of the mutineers.

Bligh's account of this last perception is confirmed by Captain Beechey's narrative signed by Alexander Smith.

Edward Christian said [122] "a short time after it had quitted the ship, Christian declared that he would readily sacrifice his own life if the persons in the launch were all safe in the ship again".

It would now be helpful to summarise those aspects of the Mutiny which correspond with Fletcher Christian's response to the potential loss of an established relationship with Mauatua.

The first phase of the theory predicted that the person suffering such a loss would suffer a period of numbness up to a week long. Morrison wrote [123] that Christian said that he had been "in hell for this fortnight past". A fortnight before the Mutiny is about a week after "the Bounty" left Otaheite. This confirms that Christian began to feel acute distress about a week after he left Mauatua. This was a week before Bligh rebuked Christian at Annamooka. Bligh records Christian as saying "I am in hell" but Bligh seems to have thought then that Christian's distress was due to emotional distress at betraying his Captain, but that was only part of the story. John Fryer gave evidence on the 22nd of October 1790 at Bligh's Court Martial on the loss of "Bounty" that Christian said that "he had been in hell for a week", but Fryer thought that Christian's distress was due to the rebukes which Christian received a week before on Annamooka. Later, Fryer inconsistently and maliciously attributed the following words to Christian speaking with Bligh "I have been in hell for weeks with you". Morrison seems to have recorded what was said without explanation or understanding, but it turns out to be important evidence towards confirming the first phase of "numbness" in this case.

The second phase of "yearning and searching" was well illustrated in the last chapter with Christian planning to go back in search of his loved one by means of a plank and a few stays as paddles. Morrison wrote "Stewart begg'd him (Christian) not to

---

[122] Minutes of Court Martial 12.8.1792 Appendix S. Barney London 1794.
[123] Morrison Journal ML Safe 1/42

attempt swimming away". Clearly Christian's messmate thought that the plan of using a plank was no better than swimming in shark infested waters and amounted to a counsel of despair.

There is much evidence to show Christian's anger and aggression in the face of Bligh's implementation of the purposes of the voyage which frustrated Christian's search for and desire to return to his loved one. Christian uses the unspecific abuse of the word "villain" in expressing his anger against Bligh and he exaggerates the treatment and entirely distorts his position vis-a-vis Bligh in the words "used like a dog all the voyage". On the matter of aggression, Christian at an early stage in the Mutiny secured the arms chest and used the threat of arms against the officers and loyal crew members. He threatened Bligh's life: "... not a word, or death's your portion". However, there are many signs of Christian's ambivalent attitude to Bligh and those crew members loyal to Bligh. Christian agreed to the use of the launch rather than the cutter which was in a dangerous condition. He agreed that a wide variety of supplies, not immediately required for "Bounty", should be put in the launch. He overruled Churchill in his argument with Purcell over whether the Carpenter's tool chest should go in the launch, while insisting that the Carpenter's Mates and the Armourer should remain in "Bounty".

He allowed Bligh his journals, his Commission and his uniform, but he insisted that all maps remained for his own use. Of particular importance was the gift of his own sextant to Bligh. As the launch was leaving, four cutlasses were dropped into the boat but this may not have been on the instructions of Christian.

The third phase of the theory is concerned with "disorganisation and despair". We noted previously that Bligh on Annamooka sent Fryer to support Fletcher Christian in his supervision as Christian was not functioning as efficiently as Bligh might have expected. We noted also the oscillation or substitution between the phases. The third phase is well illustrated by the incident in which Christian tied a lead weight beneath his shirt to ensure his own destruction in case of the failure of mutiny. His plan to use a plank to reach an island about thirty miles away in shark infested waters was, as we have seen, a counsel of despair.

There is therefore good evidence to support the three phases of the scientific psychological theory of the reactions to separation and potential loss of an established loving relationship.

It is relevant that Fletcher Christian chose to approach Matthew Quintal first among all others because he thought Quintal alone among the crew had developed a serious attachment.

It is also relevant that Fletcher Christian continued to use the Tahitian word for silence "Mamoo" even when talking to Bligh more than three weeks after leaving Otaheite.

The case is overwhelming that Fletcher Christian was suffering the pangs of the potential loss of his loved one and of the ambivalence of both having a regard for and antipathy against Bligh and those crew members supporting the Captain. He was also exhilarated by the Mutiny in spite of being particularly short of sleep. The Mutiny is explainable in these terms, without having to presume that Bligh was cruel.

Fletcher Christian had been faced by a terrible dilemma. "Hell on earth" may be described, by George Meredith for instance, as the betrayal of a loved one, or again may be described as betrayal of a friend. Fletcher Christian had to choose between betrayal of a loved one and betrayal of a friend; either way he was in hell. It was not however an entirely free choice, because the psychological attachment to his loved one was more potent, leading to the betrayal of his friend and patron.

CHAPTER 10

The Epic open boat voyage to Timor
28.4.1789 – 14.6.1789

The launch into which Lieutenant Bligh and eighteen of the crew had been set adrift had a design capacity of only fifteen. Its dimensions were 23 ft long, 2 ft 9 ins deep, and 6 ft 9 ins wide at its maximum. It was overloaded to within 7 inches of the gunwhale; the supplies included 150 lbs of biscuit, 16 pieces of pork @ 2 lbs per piece, 6 quarts of rum, 6 bottles of wine and 28 gallons of water.

In the face of the disaster of losing his ship, it is interesting to read in the log of Bligh's reaction: "I had scarce got a furlong on our way when I began to reflect on the vicissitudes of human affairs; but in the midst of all I felt an inward happyness and peculiar pleasure which prevented any depression of my spirits; conscious of my own integrity and anxious solicitute for the good of the service I was on. I found my mind most wonderfully supported and began to conceive hopes notwithstanding so heavy a calamity to be able to account to my King and country for my misfortune...".

Making for the island of Tofoa the smoke from whose volcano could be seen above the horizon, the launch reached the island by 7pm that evening. A landing was made next morning but food and water were not easy to obtain. On the 2nd of May, an increasing number of natives began to appear and some tried to draw the launch ashore until Bligh brandished a cutlass. After having a meal with some chiefs, Bligh retired to the launch as natives began knocking stones together preparatory to an attack by about two hundred natives. John Norton, the quartermaster was killed as he attempted to return to free the mooring rope of the launch. Some clothes were thrown overboard to distract the pursuers until the chase was given up.

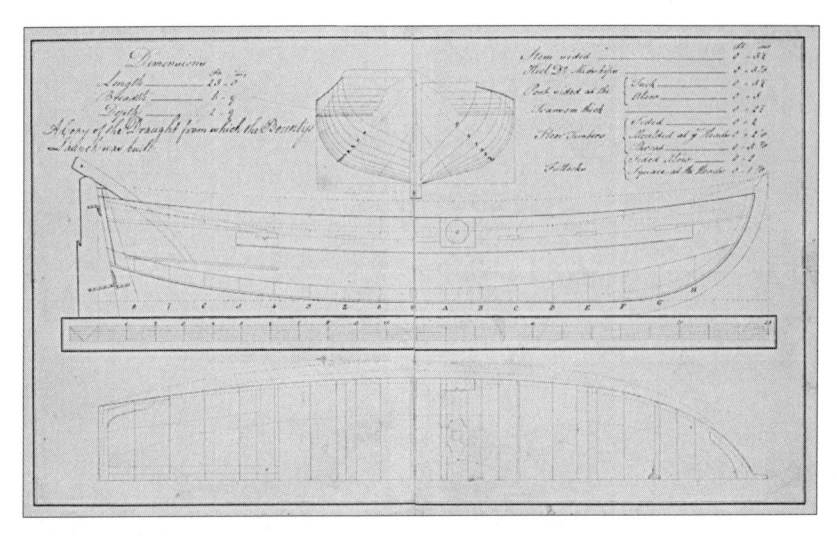

"Bounty" launch Plans
Kind permission of the Mitchell Library, State Library of New South Wales

Bligh decided against a visit to another island Tongataboo after this experience. He discussed the situation with the crew of the launch and all agreed to stretch out provisions normally appropriate for five days to eight weeks. Bligh estimated a distance to Timor as 1200 leagues or 3600 miles, a very accurate estimate considering he had no charts.

The allowance [124] of bread amounted to the equivalent weight of one pistol ball three times a day, (twenty five pistol balls weighed one pound), while water amounted to a quarter of a pint per day.

The morning after leaving the island of Tofoa, the sky was red and warned of bad weather. High seas broke over the stern of the launch causing much exertion in baling and leaving everyone in soaked clothing. Nights were cold.

On the 4th and 5th of May, the launch reached uncharted parts of what are now the Fiji Islands. Without arms, it would have been foolhardy to attempt a landing. A Historian of Fiji explains [125] why: "... on its high volcanic peaks were always sentinels watching for

---

[124] "A Narrative..." William Bligh 1790.
[125] "The Hill tribes of Fiji". A B Brewster 1922

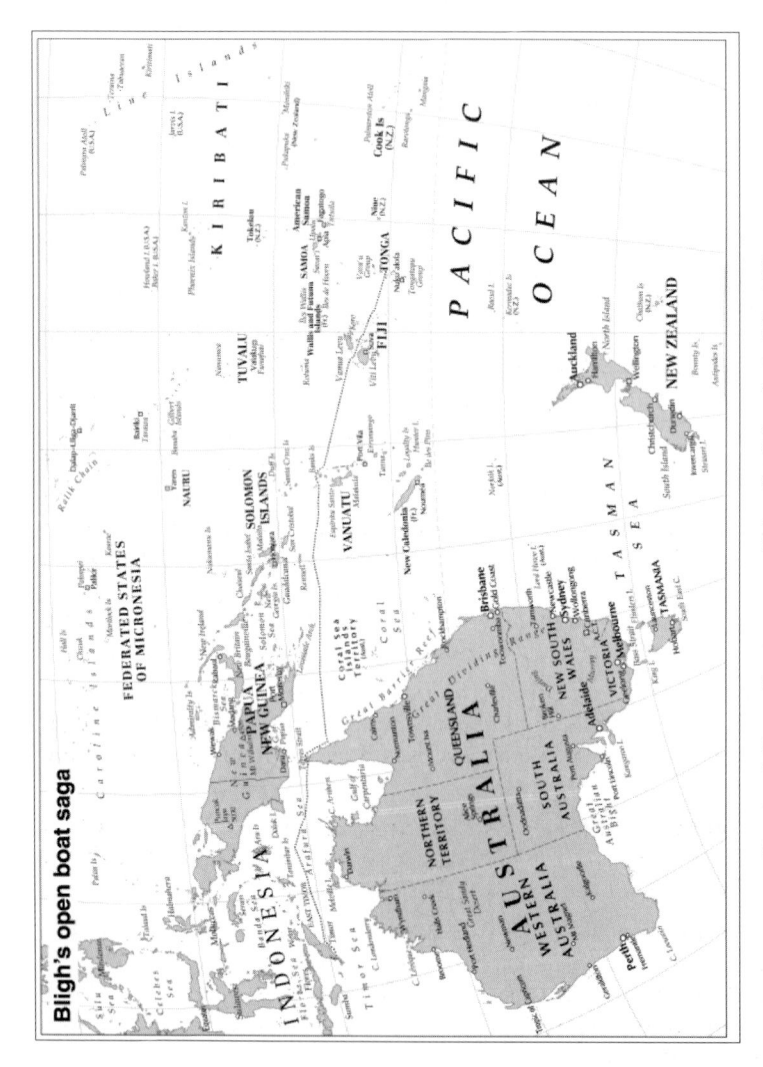

Route of Open Boat saga – Friendly Islands to West Timor
© Bartholemew Ltd. 2000. Reproduced by permission of Harper Collins Publishers

The Epic open boat voyage to Timor

canoes or other craft in distress. Such were lawful prey 'those with salt water in their eyes' being doomed by the ancient law to the bamboo knives, the heated stone oven and the cannibal maw...". The historian adds: "For many years I was a Stipendiary Magistrate for that part of the island and the chart ('Voyage'... W Bligh 1792) is a perfect sketch of that particular spot and corresponds accurately with the ordnance map".

The launch was pursued by two large sailing canoes but managed to escape.

Bad weather continued and, on the 11th of May, seas broke right over the launch. They were close to catastrophe. By the 20th of May, signs of extreme hunger were evident. On 21st May, Bligh composed a special prayer to maintain hope and raise morale. On the 22nd of May, the weather was so bad that Bligh had to let the launch run before the sea to avoid capsizing. Bligh pointed out to the crew that they were all better off and made better progress in bad weather. On the 25th of May, the bad weather abated and the sun shone. That day, a noddy, a sea bird, probably indicative of the proximity of land, was caught and shared among the crew. Another bird, a booby, was also caught later that day and Bligh reserved the blood of that bird for three of the crew who were most distressed. In spite of additional food becoming available, Bligh decided that one of the three meals per day must be cut to enable them to reach Java, if they were not able to get help in Timor.

On the 27th of May, the sunny weather began to have its effect [126] ".... unhappily we found ourselves unable to bear the sun's heat; many of us suffering a languor and faintness which makes life indifferent."

Early on the morning of the 28th of May, the sound of the sea on the Great Barrier Reef off Australia (New Holland) was heard. Next day, an opening in the reef was found.

Bligh writes [127] of their physical condition due to hunger and the effects of the sun: "The general complaints of disease among us were a dizziness in the head, a great weakness of the joints and violent tenesmus, most of us having had no evacuation by a stool since we left the ship".

---

[126] "Narrative..." William Bligh p42 1790.
[127] "Narrative..." William Bligh, p48 1790

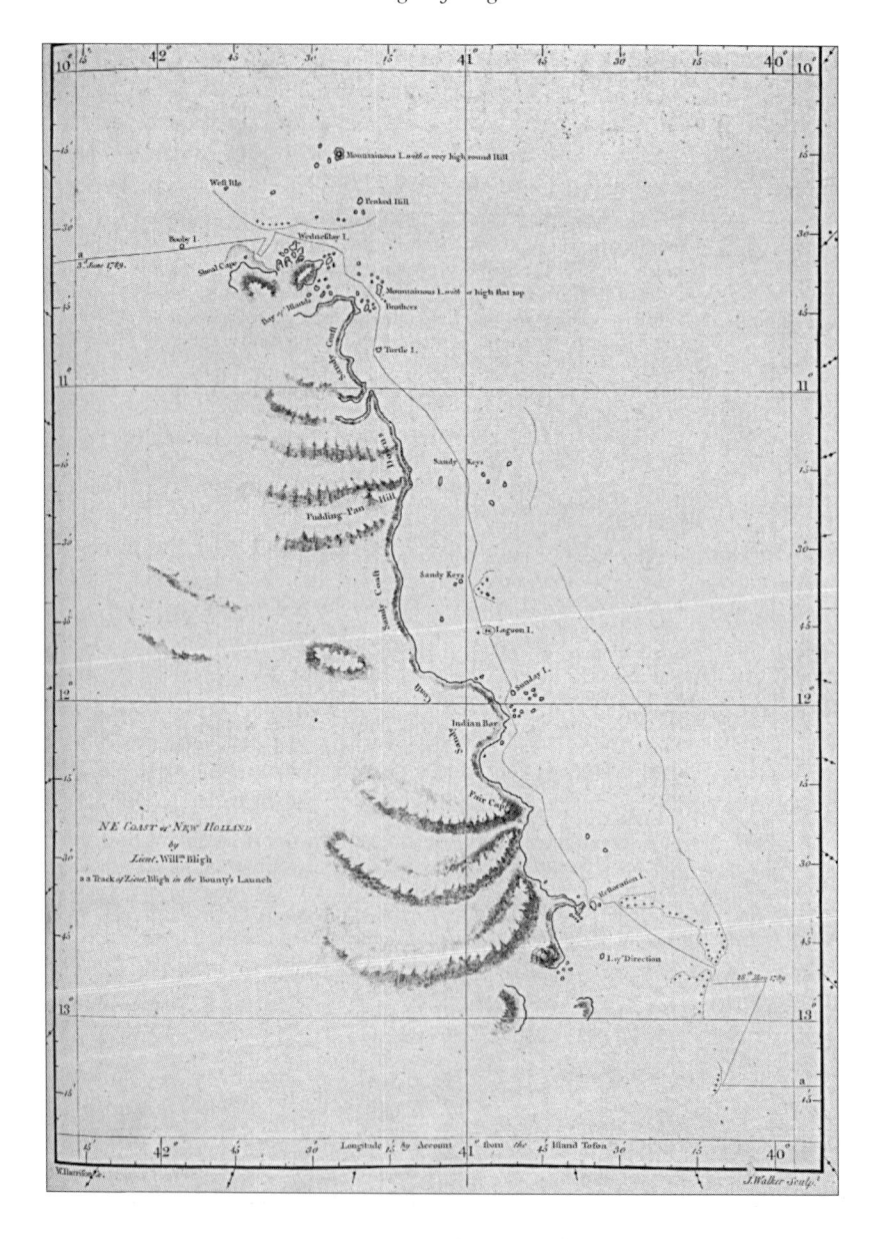

Bligh's sketch of part of the N.E. Coast of Australia during the Open Boat voyage by permission of the British Library 1007628.011

The Epic open boat voyage to Timor

Bligh's painting of a Noddy bird
By kind permission of the Mitchell Library,
State Library of New South Wales

Bligh's painting of a flying fish
By kind permission of the Mitchell Library,
State Library of New South Wales

Landings were made on islands rather than the mainland. On the 30th of May at Restoration Island, named by Bligh after the Restoration of Charles II, oysters were found and a pint of stew per person was made available. The Lieutenant and the Master had words about the amount. On examination of the stores, Bligh found to his consternation that much of the remaining pork had been pilfered. A well was dug and fresh water was used to fill up their storage vessels to 60 gallons.

Native fireplaces were discovered and twenty natives were seen on the mainland shore.

After landing at Sunday Island, Bligh ordered two parties to gather food and one party to stay by the boat. Some "declared [128] they would rather be without their dinner than go in search of it". Fryer suggested that each man should eat what he collected, but this was unfair on those most affected by the ordeal.

At this place another incident occurred, recorded in the log: "The carpenter began to be insolent to a high degree and at last told me with a mutinous aspect he was as good a man as I was – I did not just now see where this was to end. I therefore determined to strike a final blow at it and either to preserve my command or die in the attempt, and taking hold of a cutlass I ordered the rascal to take hold of another and defend himself. The Master now instead of backing his commander and seizing the villain of a mutineer called out to the boatswain to put me in arrest ... I told the master that if he ever presumed to interfere while I was in the execution of my duty and that should any tumult in future arise I would certainly instantly put him to death... He now assured me that on the contrary of opposing I might rely on him to support my orders and directions for the future...." Fryer claimed that he himself had been joking and goes on to say that Purcell explained to Bligh what he meant, to which Bligh replied "Well then, if you have not any meaning in what you said I ask your pardon".

On the same day, Bligh lists in his log men who did not give him "uneasyness". They were: Nelson, Samuel, Hayward, Peckover, Ledward, Elphinstone, Hallet, Cole, Smith and Lebogue.

A canoe 33ft long and 3ft at its maximum breadth capable of transporting about twenty men was found on that island. A party of seven black naked natives with a larger number at a greater distance was seen beckoning on the mainland.

---

[128] Ibid p55

The Epic open boat voyage to Timor

At Lagoon Key, the botanist Nelson was badly affected by the sun, temporarily losing his sight and being unable to walk, others became ill from eating poisonous berries.

At the same time, the Master unnecessarily put the security of the crew at risk. Bligh writes: "When I found all the grass set on fire, owing to the master while I was away insisting on having a fire to himself, notwithstanding Mr Peckover and Mr Samuels had remonstrated with him and told him of the consequence and he knew my particular orders..."

On only one occasion did Bligh personally deal out summary punishment. He had sent out a party to catch birds for food when Robert Lamb, the butcher, left the party, caught and ate nine birds and in doing so frightened off other birds so that only twelve were caught. Bligh admits that "On the return of the offender, I gave him a good beating".

Bligh and his crew stayed six days on the islands between Australia and the Barrier Reef. He anticipated that it would take eight to ten further days to reach Timor. They had passed the entrance to Endeavour Straits which he called the Bay of Islands and proceeded on the 4th June to Wednesday Island, the most northerly land point before turning West.

On that day, Bligh in his log rejected cannibalism "the necessity of destroying one another for food" on the ground that they would all agree to "death through famine".

Bligh had refused to increase the bread ration but on 6th of June he discovered that clams had been pilfered from the sea store. He was however sufficiently worried about the physical condition of his men to restore the third meal of the day next day.

He wrote [129] of the 8th of June "... Mr Ledward the surgeon and Lawrence Lebogue, an old hardy seaman, were giving way very fast. I could only assist them by a teaspoonful or two of wine which I had carefully saved, expecting such a melancholy necessity".

On the 9th of June, Bligh himself was violently sick. On the 11th of June, he wrote [130] "I had great apprehensions that some of my people could not hold out. An extreme weakness, swelled legs,

---

[129] "Narrative..." William Bligh p70 1790
[130] Ibid p72

hollow and ghastly countenances, great propensity to sleep with an apparent debility of understanding, seemed to me melancholy presages of their approaching dissolution ... but the boatswain very innocently told me that he thought I looked worse than anyone in the boat. The simplicity with which he uttered such an opinion diverted me and I hold good humour enough to return him a better compliment".

It is revealing that Bligh could still retain a sense of humour in such appalling conditions.

On the same day, Bligh recorded in his log that he told the crew that they were within 100 miles (about 33 leagues) of Timor. This produced "a Universal joy and satisfaction". As he was unable to calculate longitude accurately with the instruments he possessed, it was fortunate that he was actually about 60 miles away.

On the 12th of June, they first [131] sighted Timor. Heavy surf made landing dangerous and the log reads "the master now led the carpenter to join him in a murmur that I kept them from landing and that we had left a probable place to have got supplies... I assured them I would give an opportunity to land on the very place and gave the master and carpenter leave to land, but neither of these chose to venture out..." When they were able to land they met five Malays, one of whom agreed to act as pilot to take them to Coupang.

On the 14th of June, they reached that port.

This incredible journey of 3618 miles, averaging 90 miles per day, took 41 days.

It was described by Dr Mackaness in a number of ways: "the longest and most arduous boat journey in naval history" [132], "a boat voyage which for length, privation and heroism is unparalleled [133], ".... in the history of deep sea navigation... an epic, one of our greatest epics of the sea. The story told in Bligh's log books is worthy to stand for ever in the front rank of maritime exploration and adventure". [134]

---

[131] Ibid p73
[132] "The Life of Vice Admiral Bligh" G Mackaness Ch XIX 1931
[133] Ibid Ch XIV 1931
[134] Ibid, Ch XIV 1951

There is no doubt as to who is foremost among the heroes in this open boat epic.

One of William Bligh's Prayers:

> Continue O Lord we beseach thee, through the mediation of our blessed Saviour Jesus Christ, this thy goodness towards us, strengthen my mind and guide our steps. Grant unto us health and strength to continue our voyage, and so bless our miserable morsel of Bread, that it may be sufficient for our undertaking.

CHAPTER 11

The mutineers on Tubuai and Otaheite
28.4.1789 – 23.9.1789.

By 9am on the same day following the mutiny, Christian changed course from WNW towards the island of Tubuai (Toobouai) en route for Otaheite, using the easterly trade winds to approach Otaheite from the east. Morrison confirms that Christian's destination was Otaheite.

Christian appointed George Stewart his second-in-command and set two watches only, one in his own charge, the other in the charge of Stewart. He appointed James Morrison as boatswain and storekeeper, Thomas McIntosh as carpenter and John Mills as gunner. He transferred the keys of the arms chest from Joseph Coleman, the armourer, to Charles Churchill and had an arms chest put in Churchill's charge.

A month later, "Bounty" reached Tubuai. George Stewart approached in a boat ahead of "Bounty", but met with a hostile reception and one man in the boat with Stewart was wounded. Tubuaian warriors hoped to surprise "Bounty" while some of their womenfolk were being entertained on board, but they desisted as their ruse was observed. Christian used the four pounder gun to prevent native canoeists stealing an anchor buoy and followed up this action by a musket attack on warriors resisting a landing. 12 natives were killed and many wounded. The crew agreed to call the place Bloody Bay.

This visit to Tubuai was unsurprisingly short and by the 6th of June, "Bounty" had reached Otaheite and Christian was reunited with Mauatua, his "Isabella".

Christian lied about what had happened: "We had met Captain Cook, who had taken Mr Bligh and the others with the plants and the long boat and had sent us for hogs, goats etc for a new settlement which the King had sent him to make which he described to be on New Holland".

Otaheite had previously been charted and was on trade routes. It was therefore dangerous for the mutineers to stay there long with "Bounty". They left in about ten days, with "9 (native) men, 8 boys, 10 weomen and one female child". Among the ten women was Mauatua. It is significant that Christian's party was able to attract so few Tahitian women, even less than the number of Tahitian men who went with them. This strongly supports the view that previous attachments were voluntarily renewed, but a small number of women appear to have been taken under duress, as Heywood said most went voluntarily.

Tubuai was reached again on the 23rd of June. Christian's plans at this time were later told [135] to Bligh by Mary, the wife of Thomas McIntosh: "Christian's intentions were to settle in that island - Tobooi- and he had begun to build houses and a battery there to defend himself with the ship's guns. Two principal chiefs on the island on seeing these proceedings objected to his staying longer..."

Christian had to take measures against two of the crew, Matthews Quintal and John Sumner, for being absent from the ship without leave. They were put in irons.

An ambitious fortification, about 50 yards square and protected by a deep ditch, was planned and called Fort George, but in the meantime there was trouble with the natives. Christian's party shot one Tubuaian and later a Tubuaian chief's house was burnt.

Within a fortnight of landing, relationships and discipline were in serious trouble: "drunkenness, fighting and threatening each other's life was so common that those abaft were obliged to arm themselves with pistols" [136].

Morrison [137] claimed that he put to Stewart a plan to use the cutter to escape to Otaheite but Stewart said he and Peter Heywood had already formed such a plan. Christian delayed repairs to the cutter to forestall such an attempt.

---

[135] HMS Providence log 2.5.92.
[136] Heywood's Journal p2 (6.7.89)
[137] Morrison's Journal p72 ML Safe 1/42

The situation for the mutineers continued to deteriorate [138]: "On 1 Aug a party went on shore to get wives by force, but they met opposition from the Natives, one of whom was shot and another run through with a bayonet... the discontented party proposed to make slaves of the Otaheitans and cast lots for them, or land and destroy the Natives to procure women by force, but Christian wd (would) not agree to either scheeme and work at the fort was now discontinued".

Kennedy (1989) writes that Christian did not like the proposal to put his Isabella (Mauatua) into a lottery along with the other Tahitians.

Discontent about women continued for a further month. Christian was pressed to find a solution and held a hopefully grog-free meeting but some members of the crew broke into the grog store. The meeting lasted three days without a decision. A further meeting on "Bounty", at which a decision to move to Tahiti was overuled, was followed by another meeting the next day at which, by a show of hands of the Europeans, 16 voted to return to Tahiti and eight to stay with Christian in "Bounty".

Before "Bounty" left, some members of the crew ashore were waylaid by natives and beaten up. A punitive force was ambushed by a force of 700 natives but managed to drive off its attackers. Next day, there were battles in which 60 native men and 6 women were killed with many others wounded as well.

Six natives men including a chief and 12 women including Mauatua left with "Bounty" for Otaheite.

Morrison explains [139] what happened when they reached Otaheite: "It being late before everything was landed, Mr Christian told us he intended to stay a day or two and hoped that we would assist him to fill some water, as he intended to cruise for some uninhabited island where he would land his stock – of which the ship was full, together with plants of all the kinds that are common in these islands – and set fire to the ship, and where he hoped to live the remainder of his days without seeing the face of a European, but those who were already with him..."

---

[138] Heywood's Journal p3
[139] Morrison's Journal p100 ML Safe 1/42

Sixteen Europeans did in fact leave "Bounty" on arrival at Tahiti, while Christian and eight Europeans prepared to stay with the ship. Christian organised a farewell celebration that evening on "Bounty", a celebration designed to entrap some Tahitian males to provide sufficient crew to sail "Bounty" safely, but more importantly to entrap sufficient Tahitian females to make wives for his European crew.

That night, Christian cut the anchor cable and sailed.

CHAPTER 12

Aftermath of the Epic open boat voyage
14.6.1789 – 15.12.1790.

William van Este, the Dutch Governor at Coupang, offered Bligh and his crew hospitality and help. A house was obtained by Bligh, but he insisted that his crew should be accommodated in as good circumstances and asked that the Governor should "lodge them all with me". [140]

Bligh wished to give the Governor a present in return and asked William Purcell, the carpenter, to give him some chalk, but the carpenter refused. Purcell was sent to be detained by Captain Spikerman on a Dutch ship for a while.

By the 22nd of June, it was noted that the hollow and ghastly countenances of the crew were lost.

Bligh decided to purchase a 34ft schooner which was called "Resource", to ease the discomforts of the journey to Batavia in Java from where a ship for England could be found.

During July, Bligh was at odds on a number of occasions with the Master, John Fryer. On the 6th of July, Bligh wrote "I directed the master to attend and see that the carpenter did not loiter away his time and report to me if, when I was absent, he saw anything doing he thought was contrary to my directions, when I received for answer that he was no carpenter and did not understand that he had a right to attend to it; but that at any rate he would have an order first...."

Of the 7th of July, he noted in the log: "Robert Tinkler, the master's brother-in-law, having behaved saucy and impertinent to the boatswain received some little chastisement for it upon which it

---

[140] "Narrative...." William Bligh p81 1790

appears the master interfered and ordered him, Mr Tinkler, to stick his knife into him. As soon as I became acquainted with this matter I as publicly reprimanded the master, making him responsible and equally criminal with Robt Tinkler in case any such violence is committed."

Of the 9th of July, he added "the masters insolence and neglect induced me to give him written orders to attend and report to me the progress of the outfit of 'Resource'."

John Fryer used devious channels to get at Bligh. He prevailed indirectly on the Governor to require more than Bligh's signature on requisitions. Captain Spikerman's wife was the sister of the Governor's wife and by such influence Fryer was able to make trouble for Bligh, particularly as the Governor was seriously ill. However, the Governor's second in command Mr T Wanjon was also his son-in-law and he was prepared to accept Bligh's signature alone for requisitions rather than receipts.

On the 20th of July, David Nelson, the Botanist, died [141] of an "inflammatory fever". Bligh is generous in his tribute to this man: "it bears very heavy on my mind, his duty and integrity went hand in hand, and he had accomplished through great care and dillegence the object he was sent for, always forwarding every plan I had for the good of the Service we were on. He was equally serviceable in my Voyage here in the Course of which he always gave me pleasure by Conducting himself with Resolution and integrity".

On the 19th of August, Bligh wrote a letter to his wife explaining what had happened:

"My dear Betsy,

I am now in a part of the world that I never expected, it is however a place that has afforded me relief and saved my life, and I have the happiness to assure you I am now in perfect health. That the chance of this letter getting to you before others of a later date is so very small I shall only give you a short account of my arrival here. What an emotion does my heart and soul feel that I have once more an opportunity of writing to you and my little Angels, and

---

[141] "Narrative...." William Bligh p85 1790

particularly as you have all been so near losing the best of friends – when you would have had no person to have regarded you as I do, and you must have spent the remainder of your days without knowing what was become of me, or what would have been still worse, to have known that I had been starved to Death at Sea or destroyed by Indians – All these dreadful circumstances I have combatted with success and in the most extraordinary manner that ever happened, never dispairing from the first moment of my disaster but that I should overcome all my difficulties. Know then my own Dear Betsy, I have lost the Bounty..."

"Resource" and "Bounty's" launch left Coupang on the 20th of August. Sourabaya was reached on the 12th of September and it was here that their stay was prolonged by a number of incidents. Bligh was embarrassed at the official leaving ceremony when his crew failed to accompany the boat on which he was travelling with the Dutch Commandant back to "Resource". Thomas Hayward failed to get the cooperation of the other members of the crew.

When two men, John Hallet, Midshipman, and William Elphinstone were found drunk, Bligh asked John Fryer, the Master, if they were drunk or ill. Fryer replied "Am I a doctor? Ask him what is the matter with them". Bligh said "What do you mean by this insolence?" to which Fryer answered "It is no insolence – you not only use me ill, but every man in the vessel and everyman will say the same".

Bligh describes further trouble: "the cause was that the Opperhooft (Governor) had sent me vegetables and other things by his slaves to be carried to the boat, but meeting with these people at the house they were drinking at, they detained the things there and the slaves returned to their master, of course it rested with themselves to get the things to the boat, which it appears they paid a penny for". It was for this payment that the Master and Carpenter promoted disorder.

Bligh arrested both of them and hailed the Commandant to return to investigate the matter. Bligh tells us of what he learnt from the Commandant: "my officers and men spread a repoart that I should be hanged or blown from the mouth of a cannon as soon as I got home – alarmed at such a disgraceful account, I desired that everyone might be asked if he said it". William Purcell was named as the source of the report. Bligh now adds "I desired the Commandant to make enquiry who had any complaints against me". The complainants had an opportunity of being heard independently by the Governor. John Hallet, Midshipman, Thomas Ledward, the Surgeon, and William Cole, Boatswain, took the opportunity offered to them. John Fryer, the Master, and William Purcell, Carpenter, who were in detention would also be given opportunity to make complaints.

Hallet complained of a beating for not getting into a boat. He agreed that Bligh was not brutal or severe, that he had taken "every pains to preserve the ship's company" and that it was not possible for Bligh to have retaken "Bounty" during the Mutiny. Ledward complained that he had been refused permission to go ashore on one occasion. Cole wished to say that he had no complaint.

The complaints made by Fryer were indeed serious: Firstly, he accused Bligh of "extravagant charges to Government". Fryer produced a document signed by William Van Este at Coupang to this effect. Bligh was able to rebut these charges by showing "receipts and vouchers signed by the master and the boatswain and witnessed by two respectable residanters".

Secondly, Bligh was accused by Fryer "that I had given my ship's company short allowance of yams and therefore they had taken away the ship". "The carpenter asserted also that the cause of the ship being taken was owing to my stoping provisions".

Bligh wrote of these complaints in these words: ".... for all such stoppages, every seaman receives money for it on their return to England – It, however, is sometimes necessary for the good of the service and at this time, I found it absolutely so, to give $^2/_3$ allowance of bread because that article I was short of in proportion to other species of provisions and I had to guard against a failure of making my passage through Endeavour Streights –"

"As to yams – it happened that on my arrival at the Friendly Islands our stock of plantains, ferra and yams was so far expended that only 1½ lbs were issued to each person for that day, but the day following we had abundance of everything and, from my departure to the time of the mutiny, 2lbs of yams each day were served to every individual which is legal and sufficient for any man whatever, but in all my weights all dirt, decayed parts and everything not eatable was carefully thrown away, so that it was ever a principal with me that weights should be real, that my people might suffer no loss. Conscious therefore of my integrity, these assertions gave me little concern".

Fryer acknowledged that his complaints had come to nothing and on the 16th of September wrote to Bligh asking "if matters can be made up". His apologies on this occasion were not accepted and Bligh said he was too busy to deal with the matter. Fryer was now prepared to "make every concession...". Bligh however asked for such concessions by letter.

On the 17th of September, "Resource" and the launch finally left Sourabaya with an escort kindly provided by the Governor to secure them against pirates.

Batavia, further west, was reached on the 1st of October. Here Bligh became seriously ill with a fever and was advised by the Surgeon General to leave as soon as possible.

On the 10th of October, Thomas Hall, the cook, died of fever.

Bligh sold "Resource" and "Bounty's" launch for a considerable loss on what he had had to pay for "Resource". He also wished to provide money for those going home on a ship later than the one on which he was to travel. His requirement for security caused some concern. Ledward, the Surgeon, wrote [142] to an uncle: "There is one thing I must mention which is of consequence; the captain denied me, as well as the rest of the gentlemen who had not agents, any money unless I would give him my power of attorney and also my will, in which I was to bequeath to him all my property, this he called by the name of proper security. This unless I did I should have got no money, though I showed him a letter of credit from my uncle and offered to give him a bill of exchange upon him..."

Bligh embarked on the Dutch ship "Vlydte" on the 16th of October. Within a fortnight, William Elphinstone and Peter Linkletter had died of fever at Batavia. Of those returning home later, Robert Lamb, the butcher, died on the passage home.

In his "Voyage to the North Pacific" 1790, George Vancouver lists [143] a Mr Ledward as Surgeon among his crew members, but the

---

[142] Notes and Queries 1903 9th Series vol xii.
[143] "Bligh" Gavin Kennedy Chap 14 1978

Reverend James Bligh, Headmaster of Derby Grammar School and six years younger than William Bligh, wrote that Ledward died in a Dutch vessel which foundered between Batavia and the Cape of Good Hope.

Bligh reached Portsmouth on the 14th of March 1790. He was soon to see his twin daughters Frances and Jane who had been born and baptized in Wapping while he had been away. On his return he put the finishing touches to his "Narrative" of the Mutiny and Open-boat journey and was able to announce a publication date for "the Narrative" on the 1st of April 1790.

Bligh has been criticised for what he wrote to members of the Heywood family on his return, when they wrote to him. Heywood's mother wrote in March 1790.

It must be remembered that Bligh considered Peter Heywood, although at the time of the Mutiny only seventeen years old, to be one of the leaders of the Mutiny. Heywood was certainly a close friend of Fletcher Christian. William Purcell's evidence was that Heywood was armed with a cutlass at one stage during the mutiny while Thomas Hayward's evidence was that Heywood was given an opportunity to go into the open boat but did not avail himself of the opportunity. As a result of the Mutiny, Norton died on Tofoa Island, while Nelson, Hall, Linkletter and Elphinstone died in the East Indies and Lamb died on the journey home after the Open-boat voyage.

Bligh wrote to Heywood's widowed mother: "His baseness is beyond all description, but I hope you will endeavour to prevent the loss of him, heavy as the misfortune is, from afflicting you too severely. I imagine he is, with the rest of the mutineers, returned to Otaheite". To Peter Heyward's uncle, Bligh wrote: "His ingratitude to me is of the blackest dye, for I was a father to him in every respect..."

In August, Captain Edward Edwards was appointed to go in pursuit of the mutineers. On the 22nd of October 1790, the Court Martial for the loss of "Bounty" was held. Each surviving member of the Open-boat journey was asked if they had any objection or complaint against Lt Bligh. They each swore that they had not. Bligh, who had been the first witness, did however lay a complaint against William Purcell, the Carpenter, and the court heard the case against Purcell on the same day. The six charges [144] against Purcell were: 1. His refusal, while at Adventure Bay, to assist in hoisting water out of the hold. 2. His refusal to take anti-scorbutic medicine. 3. His refusal to cut a grinding stone for one of the chiefs. 4. His insubordination on Sunday Island. 5. His refusal to give a piece of chalk to the Governor at Coupang when ordered to do so. 6. General charges of disrespect and misconduct.

Purcell's case was part proved and he was reprimanded.

Bligh was honourably acquitted. On the 14th of November 1790, he was promoted as Commander and given charge [145] of the sloop Falcon (14 guns).

On the 15th of December 1790, he was again promoted to the rank of Post Captain attached to HMS Medea; the requirement of three years service in his present rank being dispensed with as a mark of special favour.

---

[144] PRO Admiralty 1/5328
[145] PRO Admiralty Log 51/337

CHAPTER 13

The Pitcairn mutineers
23.9.1789. – 1800

"Bounty" left Otaheite with a complement of thirty five persons. This was made up of nine European mutineers, four Otaheitan males, two Tubuaian males and nineteen native women including Mauatua, Christian's Isabella, and a native child belonging to William McKoy's consort.

The mutineers who chose to go with Christian were: Edward Young, Midshipman; John Williams, AB; Matthew Quintal, AB; John Adams (alias Alexander Smith), AB; William McKoy, AB; Isaac Martin, AB; John Mills, Gunner's Mate and William Brown, Botanist's Assistant.

The Otaheitan males were called Temua (Teimua or Timoa), Menalee (Manarii or Manale), Nehow (Niau or Nehou) and Tetaheite (Tetahiti). The Tubuaians were called Talaloo (Tararo or Taaroamiva, younger brother of Chief Taaroa) and Ohoo (Oher, Ohuhu or Oopee).

We learn of the journey in "Bounty" at this time from Jenny (Teehuteatuaonoa), consort of Isaac Martin. She left Pitcairn in "Sultan" in 1817 and told [146] her story to Captain Peter Dillon of "Research" in Otaheite sometime between 1826 and 1828: "... only nine (Europeans) were left on board, attracted by the native females who were in the ship about nineteen in number... the mutineers cut the cable ... four natives of Otaheite and two Tabouaian [1] men were then on board ... one of the women leaped overboard ... close

---

[146] "Narrative of a Voyage" Captain P Dillon London 1829. Also United Services Journal 1829 vol ii p589. "Jenny" does not thereafter distinguish between Tubuaians (Tabouaians she calls them) and Otaheitans. She calls them Otaheitans.

in with the island of Eimeo. A canoe shortly afterwards came off and six of the women who were rather ancient were allowed to depart in her; twelve then remained on board ... after many days had elapsed a small island was discovered called by the natives Purutea ... one of the natives ventured on board and was much delighted at beholding the pearl shell buttons on the jacket of Captain Christian, who, in a very friendly manner gave the man the jacket. The latter stood on the ship's gunwhale, showing the present to his companions, when one of the mutineers shot him dead. He fell into the sea. Christian was highly indignant at this, but, having lost all authority could do nothing more than reprimand the murderer severely...."

Fletcher Christian sailed "Bounty" through some of the Tongan Islands and then reached Ono-i-lau in the Southern Lau group of the Fijian Islands. From there, Christian sailed in an initial south easterly direction but thereafter looping in search of Pitcairn Island.

Among the books which Christian found that Bligh had left on "Bounty" was "Accounts of Voyages ...." vol 1 1773 by Hawksworth. This book included an account of the voyages of Captain Carteret in HMS Swallow in the period 1766-1769. Carteret had discovered and named the uninhabited island of Pitcairn after the midshipman who first sighted it. Carteret however unfortunately mischarted its position. After much searching, Fletcher Christian finally located Pitcairn Island in January 1790.

As John Adams (alias Alexander Smith) is the main source of information about what happened on Pitcairn, it is important that his previous conduct is understood. We learn [147] that he and his brother were orphans brought up at the Poor-house in Hackney, East London. His father had been a coal merchant's servant, who was drowned in the Thames. John Adams had two older sisters while his brother was younger. It is not known when or if John Adams married his wife Hannah, but a daughter was baptised a fortnight after Adams joined "Bounty". When John Adams signed on for "Bounty", he used the alias Alexander Smith, as he had apparently defected from another ship. Evidence sworn at the Court Martial of those mutineers apprehended indicated that Adams was one of the most prominent of the mutineers and had

---

[147] Anonymous letter dated Hackney 4.11.1818, to Gentlemen's Magazine, quoted by Mackaness Chapter XXI 1951

stood as an armed sentry over Bligh. John Adams denied all complicity in the mutiny. He did however admit that fearing that he might be on the weaker side, "he turned out again and went for a cutlass".

A further source of information is the Pitcairn Island Register. It is significant that this records that all adult native males had died before the end of 1793.

The first contact with those mutineers who landed on Pitcairn was in February 1808 [148], when the American vessel "Topaz" from Boston under Captain Folger who was searching for seals landed there. He reported in a log that the population there was now thirty five people (1 male, 8 female and 26 children) and various inconsistent reports including one that about four years after the mutineers landed, their servants attacked and killed all the English, excepting the informant and he was severely wounded. The same night, the Otaheitan widows arose and murdered all their countrymen.

The next contact with the settlement took place in 1814; the American armed vessel "Essex" was interfering with British trade in the South Seas and HMS Briton under Captain Sir Thomas Staines and HMS Tagus under Captain Pipon were sent to prevent this.

Staines reported [149] back "... a son of Christian was the first born on the island now about 25 years of age named Thursday October Christian; the elder Christian fell a sacrifice to the jealousy of an Otaheitan man within three or four years after their arrival on the island. The mutineers were accompanied thither by 6 Otaheitan men and twelve women... five of the latter died at different periods... leaving seven women of the original settlers".

Pipon wrote [150]: "It appears that this unfortunate ill fated young man (Fletcher Christian) was never happy after the rash and ill considered step he had taken, but always sullen and morose, a circumstance which will not surprise anyone; this moroseness however led him to many acts of cruelty and inhumanity which

---

[148] Quarterly Review – February 1810.

[149] Quarterly Review 4/1815 p377/8

[150] "Interesting Report..." P Pipon, Banks Papers, Brabourne Collection ML A77 Series 71.05/CY3011/322-333

soon was the cause of his incurring the hatred and detestation of his companions here: one cannot avoid expressing astonishment when you consider that the very crime he was then guilty of towards his Companions who assisted him in the Mutiny was the very same they so loudly accused their Captain of ... for what we could learn he was shot by a black man while digging in his field and almost instantly expired. This happened about 11 months after they were settled in the island but the exact dates I could not learn ... Christian's wife had paid the debt of nature and as we have every reason to suppose sensuality and a passion for the females of Otaheite chiefly instigated him to the rash step he had taken, so it is readily to be believed he would not live long on the island without a female companion. Consequently after the demise of his wife, he forcibly seized on one belonging to one of the Otaheitan men and took her to live with him. This exasperated them to a degree of madness, open war and every opportunity sought to take away his life and it was effected whilst digging in his own field..."

In 1817, Captain Amasa Delano, a friend of Captain Folger wrote [151] "... they lived under Christian's government several years after they landed; that during the whole period they enjoyed tolerable harmony; that Christian became sick and died a natural death... the account of Lt Fitzmaurice as he professed to receive it from the second mate of 'the Topaz' is that Christian became insane and threw himself into the sea. The Quarterly Reviewers say that he was shot dead while digging in the field by an Otaheitan man, whose wife he seized for his own use. Neither of these accounts is true ... from the authority of Captain Folger."

A further account of the settlement at Pitcairn stemmed from the visit of Captain Beechey in HMS Blossom [152] in 1825.

That part of his story concerning Pitcairn was signed by John Adams and is in much greater detail than previous accounts. Captain Beechey was able to assure Adams that no action would be taken against him. The account tells of the burning of "Bounty" a short while after their arrival in Pitcairn by Matthew Quintal. The land was divided only among the nine European males, while the

---

[151] "Voyages and Travels of Amasa Delano" Delano 1817, reprinted in the Quarterly Journal of Science and Art 1819 vol V part i, article VIII.
[152] "Narrative of a Voyage..." F W Beechey, London 1831

native males were made to serve the Europeans. Each European had a native female consort while only one native (Talaloo) had his own female consort. This meant that only two native females were available for the other five native males. The situation was exacerbated after about a month when William's consort fell from a cliff while collecting birds' eggs and died. After two years, Williams threatened to leave the island unless he was given a native female consort. Christian agreed that a native consort (belonging to Talaloo) should be given to Williams and an armed party was on hand to enforce it. There were a number of conspiracies, but Christian, when warned by a native female, challenged Ohoo with one of these. Ohoo and Talaloo fled to the woods where later the other native males were prevailed upon to kill them. There were then some two years of peace. It was the cruelty of Quintal and McKoy which triggered a conspiracy by the remaining native males to kill all the Europeans. Temua and Nehow were to abscond, taking guns, while Tetaheite was to borrow a gun to shoot wild pig. Williams was shot, also Christian. Quintal told Mills that he heard groans and that "there was surely some person dying". Mills answered "it is only Mainmast (Christian's consort) calling her children to dinner." Williams and Christian were killed also Mills, Martin and Brown. McKoy and Quintal fled to the woods. Adams was lucky to survive a shot which entered at his right shoulder and left beside his throat. Young was hidden by a native woman.

At this point, the four remaining native men quarrelled among themselves about women. Menalee killed Temua and fled to the woods to join McKoy and Quintal. Adams went to Quintal and McKoy to persuade them to kill Menalee as a condition of them rejoining Young and Adams. They agreed to kill Menalee, but declined the invitation to rejoin the other two remaining Europeans while the two native males with Young and Adams were alive. Young prevailed upon his consort to kill Tetaheite, while he himself killed Nehow.

With the death of all the native adult males, the native females were burdened with those tasks previously undertaken by the native males.

The native females then were sufficiently disillusioned to think of building a boat to escape from the island. A boat was built, but capsized before its purpose could be achieved.

After some years, Quintal constructed a still to produce alcohol from local tree roots. McKoy overindulged himself with alcohol, producing delirium. His weighted body was found at the foot of a cliff and it was believed that he committed suicide. Towards the end of the decade, Quintal's consort's body was found at the foot of the cliffs and it was believed that she had fallen collecting bird's eggs. Another source quoted [153] by Darby said that Quintal's consort committed suicide after Quintal bit off her ear.

Quintal now wanted a consort who was in the possession of one of the two remaining European males, otherwise he threatened to kill each of them. Adams and Young decided that Quintal must die and he was killed with a pole-axe. Young died of asthma a little while later, leaving Adams as the sole remaining adult male and European left.

For about a further thirty years, Adams presided over the island with a touching benevolence, rooted in the Christian principles which he learnt in the Poor-house at Hackney.

Mauatua was expecting Fletcher Christian's third child (Mary Ann) at the time of the massacre. Other accounts say that she bore Edward Young three children after this and that she was the consort whom Quintal demanded for his own.

Before concluding this episode of the mutineers on Pitcairn, it is necessary to discuss two claims about Fletcher Christian.

Letters from Mr Fletcher Christian containing a Narrative of the Transactions on board HM ship Bounty before and after the Mutiny with his subsequent Voyages and travels in South America were published in London in 1796. Dr Mackaness wrote [154] "James Bonwick (author) pronounced them a 'vulgar forgery', an opinion with which we may agree". Other biographers have concurred with this view.

The second claim was made by Peter Heywood who thought he saw Fletcher Christian in Plymouth sometime after the mutiny. No other evidence supports this speculation.

The life on Pitcairn following the Mutiny has been described as "hell" [155] for the mutineers and certainly for the natives who

---

[153] "Who caused the Mutiny on the Bounty". M Darby Ch 14 1965
[154] "The Life of Vice Admiral Bligh" G Mackaness Ch XIII 1951.
[155] "Bligh" G Kennedy, Ch 21 1978

The Pitcairn mutineers

accompanied them. Beechey's evidence says that Fletcher Christian either promoted or agreed to the denial of a share of land to the native males and to their virtual enslavement. He was a party to the armed abduction of a native female from the only native male with his own consort. Fletcher Christian's incompetence and the cruelty of his men triggered off mutual genocide between the mutineers and the native males. It cost, in that decade on Pitchairn, the lives of all the native adult males and all but two of the Europeans.

One account[156] asks whether it was Christian's remorse for what had happened because of the mutiny on "Bounty" that Fletcher Christian made a twice daily recitation of the prayer of the prodigal son compulsory during his leadership. That prayer has the words: "I will arise and go to my father and say unto him: 'Father, I have sinned against Heaven and before thee and am no more worthy to be called thy son'."

In his poem "The Island or Christian and his Comrades" written in 1823, Lord Byron was outspoken in his judgement on Christian and his companions.

Canto IV Verse XI

"No nations eyes would on their tomb be bent,
No heroes envy them their monument;
However boldly their warm blood was spilt,
Their Life was shame, their Epitaph was guilt.
..."

The most likely explanation from information given by Glynn Christian[157] concerning Fletcher Christian's death and burial is that after being shot, disfigured and decapitated, his body and those of Europeans killed in the massacre were left to rot for more than six months at the behest of the native women. Fletcher Christian's head and body were then put in an unmarked pit a little way up Look Out Point near a now dried-up pool.

---

[156] "Mr Bligh's bad language". G Dening p310 '92.
[157] "Fragile Paradise" G Christian p242, Hamish Hamilton 1982.

CHAPTER 14

Pursuit and Court Martial of some mutineers and its aftermath
23.9.1789 – 1793

A month before [158] the mutineers and others with them arrived in Otaheite for the last time and before Christian and eight mutineers left in "Bounty", the brig "Mercury" under Captain Cox touched at Otaheite. He met Tinah, the Regent, and gave him a picture of the death of Captain Cook. Cox contradicted the previous claim by David Nelson that Bligh was the son of Captain Cook by saying that the real son of Captain Cook was in England. Naturally, Tinah was upset that he had been misled.

An Able Seaman called Brown was abandoned by Cox on the island after Brown had knifed another member of the crew. There were therefore seventeen European males including Brown of those who chose to stay or were abandoned there.

James Morrison claims that he made a plan to build a boat, ostensibly to sail around the island, but in reality to escape to Timor or the north west coast of North America.

The building of the boat about 30ft long named "Resolution" was begun in November 1789 and ten of the seventeen Europeans were apparently associated with the project. Seven and a half months later, the boat was launched. The use of matting rather than sail cloth restricted the possibilities of the use of the vessel.

In the summer of 1790, Captain Edward Edwards was appointed to command the frigate "Pandora", 24 guns, to go in pursuit of the mutineers. Edwards was a man who had experienced a mutiny seven years before on HMS Narcissus when six men were hanged.

---

[158] Marginal note to Morrison's Journal ML Safe 1/42

He took [159] with him as 3rd Lieutenant, Thomas Hayward, who survived the open boat voyage with Bligh.

Meanwhile, some mutineers on Otaheite behaved outrageously. Thompson raped an Otaheitan's wife and was himself attacked in retaliation. He shot and killed a man carrying a child who also died and he wounded others. Thompson, Churchill and Brown went to live in the south of the island, largely out of contact with the others.

Churchill was said [160] to have shot two islanders merely "for frightening away ducks which he was about to shoot at". It is surprising therefore that we hear that Churchill was given on the death of his tyo (special male companion) the sovereignty of part of the island by the natives. Thompson however killed Churchill because he said that he had found that Churchill had stolen a musket from him. The natives killed Thompson in retaliation.

In the autumn of 1790, some of the mutineers became involved in civil disputes between native chiefs. Morrison admitted that this resulted in a "great slaughter".

Captain Edwards in "Pandora" reached Otaheite on the 23rd of March 1791 by way of Cape Horn.

Coleman swam out to the ship, while Heywood and Stewart gave themselves up.

Some of the mutineers in the ship "Resolution" eluded capture for a while. The natives however took temporary possession of "Resolution" and threw three of the mutineers overboard. Six Europeans then took to the woods, but were tracked down by Lt Hayward and brought back to "Pandora". Brown was signed on, while the other fourteen remaining Europeans were handcuffed.

The mutineers and those with them had by then been on Otaheite for about eighteen months. A number of them had developed potentially long term relationships with native women. Stewart, McIntosh and Skinner each had a daughter, while Burkitt and Millward each had a son. It is significant [161] that Stewart's consort, Peggy, as he called her, died of despair or "a broken heart"

---

[159] "Voyage of HMS Pandora" E Edwards and G Hamilton – notes by Basil Thomson, London 1915.
[160] Morrison's Journal p 125a ML Safe 1/42
[161] "The Life of Vice Admiral Bligh" G Mackaness Ch XX 1931

within two months after "Pandora" left, with Stewart confined and under arrest on a capital charge.

The method of confinement was intimidating. Edwards had a structure 11ft by 18ft erected on the deck of "Pandora" with two 9 inch square ventilation holes and an entrance about 18 inches square. This small structure confined the fourteen prisoners and has been called "Pandora's Box".

"Pandora" left Otaheite to search for "Bounty" early in May. Henry Hillbrant, one of the prisoners, told Edwards that Christian had mentioned that he was proposing to sail to an island now in the Union Group. Edwards checked this out without finding "Bounty", but did find some flotsam, clearly belonging to "Bounty".

Within a month of leaving, "Pandora" suffered the loss of its jolly boat with five of its crew. About a further month later, "Pandora" was separated from "Resolution" and its nine crew members; "Resolution" also missed the rendezvous planned in the event of separation. "Resolution" did however survive to spend five weeks on Fiji and discover new parts of it, reach New Holland (Australia) and fall in with a Dutch vessel west of Endeavour Straits. This was an amazing achievement, but it was a larger boat, with fewer people to feed and its personnel had firearms, navigational instruments and maps when compared with Bligh's open boat voyage.

At the end of August, "Pandora" was holed on the Great Barrier Reef. Edwards had insufficient boats to cope, particularly after losing the jolly boat and being separated from "Resolution".

Peter Heywood, one of those confined, described [162] what happened to the prisoners: "(Edwards) sent the corporal and armourer down to let some of us out of irons; but three only were suffered to go up, and the scuttle then being clamped on ... the armourer had only time to let two persons out of irons, the rest except three letting themselves out; two of these three went down, and the third was picked up".

Stewart and Sumner died after being struck by debris in the water. Skinner was drowned in the sea and Hillbrant was drowned

---

[162] "A memoir of the Late Captain Peter Heywood RN" E Tagart p35 London 1832.

in "Pandora's Box" [163]. More than thirty crew members were also drowned. Ninety nine men including ten prisoners were rescued in four boats and made for Coupang in Timor which was reached in mid September, after a three day stay on an island off New Holland and fourteen days at sea. They reached Samarang at the end of October where they met up with the crew of "Resolution" and proceeded to Batavia, reached early in November. They left in the Dutch ship "Vreedenberg", conditions on which were described vividly by Morrison, one of the prisoners: "Our lodgings were none of the best, as we lay on rough logs of timber, some of which lay some inches above the rest and which a[s] small portion of cloathing would not bring to a level, the deck above us was also very leaky, by which means we were continually wet, being alternatively drench'd with salt water, the urine of the hogs or the rain which happened to fall."

The prisoners were transferred to HMS Gorgon at Cape Town and reached England on the 18th of June 1792. Two days later, they were transferred to HMS Hector to await a Court Martial.

A key figure behind the scenes in the drama of the Court Martial of the mutineers was Captain (later Admiral) Pasley who married [164] a sister or cousin of Peter Heywood who was on trial. Kennedy describes [165] the relationship differently and says that Commodore Pasley -an uncle of Peter Heywood – at first wrote to Nessy, Peter's sister "... Your brother appears by all accounts to be the greatest culprit of all, Christian above except". Pasley saw to it that Heywood had a legal adviser who advised him to petition [166] the Lords Commissioners of the Admiralty to grant a speedy trial. Pasley also personally interviewed a number of "Bounty's" crew to find witnesses unfavourable to Bligh for any reason.

On the 14th of July 1792, Peter Heywood wrote [167] a letter to Mrs Bligh noting her husband's miraculous escape, but protesting innocence of support for the mutiny.

---

[163] Morrison's Journal p189/90 ML Safe 1/42 pp190-191
[164] The Farington Diary Vol 1 p56 quoted by Mackaness Ch XXII 1931
[165] "Bligh" G Kennedy Ch 17 1978
[166] "A memoir of the late Captain Peter Heywood RN" E Tagart p62/3 1832
[167] "Bligh" G Kennedy, Ch XXII 1978

A 19th century author, Judge McFarland, is outspoken [168] on this Court Martial, he wrote: ".... indeed it is almost impossible to imagine a more pitiable or censurable parody upon the administration of justice than was involved in the absence of Bligh". McFarland was speaking of the difficulties of the defendants, but the difficulties being stored up for Bligh had also to be considered.

The Admiralty had chosen to send him on the 2nd Breadfruit Voyage which meant that he was not able to be present at the Court Martial, but he did leave affidavits exonerating four of those charged, namely Coleman, Norman, McIntosh and Byrne.

The Court Martial was presided over by Vice Admiral Lord Hood and eleven Captains sat with him. Among the Captains were Captain Montagu a friend of Pasley and Captain Bertie, related [169] to Peter Heywood's family by marriage.

Although Purcell, "Bounty's" Carpenter, gave evidence [170] that Heywood was armed with a cutlass, Heywood's written statement read out to the Court claimed as mitigating circumstances extreme youth and the fact that he lost his head.

Fryer, "Bounty's" Master, said [171] he advised the loyalists that "if you are ordered into the boat, say you will stay on board. I flatter myself we shall restore the ship in a short time".

Both Heywood and Morrison in their statements referred to Fryer's plan and none [171] of those on trial for their lives used ill treatment by Bligh as a defence.

The verdict of the Court was that the four men subject of Bligh's affidavit were acquitted and that the other six men were guilty of mutiny with a recommendation of reprieve for Heywood and Morrison "in consideration of various circumstances".

It is very probably that the "various circumstances" involved the threat of a counter Court Martial from both Heywood and Morrison.

It must be remembered that Bligh had received promotion under special circumstances at the end of 1790 and it would have been

---

[168] "A Mutiny in the Bounty" A McFarland p75 Sydney 1884.
[169] "A Memoir of the late Captain Peter Heywood" E Tagart p64 1832
[170] Ibid p96
[171] "Who caused the Mutiny on the Bounty" M Darby Ch 13 1965

embarrassing for both the Crown and the Admiralty to instigate a Court Martial against Bligh and to wait for his return. The international situation, particularly relating to France following the Revolution, was uncertain at this time and the morale of the Navy was problematical due to the effects of inflation on pay.

It was very likely indeed that the Court Martial lawyers knew that Morrison was busy writing a "Memorandum..." which purported to provide information on which a counter Court Martial might be based.

Muspratt, one of the six convicted mutineers, won a reprieve on a technicality. His advocate had asked that the Court should first acquit Norman so that he could have been available to be cross-examined.

Morrison sent his "Memorandum" with a letter [172] dated 10th October 1792 to the Reverend Howell, a priest who helped him to edit his writings.

The Royal reprieve for Heywood and Morrison was announced on the 24th of October.

Three mutineers, (Burkitt, Ellison and Millward) were hanged on "HMS Brunswick" on the 29th of October with its menacing "yellow flag flying".

Lord Hood offered Pasley the opportunity of Heywood being given a place on his flagship, but Pasley declined the offer and made a place available for him on his own ship "HMS Bellerophon".

On the 5th of November, Heywood wrote [173] to Edward Christian, Fletcher's brother, proposing a meeting and writing of Fletcher Christian as a "man of strict honour, adorned with every virtue and beloved of all – except one whose ill report is his greatest praise – who had the pleasure of his acquaintance". In the same letter, Heywood attempts to rubbish Bligh's accounts of the Mutiny ("the Narrative..." 1790 and "the Voyage..." 1792) as "false reports of slander and vile suspicion". This letter without disclosing its author was passed by the recipient to the press and was published in the Cumberland Package and Whitehaven Advertiser on 20th

---

[172] "Memorandum and letter" James Morrison ML Ms
[173] Banks Papers A78-4 p2

November 1792 to bolster local support for Christian. Professor Edward Christian now seems to have fallen out with Heywood. The Professor's objective appears to have been to denigrate Bligh as a means of providing reasons for the rehabilitation of the name of Christian and to provide arguments in mitigation of Fletcher Christian's conduct in case of his arrest. This involved ensuring that an account of the Court Martial was published to which Professor Christian would provide an Appendix. Professor Christian's uncompromising objective is likely to have threatened Heywood's position, by compromising Heywood's sworn statements about his role in the Mutiny and drawing attention to Purcell's statement that Heywood was armed in the Mutiny.

On the 25th of November 1792, the Reverence H Howell wrote [173] to Captain Phillips who was then working for Sir Joseph Banks about the progress of Morrison's Journal: "Morrison is getting forward with his publication which will be ready for the press in about 6 or 7 weeks... It will consist of a very particular and diffuse account of the proceedings of Christian and his party after the Mutiny".

On 12th December, Phillips sent [174] Banks a manuscript copy of Morrison's "Memorandum" which was concerned with the Mutiny and its antecedents. It is likely that Howell and Morrison would have been warned that publication of "the Memorandum" or of "the Journal" which included information from the "Memorandum" would lead to legal proceedings.

Meanwhile, Professor Christian set about generating information for his Appendix, while Stephen Barney, Muspratt's Attorney, worked on a selection of "the Minutes of the Court Martial".

Professor Christian decided to set up a private "Court of Enquiry" purporting to be unbiased. There were twelve members, as if a jury of twelve good men and true, but of the eleven members, excluding the Professor himself, it has been shown [175] convincingly that at least nine members had connections or friendships with Christian's family. This was therefore nothing less than a travesty of an independent enquiry.

---

[173] Banks Papers A78-4 p2
[174] BM Add Ms 33.9.79 quoted by Kennedy
[175] "Bligh" G Kennedy Ch 21 1978

Professor Christian indemnified Barney against damages and arranged many statements damaging to Bligh that were not attributable so that Bligh could not take successful proceedings against named persons. The intention was to provoke Bligh into legal proceedings which could not be won.

The activities of Professor Christian had a dramatic effect in poisoning Bligh's reputation so that when Bligh returned in 1793 from the 2nd Breadfruit Voyage, the First Lord of the Admiralty, Lord Chatham, brother of the Prime Minister William Pitt the Younger, would not meet him.

Bligh by Bligh

Table 1

Ch 14. Pursuit and Court Martial of some Mutineers and its aftermath

23.9.1789
Christian and eight mutineers leave Tahiti for last time.
Summer 1790
Captain Edwards appointed to "Pandora".

22.3.1791
"Pandora" reached Tahiti
August 1791
Loss of "Pandora"

18.6.1792.
Some recaptured mutineers reach England

12-18.9.1792.
Court Martial on charges of Mutiny
24.10.1792
Royal reprieve for Heywood and Morrison
29.10.1792
Execution of three mutineers
1793 Professor Christian's unofficial court of enquiry

September 1793
Lord Chatham refuses to meet Bligh

Ch 15. 2nd Breadfruit Voyage and its aftermath

October 1790
Bligh's Court Martial on the loss of "Bounty"
December 1790
Lord Auckland authorises Voyage.
March 1791
Bligh nominated to lead Voyage
Summer 1791
Voyage begins
April 1792
"Providence" reaches Otaheite

20.7.1792
"Providence" leaves Otaheite

Early 1793
Breadfruit plants left in the West Indies
7.8.1793
"Providence" returns to Deptford, Duke of Clarence visits the ships
Early 1794
Edward Christian's "Appendix" published
Late 1794
Bligh's answer to the Appendix
Early 1795
Edward Christian's short reply to Bligh's answer
29.4.1795.
Bligh appointed Captain of "HMS Calcutta"

CHAPTER 15

The 2nd Breadfruit Voyage and its aftermath
29.12.1790 – 1795

At the end of December 1790, Lord Auckland wrote to Sir Joseph Banks authorising the 2nd Breadfruit Voyage. Bligh was put on half pay on the 8th of January 1791 following his promotion and this might have been arranged to free him to take charge of the forthcoming Voyage. It was probably a result of the House of Assembly, Jamaica, canvassing for Bligh to lead the 2nd Voyage that they voted him a gratuity of 500 guineas.

On the 21st February, Ann, the sixth daughter of William and Elizabeth was born and she was baptized on the 19th of March at St Mary-at-Lambeth as her parents had by then moved to 14 Moor Place, Lambeth. It must have been a great disappointment to the family that Ann was mentally handicapped and epileptic.

In March, the Admiralty sanctioned the Voyage, nominated Bligh as being in charge and asked him to find a vessel. His instructions included an examination of Torres Strait, though this was a potentially disastrous instruction. Due to the unknown dangers of the Strait, it was sufficient surely in such an enterprise to navigate through the Strait without taking unnecessary risks.

Bligh asked for and received not merely a new vessel "Providence", of 420 tons, but also an escort, the brig "Assistant", of 110 tons.

Royal approval for the Voyage was given in the same month, so Bligh was formally committed to the Voyage and to the inevitability of being out of the country if the mutineers were brought back and tried.

In April [176], Bligh was posted as Captain of "Providence". He chose as his Second in Command, Lieutenant Nathanial Portlock

---

[176] PRO Admiralty log 51/1507

who had been Master's Mate in "Discovery" during Cook's third voyage to the South Seas and who became, following the death of Cook, Master's Mate in "Resolution" where Bligh was Master. Portlock took charge of the escort "Assistant". The First Lieutenant in "Providence" was Francis Godolphin Bond, the son of Bligh's half sister; Lieutenant Pearce was in charge of two marine non-commissioned officers and fifteen marines; the third Lieutenant was George Tobin, an officer in whose career Lord Nelson took an interest, as Tobin was a relative of Lord Nelson's wife.

One of the Midshipmen on the Expedition was Matthew Flinders, previously a Midshipman on Captain Pasley's, "HMS Bellerophon". What is now clear is that Pasley, a relative of Heywood, secured the placement of Flinders as a means of keeping an eye on Bligh to obtain information which might damage Bligh and which might be used in mitigation of Heywood, in case Heywood returned to England to be accused of mutiny. Pasley wrote [177] to Flinders on the 3rd of June 1791: "All that I have to request, in return for the good offices I have done you, is that you never fail writing me by all possible opportunities during your voyage; and that in your letters you will be very particular and circumstantial in regard to everything and place you may chance to see or visit, with your own observation thereon...."

On the 17th of July 1791, Bligh wrote to Sir Joseph Banks: "Should Peckover, my late Gunner ever trouble you to render him further services I shall esteem it a favor if you would tell him I informed you he was a viscious and worthless fellow – He applied to me to render him service and wanted to be appointed Gunner of Providence, but as I determined never to suffer an officer who was with me in the Bounty to sail with again, it was for that cause I did not apply for him".

It was probably about this time that Captain Riou, previously a Midshipman in Cook's third voyage to the South Seas and known to Bligh, asked for a reference for John Fryer. Bligh wrote [178] "Riou applied for Fryer and I refused to give any a good Character...."

The Voyage began on the 3rd of August 1791. As "Providence" reached warmer weather, Bligh became so ill with an illness "of a

---

[177] "The Life of Vice Admiral Bligh RN" G Mackaness Ch XXIII 1951
[178] "Remarks of Captain Bligh on the Court Martial" ML Safe 1/43

nervous kind" that Edward Harwood, surgeon of "Providence", wrote to Mrs Bligh on the 13th of September on his behalf. Lt Portlock was transferred back to "Providence", while Lt Bond was put in charge of "Assistant". However Bond was dissatisfied with his "secluded life and the loss of his merry messmates". By late September, Bligh was well enough to carry out his duties, but a full year afterwards he wrote of this continuing illness. In the late 20th century, the illness appears to have some of the characteristics of "post traumatic stress disorder". The stress of the Mutiny and the open boat journey had probably affected Bligh despite his acknowledgement of considerable psychological reserves. It is interesting that the effects were delayed until Bligh experienced similar conditions to those he experienced just prior to the Mutiny and until he had the time and privacy to recall those events.

On the 30th of October, a week before landing at the Cape, the Quartermaster was guilty of insubordination to the Commander's Mate and had assaulted the Boatswain's Mate for which he received 30 lashes. Bligh had been once again faced with having to order disciplinary measures to support others.

Lt Tobin [179] writes amusingly of some of his brushes with authority: "A few passing squalls had taken us within board as well as without, but by clewing up in time (shortening sail) without any serious mischief". He wrote confidentially to his brother about his Captain "... in her commander I had to encounter the quickest sailor's eye, guided by a thorough knowledge of every branch of the profession necessary on such a voyage... It is easy of belief that on first joining a man of such experience my own youth and inferiority were rather busy visitors. They were, but we had by this time crossed the equinoctial and were about doubling the Cape together and I had courage to believe that my Captain was not dissatisfied with me..."

In early February 1792, the Expedition reached Tasmania. Bligh would have been surprised to know that Adventure Bay is on Bruny Island and not part of the mainland of Tasmania as he thought or that the Tasman peninsular was part of the mainland Tasmania and not one of a number of islands, as he also thought. Bligh left there a variety of fruit trees, fruiting plants and herbs

---

[179] Quoted in "Life of Vice Admiral Bligh" G Mackaness Ch XXIII 1951

including apple, pomegranate, fig, quince, strawberry and rosemary. He reproached himself for not digging for potatoes which he had planted on his earlier visit. Bligh, Tobin and George Holt, a Midshipman, made a number of water colour paintings largely of wild life seen on the Voyage.

On the 10th of April 1792, the Expedition reached Otaheite. Bligh renewed his friendship with Tinah (Tynah) and Iddeah. Within the month, Bligh had been invited by the Regent to see the Great Temple and to take part in a religious ceremony. Bligh describes this in some detail: "The Morai or temple where the ceremony was held was an oblong pile of stones about ten yards long and fourteen feet high – on top of which were about fourteen rude ornaments, some resembling a man and some a bird. The whole range of them was called the Tebboo – taboo – ataiah. I interpret this as meaning Great Temple or principal place of worship ... Tootaha – the High Priest – was at prayers and the Etuah – God – laying before him wrapt in red cloth. To the right of it lay the dead body of a man wrapt in the plaited branch of a cocoa-nut tree and tied to a pole by which means the body was carried about."

"To the right of the priest were two drums and a distance of twenty yards off was the Evatah or altar, on which there were lying twenty nine dead hogs and a turtle. Two priests assisted Tootaha at the ceremony as well as two inferior people of that order. After the first prayer upon our arrival, the bundle called the Etuah was untied and exposed. The Marro Oorah or feather belt was taken out of another bundle and spread out, so that I could see every sacred thing they had."

"The Marro Oorah or feather belt is put on the Erree ra high -Boy King- when the sacrifice is made and the eye presented. It was twelve feet long. One half was made with yellow feathers, traced with red feathers, the other half was simply of red English bunting – it was not neatly made or in any way elegant."

"The red bundle or Etuah which they call Oro was nothing more than a number of yellow and red feathers and four rolls eighteen inches long plaited over cocoanut fibres, and to these they give the name of some inferior deities.... Tootaha now began a prayer, it was very long and had many repetitions, so that the retentiveness of this man's memory is not so extraordinary. Taking up his prayer in all its various changes and repetitions, the whole amounted to this: we have sacrificed a man. We have presented one of his eyes to thee as a token of thy power and one to our king, because it is by thy will he reigneth over us. We display our feathers. We present our hogs to thee. We do this, O Oro, because we know thou delightest in it. Our wish is to do as thou desirest. Prosper therefore our undertakings. Let us conquer our enemies and live in plenty."

"After this, one of the hogs was burnt and cut up and the remains brought to the Morai. This appeared to me to be particularly the offering of my friend Tynah. Another prayer was pronounced in favour of King George, myself, and the people who were with me in the ships. Drums were beat at intervals and the hogs laid on the Evatah or altar and the body buried by the side of Morai."

"The Marro was tied up in one bundle, the Etuah in another, and carefully covered over with a piece of red English cloth and the ceremony ended. There were not many people present and, among those that were, I saw no grave or serious attention. Otoo (Tynah's father) was carried about on a man's shoulders, talking to us and playing his tricks during the whole time of the devotion. The priest himself, the moment he had done prayers, began to joke in an obscene manner."

Early in May, Bligh records that he met Mary, the native consort of McIntosh, one of "Bounty's" crew who had been taken away in "Pandora" but for whom Bligh's affidavit secured him his acquittal. Mary told him that he had been well spoken of by McIntosh, Coleman, Hillbrant, Norman, Byrne and Ellison, but significantly Stewart and Heywood were not listed with them.

On the 20th of June, Bligh wrote an appreciation of his Second in Command, Lt Portlock in his log "... Lt Portlock whose alertness and attention to duty makes me at all times think of him with regard and esteem."

The plants that were taken on the return journey consisted of 2126 breadfruit plants, 472 other plants and 36 curiosity plants making a total of 2634. This was a formidable responsibility for the two botanists, as more than twice the number of breadfruit plants were being taken compared to the 1st Voyage.

The ships left Otaheite on the 20th of July 1792 less than three and a half months after their arrival. This was made possible by scheduling the time of the stay at Otaheite to a growth period of the breadfruit and to a period when the breadfruit plants could be moved in their pots.

Tobin tells us that Bligh took extra precautions to ensure the success of the expedition after leaving Otaheite by posting an extra warrant officer to each watch.

The journey back took the ships to Fiji where Bligh listed 28 islands. Lt Portlock made the following claim for Bligh: "Tasman it appears, in 1643, fell in with the eastern or small cluster of this group and gave it the name of Prince William's Isles, but certainly Captain Bligh is the discoverer of the western or large group". Bligh's description of dwellings on the Fijian Island of Ngau is interesting: "It is an uncommon sight in this sea to see well-built villages on an eminence, but here was a considerable one delightfully situated on the brow of a hill amidst a charming grove of trees. The houses were thatched all round the sides and tops with one opening or doorway. Some of them resembled those of the Friendly Islands with the roofs exceedingly overhanging the base and sides inclined outwards so that the floor is considerably less than the bounds of the roof. Others were like the Sandwich Islands houses..."

At the end of August, they sighted the coast of New Guinea and were soon to begin the navigation of Torres Strait. Lt Tobin nearly came to grief when he and his companions in a ship's cutter were attacked by native canoes. Afterwards nine canoes with about a hundred native warriors attacked the larger ships where a quartermaster died later from a poisoned arrow and another crew member lost the use of his arm.

Gales one night added to the danger of "rocks all round and a dreadful tide running". Of one incident, Bligh wrote "I furled all sails and also came to anchor. To my horror when the half cable came out it had the dog stopper on which although I cut it immediately and let go a second anchor I only had it just in my power to save the ship from the rocks..."

By the 20th of September, there was no land or shoals to the westward and they were through the Strait.

Matthew Flinders wrote [180]: "This was accomplished in nineteen days, the passage from the Pacific or Great Ocean to the Indian Sea;

---

[180] "A Voyage to Terra Australis" M Flinders Introduction p XXIX 1814.

without other misfortune than what arose from the attack of the natives and some damage done to the cables. Perhaps no space of 3½° in length... presents more dangers than Torres Strait; but, with caution and perseverance, the Captains Bligh and Portlock proved them to be surmountable; and within a reasonable time...."

The supply of fresh water did however become a problem at this stage and more than two hundred breadfruit plants were lost.

Bligh would have been understandably angry when he is said [181] to have discovered that someone had watered some of the plants with sea water and to have said that he "longed to flog the whole company".

If Flinders was writing such things to Pasley, it is understandable that relationships between Bligh and Flinders deteriorated when Bligh later found out what Pasley was doing.

On the 2nd of October 1792, Bligh wrote [182] to his wife Betsy from Coupang: "I am well except for a low nervous disease which I have had more or less since I left Tenariffe... This is the last voyage I will ever make if it pleases God to restore me safe to you... Next June, my dear, dear Betsy, I hope you will have me home to protect you myself – I love you dearer than ever a woman was loved – you are, nor have not been a moment out of my mind, every joy and blessing attend you my life, and bless my dear Harriet, my dear Mary, my dear Betsy, my dear Fanny, my dear Jenny and my dear little Ann. I send you all my kisses on this paper and ever pray to God to bless you – I will not say farewell to you now my dear Betsy because I am homeward bound. I shall lose no time, every happyness attend you, My dearest life, and ever remember me your best of Friends and most affectionate Husband."

Wm Bligh

On the 13th of December 1792, Francis Bond, First Lieutenant, wrote a confidential letter to his brother in which he expressed "no small disappointment to my hopes that I have not gained so much information as expected; an insurmountable bar has always lain in my way, since my pride will not allow me to receive magisterial

---

[181] "The Life of Matthew Flinders RN" E Scott p33 1914.
[182] Bligh Family Correspondence ML Safe 1/45

tuition..." He adds "...soon after leaving England, I wished to receive information from this imperious master, until I found he particularly exposed any deficiency on my part in the Nautical Art & ...". Bond found "the utmost difficulty in keeping on tolerable terms with him".

Professor Kennedy (1989) writes: "We only have a list of Bond's grievances, which do not amount to much".

Bligh showed no favouritism to his proud nephew who wrote of his uncle's "unparralled (sic) pride".

The ships reached St Helena on the 17th of December 1792 where ten breadfruit plants were left. The island of St Vincent in the West Indies was reached on the 23rd of January 1793. Bligh left more than 500 plants there and was rewarded with plate worth 100 guineas. The House of Assembly in Jamaica voted 1000 guineas to Bligh and 500 guineas to Portlock. Sir Joseph Banks informed the House of Assembly that "You have made a good man happy and a poor man comparatively rich".

The irony about the enterprise was that later the Breadfruit was not found to be sufficiently palatable and did not meet the objective for which it was brought.

The return of the ships were delayed due to the outbreak of war with France, but they were escorted back in convoy on the 15th of June 1793 and reached Deptford on the 7th of August.

The King's son, the Duke of Clarence, paid a visit to the ships before the crews were paid off.

The author, Owen Rutter, records[183] that during this second voyage lasting two years, only 12 punishments by lash were recorded, of which on only two occasions were more than 12 lashes ordered. He categorized Bligh's behaviour in terms of late 18th Century traditions as "extremely moderate".

The Kent Register of the 6th September records the paying off: "His Majesty's ship Providence... was paid off at Woolwich. It was a scene highly gratifying to observe the cordial unanimity which prevailed among the officers; and decency of conduct and healthy and respectable appearance of the seamen after so long and perilous a voyage, not one of whom but evinced that good order

---

[183] "Turbulent Journey" O Rutter. p72 (1936).

and discipline had been invariably observed. The high estimation, in which Captain Bligh was deservedly held by the whole crew, was conspicuous to all present. He was cheered on quitting the ship to attend the Commissioner; and at the dock gates the men drew up and repeated the parting acclamation".

Bligh's official report gave credit to all his senior officers and singled out some for special mention.

On the 18th of September 10 days after his official report, he wrote to the Admiralty asking them to order the Navy Board to settle arrears of pay for six seamen from "Providence" who were waiting to join other ships.

However, Edward Christian's activities had clearly been having some effect despite the efforts of Sir Joseph Banks. Bligh waited on the First Lord of the Admiralty, Lord Chatham, in vain, in spite of Lieutenant Portlock being granted an audience.

Bligh wrote [184] to the Admiralty to point out that the reduction of 2 shillings per day in his pay in lieu of profit meant that he did not clear his expenses. He did not obtain any redress, but the gratuities he received in the West Indies meant that he was not at all out of pocket; but it does point to the likelihood that his pursing was not carried out at the expense of his crew.

At this time, Bligh was able to claim the gold medal of the Society for the Encouragement of Arts, Manufactures and Commerce offered to the first person to transport six living breadfruit plants to the West Indies.

Bligh was now on half-pay and had time to catch up with what had happened at the Court Martial of the mutineers and with what Pasley and Professor Christian were doing. Bligh at some stage fell out with Flinders. In a letter to Sir Joseph Banks, Flinders wrote [185] later "perhaps he (Bligh) will see the injustice of considering me with an unfavourable eye". Banks would however have known that Pasley had used Flinders to report on Bligh. After the 2nd Breadfruit Voyage, Flinders had returned to serve under Pasley on "HMS Bellerophon" as a Midshipman.

---

[184] PRO Admiralty 1/1509 Cap B 165.
[185] HR NSW vol 6 p274

Sir Joseph Banks would have had other matters for Bligh's attention. He had received a letter dated the 16th of December 1792 from Edward Christian while Bligh was away; this letter concerned "Purcell, Fryer, Peckover, Hayward and Smith". Bligh prepared the following observations [186]: "These people had an opportunity, at the Court Martial held on the loss of 'the Bounty' and for many months after it, (until Bligh left on the 2nd Breadfruit Voyage) of declaring everything they knew; it is therefore extraordinary there should be any new assertions at this time. It appears that these People have been tampered with, for Captain Bligh tried Purcell by Court Martial immediately after the tryal for the loss of the Ship – Fryer was particularly under displeasure and Peckover received some proofs of his disapprobation, yet the latter applied to Captain Bligh to accompany him again in the Providence and received a refusal – They would therefore surely have brought forward anything they knew against Captain Bligh before the arrival of the Mutineers, if there had been any just grounds".

Before Bligh returned from the 2nd Breadfruit Voyage, Edward Christian had been involved in 1783 with his unofficial, biased, "Court of Enquiry" and he worked with a lawyer, S Barney, to prepare selective abbreviated "Minutes of the proceedings of the Court Martial held at Portsmouth... on ten persons charged with mutiny on board His Majesty's ship the Bounty". This paper with an Appendix by Edward Christian was published early in 1794.

The main thrust of the Appendix was that the Hell of which Fletcher Christian spoke was one caused by Bligh as exemplified by the insults which Christian received from Bligh in front of the chiefs at Annamooka (Nomuka).

Edward Christian claimed that this line of reasoning was supported by the fact that those with Bligh in the open boat were said to have no resentment against Fletcher Christian. Purcell, the Carpenter, was quoted [187] to show there was resentment against Bligh: "His Captain told him 'if I had not taken so much pains with you, you would never have been here'. The carpenter replied 'Yes, if you had not taken so much pains with us, we should never have been here'."

---

[186] "Remarks on Mr Christian's letters" ML Safe 1/43187 "Minutes of the proceedings..." S Barney Appendix p68 1794

[187] "Minutes of the proceedings..." S Barney Appendix p68 1794

The 2nd Breadfruit Voyage and its aftermath

A fatal flaw in the Appendix is that Edward Christian claimed that Fletcher Christian did not have a female attachment on Otaheite. He writes "The officers who were with Christian upon the same duty declare that he never had a female favourite at Otaheite nor any attachment or particular connection among the women. It is true that some had what they called their girls or women with whom they constantly lived all the time they were upon the island, but this was not the case with Christian".

Professor Kennedy wrote [188]: "This was not true; he did have a female companion and he took her to Pitcairn".

Among the draft notes to Edward Christian's letters which Bligh drafted for Sir Joseph Banks, Bligh wrote that Lebogue had believed he had seen Christian's girl on their stay at Otaheite during the 2nd Breadfruit Voyage also. Lebogue however must have been mistaken and misled Bligh into thinking that she might not have left Otaheite with Christian. However we have seen that both Joseph Coleman, the Armourer, and John Smith testified that Fletcher Christian had a girl on Otaheite before the mutiny. Coleman made it clear that this girl was the same one who went with him and Fletcher Christian to Tubuai (Tobooy) and lived with Fletcher Christian. It is also clear from her own evidence that Mauatua had gone to Pitcairn.

After returning from the second breadfruit voyage, Bligh planned to move to a new house, 3 Durham Place (now 100 Lambeth Road) which was only a short distance from Moor Place.

During 1794, Bligh worked on a response as a means of defending himself against the damage done to him by the Appendix and press reports about it.

In July 1794, Dr Harwood, Surgeon of "Providence", wrote to "the Times" in support of Bligh. In August, Bligh took affidavits from Coleman, Smith and Lebogue. On the 28th of October, Captain Lamb who had been Chief Mate under Bligh in "Britannia" in the Merchant Marine on the West Indian run before the 1st Breadfruit Voyage, wrote to Bligh: "...I saw your partiality for the young man (Fletcher Christian)... though he went about every point of duty with a degree of indifference that to me was truly unpleasant; but you were blind to his faults... in the Appendix it is

---

[188] "Bligh" Gavin Kennedy Ch 21 1978

said that Mr Fletcher Christian had no attachment among the women at Otaheite; if that was the case he must have been much altered since he was with you in the Britannia, he was then one of the most foolish young men I ever knew in regard to these."

The year 1794 saw a mutiny in "HMS Culloden" as a result of which five seamen were executed.

At the end of 1794, Bligh published in "the British Critic" his answer to the Appendix. This consisted of an introduction and fifteen detailed arguments, but it was essentially a defensive document and one calculated to avoid the legal traps which Professor Christian had laid.

Early in 1795, the Professor published "a short reply to Captain W Bligh's answer" which claimed to show that Lawrence Lebogue had committed "perjury" in denying making certain statements to his self appointed Court of Enquiry and claimed that two members of that Enquiry, who were in fact friends of the Christian family, had corroborated that claim.

If Edward Christian was trying to defend the family name against the damage done by Feltcher Christian's mutiny, then Fletcher's cousin, the Chief Justice,[189] was not exactly supporting him when he remarked that Edward Christian "operated in the full vigour of his incapacity".

By that time, Bligh was occupied in getting back into active naval service. On the 13th of April 1795, he was appointed Captain of "HMS Warley" but actually on the 29th of April 1795 was appointed [190] to the command of "HMS Calcutta", in fact, the same vessal, which was a merchant one, that Bligh had to fit out as a 24-gun armed vessel. On the 29th May, Bligh wrote to the Admiralty:

"Sir,

Whereas by letter from the Navy Board, Deptford Yard and my Commission, His Majesty's ship I command now stands under three different names, I beg leave to know under which their Lordships have been pleased that she shall be distinguished...." the answer to a higher authority was:

---

[189] "Mr Bligh's bad language". G Dening p250 '92.
[190] PRO Admiralty log 51/1102

"Inform him that the name of Warley has been changed to Calcutta".

On the 1st of August 1795, Bligh informed the Admiralty: "...Except in these particulars, the want of officers and men, His Majesty's Ship under my command is perfectly ready and fit for service."

CHAPTER 16

The distortion of "Faction" especially in films about Wm Bligh

Novels and films have contributed heavily to the development of the legend of infamy concerning William Bligh.

The treatment of Bligh in novels and films makes an interesting case-study in the uses and misuses of communication.

The books "Mutiny" in 1933, "Men against the Sea" 1934 and "Pitcairn's Island" by C B Nordhoff and J N Hall gave warning in each case that they were novels; in these cases there is a deadly mixture of fact and fiction, now called "faction". Much of the factual story had been published in 1931 in "The Life of Vice Admiral Bligh" by Dr George Mackaness, but the facts were to be poisoned with falsehoods to sensationalise the story and prepare a mix which the film industry was only too glad to exploit.

The broad distinction between fact and fiction is inadequate, because we tend to associate fact with truth and we have difficulty in talking about false facts, which almost seem a contradiction in terms.

We can however talk about true and false descriptions of fact.

There is a similar difficulty in talking about fiction. We all understand that "pure fiction" is unrelated to fact, but there are fictional descriptions which purport to be "pure fiction" but which in fact maliciously distort the truth; such descriptions could be called false descriptions in impure fiction. There are therefore false descriptions of fact and false descriptions of impure fiction.

It will be useful to examine some examples of false descriptions in two films about Bligh; the MGM 1935 film with Charles Laughton as Bligh and Clark Gable as Christian was based on a novel by Nordhoff and Hall. We are duly warned therefore that we are dealing with "faction". The following examples of false descriptions from the film give some idea of the distortion involved and of the vilification of the character of Bligh: Early in the film, Bligh is portrayed as ordering the continuation of the sadistic flogging of a seaman when the man was already dead; He is portrayed as ordering the cruel and banned punishment of "keel hauling", whereby the viction is hauled under water from one side of the ship to the keel and up the other side; He is purported to have been involved in a further flogging which resulted in death; Bligh is falsely shown to accompany Captain Edwards in HMS Pandora and to be associated with the infamous Pandora's Box. The film also involves "pure fiction" in the use of a non-historical character.

The MGM 1962 film with Trevor Howard as Bligh and Marlon Brando as Christian was also based on the novels of Nordhoff and Hall. The following examples of false descriptions compound the distortion and vilification of Bligh: Mills accused Bligh of being a thief and was flogged for it; Norman died at Cape Horn after being crushed; Bligh ordered the punishment of "keel hauling" and left the corpse to the sharks; Bligh places a ladle for water on the yard arm as a result of which a man falls to his death; and Bligh stops Christian giving water to Williams who was in a critical state.

Gavin Kennedy categorises both these films as ridiculous, but they were worse than ridiculous in the damage which they did to the reputation of Bligh and to the furtherance of the legend of infamy.

The 1984 production of "the Bounty" with Anthony Hopkins as Bligh and Mel Gibson as Christian was based on the biography "Captain Bligh and Mr Christian" 1972 by Richard Hough. This started as a genuine attempt to present the historical story, but the biographer and therefore the scriptwriters had not at that time access to the crucial psychological theory, which was only published later for general readership, that helps to interpret the key motivations of Christian prior to the Mutiny. The film recognises the existence of Mauatua, Christian's favourite, and of her relationship with Christian. It records Christian's plan to make a raft, but this is so obscurely presented that it is almost unintelligible.

Because Richard Hough, the biographer, did not fully understand the nature of Christian's psychological "hell", he tended to impute blame on Bligh to fill the vacuum. Kennedy writes interestingly: "It is not surprising that the Hollywood scriptwriters have had to use their imagination to create an image for Bligh that would justify Christian's actions".

The film later on makes much of a supposed threat by Bligh to sail home by way of Cape Horn. Bligh's course was to sail by the Endeavour Straits and then to the West Indies by way of the Cape of Good Hope.

There is still therefore scope for the record to be put straight. The two earlier films contain false descriptions concerning Bligh which are clearly defamatory, tending to damage his character, reputation and good standing.

It is surely a matter of public regret that the character of Bligh has been vilified by means of the propagation of false descriptions, made so many years after his death.

I do not comment on two Australian films made prior to those made by MGM nor on a musical staged in 1987, but all these contain gross errors at the expense of Bligh.

CHAPTER 17

The causes of the Mutiny in "Bounty"

The major explanation in this book of the cause of the Mutiny in "Bounty" is that Fletcher Christian had to get back to Mauatua.

Late 20th century scientific psychological theory predicts the reaction to the threatened loss of a potentially long-term relationship, particularly the phases of searching for the loved one and despair at not being reunited. The further reaction of anger and accusation by the searcher (Christian) against the person (Bligh) mainly frustrating the searching for the loved one was predicted also. The reaction was further complicated by the regard which the searcher had previously for the person frustrating the search. This ambivalence resulted in acts of kindness (such as the offer of a sextant, a vital navigational instrument) interspersed with acts of an almost lethal kind (such as threatening to kill with a bayonet and setting adrift without fire arms in an open boat).

Fletcher Christian's reaction was probably exacerbated by his psychological make-up. It is known from Bligh's description of the mutineers that Christian suffered from an unusual perspiration of his hands, possibly a sign of earlier psychological stress. It is known that Fletcher lost his father when Fletcher was only four years old and that this left his mother with severe financial difficulties such that when Fletcher was sixteen years old, his mother faced bankruptcy, leaving Cumberland to live in the Isle of Man and being bailed out by her late husband's family. However Charles Christian, a naval surgeon, asserts that his brother Fletcher was "slow to be moved".

How far was Fletcher Christian's reaction pathological? It would appear under English law at the moment [191] that grief is

---

[191] Law Report – Arbitration re Ferry "The Herald of Free Enterprise" quoted in "the Guardian" 2.5.89. p39

pathological if it is in excess of a normal grief reaction. That Fletcher's grief reaction resulted in action which was threatening to his life, in seeking to return to his loved one through shark infested waters on a raft so flimsy that it amounted to little better than swimming, is surely in excess of a normal grief reaction and is consequently pathological. In so far as Fletcher was suffering "pathological grieving", now legally [1] recognised as a mental illness, he was acting with diminished responsibility.

A little later in leading the Mutiny, as he was mentally ill, he could be said to be acting with diminished responsibility. Christian's supporters have therefore no need to scapegoat Bligh.

It will be interesting to compare this explanation with a range of explanations given over the last two centuries for the causes of the Mutiny:

William Bligh himself wrote [192]: "I can only conjecture that the mutineers had assured themselves of a more happy life among the Otaheitans than they could possibly have in England; which, joined to some female connections, have most probably been the principal cause of the whole transaction".

The following words from his log show that Bligh on reflection appreciated the power of feelings involved in the separation of those with established emotional connections: "It is therefore now not to be wondered at -tho' not possible to be foreseen- that a set of sailors led by officers and void of connections, or if they have any, not possessed of natural feelings sufficient to wish themselves never to be separated from them, should be led by such powerful inducements."

"But equal to this what a temptation it is to such wretches when they find it in their power – however illegally it can be got at- to fix themselves in the midst of plenty, in the finest island in the world, where they need not labour and where the allurements of dissipation are more than equal to anything that can be conceived".

Fletcher Christian apparently destroyed his written records in case the Mutiny should fail, so we have to rely on secondary sources for his views. According to Morrison [193], Christian blamed Bligh for the Mutiny: "Finding himself much hurt by the treatment

---

[192] "A Narrative of the Mutiny..." W Bligh 1790 p9
[193] Morrison's Journal ML Safe 1/33

he had received from Mr Bligh, he determined to quit the ship the preceding evening..."

Other commentators quoted by Darby [194] have held that Christian was looking for an excuse to get back to his mistress in Tahiti.

Both Edward Christian and James Morrison emphasise in imaginative language what they portray as the humiliation of Fletcher Christian by Bligh at Annamooka and during the incident about coconuts on "Bounty" the day before the Mutiny.

At Annamooka, Christian was clearly not operating effectively and failed to carry out Bligh's orders for which he received a dressing down. Morrison, who was writing to denigrate Bligh and probably threatened to have his Captain court martialled as a means of securing a pardon from a death sentence, made out that Bligh called Christian "a cowardly rascal".

In regard to the coconut incident, Morrison made out that Bligh called Christian "a liar". Bligh, as previously mentioned, wrote of a "public theft" and suspected that officers turned a blind eye. This explanation [195] was supported by Mr Hallet, Midshipman, and by Lawrence Lebogue, Able Seaman. This probably meant that officers were criticised in general, rather than Christian being picked on alone. It is interesting that Morrison in his Journal says that Christian said that he didn't take any, while Edward Christian said that he did take one.

Christian interprets his "hell" as being caused by Bligh, but his "hell" is interpreted by some biographers, including Kennedy [196], as one created in his own mind by himself.

Christian tries to make out that he is escaping from Bligh when, in reality, he is trying to return to Mauatua.

Dr Mackaness wrote [197] that "Except for one or two occasions when Bligh rightly had to censure him, he (Christian) had been treated with generosity and kindly consideration".

John Fryer, the Master, claimed that it was "short allowances" which caused the Mutiny when he made formal complaint against

---

[194] "Who caused the Mutiny on the Bounty" M Darby Ch 10 1965
[195] "Who caused the Mutiny on the Bounty" M Darby Ch 10 1965
[196] "Bligh" G Kennedy Ch 13 1978
[197] "The Life of Vice Admiral Bligh" G Mackaness Ch13 1931

Bligh at Sourabaya. He failed to convince the Dutch Authorities that Bligh had made extravagant charges to government or could substantiate any other complaint. Fryer then apologised. It is possible that John Fryer really did not know of Christian's relationship with Mauatua on the shore camp, because Fryer was based on "Bounty". He says that Christian did not have such a relationship, but the seamen, including Lawrence Lebogue, had better information.

It is interesting that Fryer in his journal written in 1790 mentioned only Edward Young in the coconut incident, while Morrison in 1792/3 and Edward Christian in 1793/4 made Fletcher Christian the focus of that event for their own reasons.

Bligh was clearly not satisfied with the performance of Fryer, particularly after his failure to look after "Bounty's" sails and his previous attempt to obtain a reference by threatening not to sign the warrant officers accounts.

The only reference by Edward Young, Midshipman, to the cause of the Mutiny was contained in a footnote to Edward Christian's Appendix. He is imagined to have said "Yes, it is a serious affair to be starved". There is no evidence of anything remotely like starvation relating to "Bounty's" crew and this remark must refer to Bligh's acknowledged reduction, when necessary, to two thirds of an allowance which was normally one third under consumed. The crew would have been reimbursed for the one third reduction in the allowance, as "Bounty" survivors when they returned to England were reimbursed.

William Purcell, the Carpenter, in making a formal complaint against Bligh at Sourabaya said that "Stoping provisions" was the cause of the Mutiny. Bligh's acknowledgement about allowances is relevant here.

Purcell had been obstructive at Adventure Bay, Tasmania as well as at Otaheite and he was reprimanded following his Court Martial in 1790.

James Morrison, the Boatswain's Mate, went along with Christian "...much hurt by the treatment he had received from Mr Bligh, he determined to quit the ship...". He also alleged by innuendo that Bligh was an incompetent commander and corrupt purser and that this contributed to the Mutiny. It will be useful

The causes of the Mutiny in "Bounty"

briefly to summarise the charges he made and offer comment on them:

Morrison accuses Bligh of diverting cheese and other provisions to his own household, implying theft. It was apparently a frequent practice for pursers to divert small amounts of provisions to their household before ships sailed and by careful pursing to make up the deficiency before the return to port.

John Samuel, the Captain's clerk, may have possibly diverted some provisions probably without the Captain's connivance but, being caught out, was castigated by Bligh as a "worthless clerk". However Bligh says that the cheese was stolen after the public counting out. Over the matter of the pumpkins (pumpions), Morrison implies that Bligh was unfair in the proportion of pumpkin proposed in lieu of ship's biscuit (bread). Morrison says the proportion was one pound of pumpkin for two pounds of bread. Bligh said that he offered two pounds of pumpkin for one pound of bread.

Morrison claims that beef and pork pieces were not weighed and implies that short weight was being given. Bligh insists that provisions were opened publicly for which there is evidence in the log and that they were weighed so that short weight by suppliers could be recorded. The Dutch Authorities examined his books at Sourabaya and were satisfied that complaints against Bligh relating to provisions were unjustified.

Morrison complained of the small quantity of boiled wheat and barley as well as pease and oatmeal. Such quantity he said caused commotion – "broils in the gally" – requiring supervision. Bligh claimed that the men were receiving their allowance or remuneration in lieu and he was careful of the men's health. The injuries (log 13th April 1788), received in or close to the galley, Bligh said were caused by the storm at Cape Horn and not by arguments about small quantities of food.

Morrison wrote that Bligh denied opportunities for complaint. Certainly Bligh did not allow complaints to interfere with the implementation of his orders, but he did give his crew an opportunity to raise formal complaint, as at Sourabaya. It is significant that no complaint was made against Bligh, when each member of the launch was asked just this at Bligh's Court Martial on the loss of "Bounty".

Morrison suggested that Bligh was rapacious by keeping "prime pieces" of beef and pork for his own table. Bligh denied that and referred to his instructions forbidding this. He wrote privately that he fed on the same rations as his men, only reserving poultry for his own use.

Bligh denied Morrison's charge that he served up meat from an animal that had died. Bligh claimed to have killed the animal about which Morrison was complaining and Bligh described his instructions to ensure animals were not killed indiscriminately.

It is probably true that some of the animals which were killed after being kept on board for sometime had lost weight, being described as only "skin and bone" by Morrison, but Bligh was particularly careful of the health of his crew and other food was available.

In his Memorandum [198], Morrison charged Bligh with corrupt pursing and colluding with other officers who "had in the former parts of their Voyage been base enough to sign false Survey Books and papers to the prejudice of his Majesty and Government. That it may not be supposed that this account has no foundation, the Bills drawn at the Cape of Good Hope will prove that Wm Muspratt and Thos Hayward, both belonging to 'the Bounty' have signed as respectable merchants of that place".

Bligh replied [199] "... Muspratt and Hayward signed only as witnesses in C Bligh's behalf that he payed the Money to Mr C Brandt due to him on an account with Captain Bligh to prevent by any accident his calling on Captain Bligh for a second payment – These Papers are now to be seen at the Publick Boards".

Captains were expected to buy at a discount and make a profit. When Bligh became a Post Captain for the 2nd Voyage, he became liable for a deduction from his pay to take account of this profit, but he found that the profit realised on that voyage did not cover the expenses he incurred. It seems likely that he did not use his position as purser to exploit his crew financially.

At Otaheite, Morrison charged Bligh with theft of other people's property and interfering in the "market for hogs". Following Cook's example, Bligh enforced a monopoly purchasing

---

[198] "Memorandum..." J Morrison p 39 ML Safe 1/33
[199] "Remarks..." Wm Bligh p 52 ML Safe 1/43

organisation in which William Peckover was appointed the sole trader to keep the price of goods low. He therefore threatened to confiscate and actually did confiscate goods purchased outside this framework. It was necessary for the success of the Voyage that trading disputes did not prejudice good relations between "Bounty's" crew and the natives.

Morrison criticised not only Bligh but also his officers; he wrote "the behaviour of the officers on this occasion was dastardly beyond description, none of them ever making the least attempt to rescue the ship, which could have been effected had any attempt been made by one of them, as some of those who were under arms did not know what they were about and Robt Lamb who I found centry at the fore hatchway when I first came on deck went away in the boat and Isaac Martin had laid his arms down and gone into the boat but had been ordered out again".

It must be emphasised that unarmed men were facing armed men, in spite of what Morrison said. [200] He wrote: "It will no doubt be wondered at that a ship with 44 men on board should be taken by so small a Number as 10 or 11 which were the whole that ever appeared in Arms; on that Day 10 muskets, 2 cutlasses and 2 pistols were all that appeared to have been in use when the Boat put off – But no resistance was made. It will here be asked why? It may be answered that the Officers were not on such good terms with their Commander, as to risk their Lives in his service, and the Service of their Country was not at their Hearts".

Bligh drew to Sir Joseph Bank's attention that "Among all these charges, there is not one of cruelty or oppression".

The Biographer, Professor Kennedy, wrote [201] that Morrison was unable to document or invent any action that could be regarded as a justification for Mutiny.

John Adams, alias Alexander Smith, signed in 1825 Captain Beechey's narrative to the effect [202] that Bligh had repeated misunderstandings with his officers and had on several occasions given them and the crew just reasons for complaint; yet he added that there was no real discontent among the crew, nor any idea of

---

[200] "Memorandum..." J Morrison p 37 & 38 ML Safe 1/33
[201] "Bligh" G Kennedy Ch 20 1978
[202] "Life of Vice Admiral Bligh" G Mackaness Ch xxi 1931

offering violence to the Commander. The officers, particularly the Master and Mr Christian had most cause for dissatisfaction; the latter was a protegé of Lt Bligh and unfortunately was under some obligations to him of a pecuniary nature of which Bligh frequently reminded him when any difference arose. Christian excessively annoyed at the share of blame which repeated fell to his lot "could ill endure the additional taunt of private obligations; and in the moment of excitation told his commander that sooner or later a day of reckoning would arrive".... then comes the statement by Adams that it was George Stewart who made the first suggestion to Christian that, instead of risking his life in such a hazardous attempt at escape, he should endeavour to take possession of the ship – a proceeding which would not be difficult "as many of the ship's company were not well disposed towards the commander and would all be very glad to return to Otaheite and reside among their friends in that island".

The misunderstanding to which Adams refers are largely mistakes by officers which were discovered by Bligh. It is difficult to point to the "several occasions" which are said to have given rise for complaint, apart from the articulate dressings down delivered by Bligh. It is very significant that Adams identifies that there was no real discontent among the crew or any idea of offering violence to Bligh.

There is evidence supplied by Bligh that he had made money available to Christian who was understandably hard pressed financially with a need to contribute to his mother's support. There is however no other account which says this made any difference. It is also very significant that Adams thinks that Christian was excessively annoyed at the share of blame which repeatedly fell to his lot. Clearly Adams thinks that the treatment received by Christian does not fully explain what happened afterwards. Adams does however believe there was another reason: "a moment of excitation" – a psychological cause.

Edward Christian wrote [203] that the cause of the Mutiny was the pressure that Bligh put on Christian: "... the crime itself in this instance may afford an awful lesson to the Navy and to mankind that there is a degree of pressure beyond which the best formed

---

[203] Minutes of Court Martial... Appendix p79 S Barney 1794

The causes of the Mutiny in "Bounty"

and principled mind must either break or recoil. And though public justice and the public safety can allow no vindication of any species of Mutiny, yet reason and humanity will distinguish the sudden unpremeditated act of desperation and phrenzy from the foul deliberate contempt of every religious duty and honourable sentiment; and will deplore the uncertainty of human prospects, when they reflect that a young man is condemned to perpetual infamy...".

There was a degree of pressure exerted on Fletcher Christian, not by Bligh, but by the psychological reaction of the threatened loss of Mauatua. The act of desperation and frenzy was not against Bligh but in preparing to return on the raft to Mauatua. Edward Christian does not specify what he purports as Bligh's foul deliberate contempt of every religious duty and honourable sentiment. It is difficult to specify any activity of Bligh's which could possibly constitute contempt for either religious duty or contempt for honourable sentiment.

It is ironic that the perpetual infamy which Edward Christian feared for Fletcher has been shuffled off on to William Bligh.

Captain Pipon of HMS Tagus in 1814 visiting Pitcairn Island and speaking not merely to John Adams (alias Alexander Smith) but also to women and children of the mutineers wrote [204] of Christian's "rash and inconsiderate step" and added that "sensuality and passion for the females of Otaheite chiefly instigated him to the rash step he had taken...".

In 1831, Sir John Barrow published [205] an account of the Mutiny anonymously. He summarises his understanding of the Mutiny as: "suddenly conceived by a hot headed young man in a state of great excitement of mind, amounting to a temporary aberration of intellect, caused by the frequent abusive and insulting language of his commanding officer". Barrow therefore pins the blame on Bligh and does so on the basis of his language. It is interesting to compare this with the words of Professor Scott [206]: "Had Bligh's language been the head and front of his offending, he would

---

[204] "Interesting Report ..." P Pipon, Banks Papers, Brabourne Collection Series 71.05 A77.
[205] "The Eventful History of the Mutiny..." London 1831
[206] "Life of Captain Matthew Flinders RN" E Scott p26 1914

hardly have shocked an 18th Century foc'sle". It is relevant to quote Professor Edward Christian who attributed to Fletcher Christian the words that although Bligh was very passionate, yet he (Fletcher) prided himself on knowing how to humour him.

In 1857, George Borrow, author of Romany Rye, published in the Appendix a view of the cause of the Mutiny, following his discussion with a Bounty crew member who survived in the open boat and later became a Lieutenant. He wrote "... their principal motive for doing so was an idea, whether true or groundless, the writer cannot say, that Bligh was 'no better than themselves...' the ringleaders in the mutiny were two scoundrels, Christian and Young, who had great influence with the crew, because they were genteelly connected... Bligh was not genteel by birth or money...".

It was true that Christian and Young were "genteelly connected",but the crew member was clearly distracted by Bligh's West Country accent to believe that he was somehow inferior and less well connected. The crew member would have remembered vividly the incident in which William Purcell, the Carpenter, threatened the authority of his Captain on an island off New Holland (Australia) when he said he was as good as the Captain.

In 1870, Lady Belcher, stepdaughter of Peter Heywood, Midshipman of "Bounty",published a book "Mutineers of the Bounty...". This book in the same vein as a biography [207] of Captain Peter Heywood used excerpts from James Morrison's Journal to make a case favourable to Heywood. It is interesting that Captain Beechey wrote to Peter Heywood in 1830 drawing attention to the discrepancy, concerning the role of George Stewart in stimulating Christian to Mutiny, between John Adams account which Beechey had been given in 1825 and that of Marshall's biography of Heywood, to which Heywood clearly contributed. Heywood rejected Adams' account of this and claimed that Stewart was not involved. As Heywood was closely involved with Stewart, it is understandable that Heywood wished to distance himself from any part in the stimulation of the Mutiny and to ensure that he did not go back on his word that he was not involved personally.

In 1884, Judge McFarland published [208] an account of the Mutiny and specified what he thought were its causes and regretted the

---

[207] "Royal Naval Biography" J Marshall 1825
[208] "A Mutiny in the Bounty" A McFarland Sydney 1884

absence of Bligh "whose cross-examination would have proved that his own coarseness of nature, tyrannous conduct and base outrages upon Christian and others were the occasion of the mutiny".

Apart from his swearing and his disciplinary language, biographers have not identified actions by Bligh characteristic of coarseness of nature. No specific instances of action by Bligh have been shown to have been taken which were beyond his authority and so charges of tyranny are unfounded. No specific instances of base outrages against Christian and others have been established.

Dr Mackaness [209] in 1931 and in his revised edition of 1951 wrote of what he considered to be the causes of the Mutiny: "... the affair was due at bottom to the contamination of the crew by their over-long association with the delights of Otaheite... To the major cause, we must add these others: First, the personal though temporary grievance of Christian against his commander; second, the unfortunate association in one watch of all the worst characters in the ship, mostly men who had been flogged for serious breaches of discipline; and last, the prospect of a long and tedious voyage of nearly a year in cramped quarters before they reached home".

Dr Mackaness' major cause of the Mutiny, namely the contamination of the crew by the delights of Otaheite, fails to identify the main motive force of the Mutiny, namely the leadership of Christian and it also fails to identify specifically why Christian led the Mutiny. The first subsidiary cause listed by Dr Mackaness was Christian's grievance against his commander, but Mackaness admits that "except for one or two occasions when Bligh rightly had to censure him, he had been treated with generosity and kindly consideration". His second subsidiary cause was the unfortunate association in one watch of all the worst characters in the ship. This was certainly a factor in helping Christian to subvert his watch before he was able to take control of the arms chests and thereby control affairs by armed force. As Christian had been planning desertion rather than mutiny until almost the last moment, it is unlikely that he had a hand in the choice of such a watch. It is more likely that bad characters found other bad characters more congenial, and that the better characters found them less congenial. His last subsidiary cause was the prospect of a

---

[209] "The Life of Vice Admiral Bligh" G Mackaness Ch XIII 1951

long and tedious voyage. It is unlikely that this was other than a very minor cause. Certainly, the prospect of the passage of Endeavour Straits did pose some uncertainty, but the Captain and the crew had shown at Cape Horn that they could deal with daunting challenges of navigation.

The novels of Nordhoff and Hall and the MGM films of 1935 and 1962 load all the blame on Bligh by means of fictional false statements and present a travesty of the truth. In 1965, Madge Darby published her hypothesis [210] of the cause of the Mutiny. She believed that Christian was suffering from paranoid delusions. She justifies this, not by scientific psychological explanation, but by a speculative Freudian explanation that this type of delusion could be detected from the fact that "the person who is now hated and feared for being a persecutor was at one time loved and honoured".The more modern scientific psychological explanation as proposed by this book gives a more satisfactory explanation and does not require an explanation by way of a delusion, for which there is no evidence.

In 1966, Rolf Du Rietz challenged [211] Darby's explanation by saying that the Mutiny could be largely explained in terms of Bligh's conduct and justified this explanation by reference among others to the comments of Lieutenant Francis Godolphin Bond critical of Bligh. However, it must be remembered that Bligh chose Bond, the son of his half sister, to be First Lieutenant on "Providence" during the 2nd Breadfruit Voyage. Bligh offered to train Bond but he had to be particularly careful that critics could not take advantage of mistakes made by Bond. Bligh offered him only limited "discretional judgement". It is understandable that Bond found this stifling his initiative and that Bligh's use of authority he found to be "imperious". Darby remarked that Bligh was nicknamed "the Don" by the officers of that ship, a term she notes as one of admiration. Bond was not entirely dissatisfied, saying "well informed mess mates make my moments pass agreeably, so that I am by no means in purgatory".

Darby challenged [212] Du Rietz hypothesis the same year by emphasising the views of Lt Tobin, an officer also on "Providence".

---

[210] "Who Caused the Mutiny on the Bounty" M Darby 1965
[211] "The Causes of the Bounty Mutiny" R Du Rietz (Studia Bountyana Vol 1) 1966
[212] Studia Bountyana Vol 2 M Darby 1966

Tobin wrote revealingly to Bond after the death of Bligh in 1817: "So poor Bligh, for with all his infirmities you and I cannot but think of him, has followed Portlock (Bligh's second in command on the 2nd Breadfruit Voyage). He has had a busy and turbulent journey of it – no one more so, and since the unfortunate mutiny on the Bounty has been rather in the shade. Yet perhaps he was not altogether understood. I am Sure my dear friend that in the Providence there was no settled system of tyranny exercised by him likely to produce dissatisfaction. It was in those violent tornadoes of temper when he lost himself, yet when all in his opinion went right when could a man be more placid and interesting? For myself I feel that I am indebted to him. It was the first ship in which I ever sailed as an officer – I joined full of apprehension – I soon thought he was not dissatisfied with me – it gave me encouragement and on the whole we journeyed smoothly on. Once or twice indeed I felt the unbridled license of his power of speech, yet never without soon receiving something like an emollient plaster to heal the wound. Let our old Captain's frailties be forgotten and view him as a man of science and excellent practical seaman. He has suffered much and ever by labour and perseverance extricated himself. But his great quality was foresight...". This letter is not about a man who produced a "hell" for Christian or who was solely responsible for the Mutiny. It is about a man who could be exceptionally angry when mistakes were made but who quickly relented without bearing a grudge.

In 1972, Richard Hough [213] wrote that evidence mounts that Bligh was seized by a form of paranoia which manifested itself in violent outbreaks against his officers in general and Fletcher Christian in particular.

I see no evidence of paranoia in Bligh at all nor any evidence which suggests that his mental health before the Mutiny was in any way impaired. Hough goes on to list two causes of restlessness before the Mutiny. Firstly, resentment at injustices and deprivation. Secondly, anxiety about the Great Barrier Reef and Endeavour Straits.

It is difficult to identify any injustices or deprivations about which the crew would be restless. After leaving Otaheite, one

---

[213] "Captain Bligh and Mr Christian" R Hough Ch 6 1972

seaman had been flogged at sea for neglect of duty, but Hough says that flogging itself did not create disaffection.

It is accepted that the thought of finding a way through the Great Barrier Reef and Endeavour Strait would raise some anxiety, but not of the degree which would have contributed significantly to Mutiny.

In 1978, Gavin Kennedy presented his hypothesis [214]: "the mutiny is best explained by the coincidence of the collapse in the authority of the commander and an emotional storm in an immature and possibly mentally unstable young man".

Kennedy does not make an effective case for the collapse in the authority of the commander. Bligh's authority was only taken away when he was arrested and bound under force of arms. He is right about an emotional storm in Christian, but there is no evidence that Fletcher Christian was immature. We can be sure however that Christian was actually rather more than "possibly mentally unstable" at the time of the Mutiny. Kennedy was also right in saying that Christian's "hell" was not brought about by Bligh but by himself.

Professor Kennedy (1989) wrote "the causes of the mutiny were as simple and as complicated as the fact that these two men (Bligh and Christian) clashed and one broke". This unconvincing explanation fails to consider the trauma of Fletcher Christian's separation from and potential loss of Mauatua.

The 1984 film "The Bounty" with Anthony Hopkins as Bligh was based on Hough's biography but some distortion mars the film.

The 1989 International Exhibition to mark the 200th anniversary of the Mutiny at the National Maritime Museum, Greenwich was a fine collection of documents, pictures and memorabilia of the Mutiny. The Exhibition publication "Mutiny on the Bounty" in an article by Stephen Walters gives the following cause of the mutiny: "Christian was unhappy after all the brow beating by Bligh."

"The mutiny came in a dispute over a trivial matter. Bligh publicly accused Christian of stealing coconuts... Christian refused an invitation to dinner and instead planned escape on a makeshift raft to one of the nearby (sic) islands".

---

[214] "Bligh" Gavin Kennedy Ch 13 1978

The causes of the Mutiny in "Bounty"

Stephen Walter's explanation purports to show that Bligh was largely responsible for the Mutiny and that Christian was escaping from him rather than trying to return to Mauatua.

A further question is whether Fletcher Christian was acting under the influence of drugs. During the period when Thomas Huggan was surgeon, we cannot be sure that the security of drugs was effective, so that Fletcher Christian might have been able to have access to narcotics for immediate use or storage.

On the 9th of December 1788, Thomas Huggan died in an alcoholic coma, so that Thomas Ledward, a surgeon recruited by Bligh anticipating trouble with Huggan, took over as surgeon. It is likely from that time that the security of drugs would have been more effective so that drugs would have been difficult to obtain, unless of course Fletcher had amassed a personal secret store of narcotics.

However, Fletcher Christian's behaviour exactly mirrors the behaviour of one predicted to be the subject of loss of a potentially long term loving relationship.

His behaviour, if under the influence of narcotics, would not be predicted in such diverse terms.

Dr Rina Prentice, in the Guide to the Exhibition, wrote [215]: "we have only the various biased accounts to judge from, but piecing together the versions, there seems little in the way of specific grievances or convincing charges of tyranny to be made against Bligh...".

---

[215] "Mutiny on the Bounty" International Exhibition Guide. Rina Prentice p xiii Manorial Research plc, 1989.

CHAPTER 18

A preliminary assessment of Wm Bligh following the 2nd Breadfruit Voyage.

I propose to look at some of the negative criticism, which has been directed at Bligh, to examine how fair such criticism has been.

Bligh has not been accused of barbarism in the way that Captain Cook has: Cook had mutilated the ears of natives. Nor has Bligh been accused of inhuman treatment in the way that Captain Edwards has: Edwards incarcerated prisoners in Pandora's Box. But Bligh has been described as a super-tyrant; however, practically all biographers deny that he was a tyrant, let alone a super-tyrant. One of Bligh's Lieutenants on "Providence",Lt Tobin, specifically denied that he was a tyrant.

Bligh has been called a paragon of ruthlessness and cruelty, but most biographers deny that he was either ruthless or cruel; he has even been described as "humane".[216]

He has been referred to as a bully and brow-beater of officers, crew and Otaheitan natives. Dr Mackaness however says [217] that "Bligh's punishments were not only few but mild...". Bligh required his orders to be carried out efficiently and with dispatch because an 18th century sailing ship required everyone to do what they were told or disaster could very quickly overtake everyone. Beyond his requirement to obey orders, Bligh was not a bully. However he was severe on those who failed to obey his orders and those who did fail felt his sharp tongue. He did not brow-beat Otaheitan natives; in fact he handled his relations with the Regent Tinah diplomatically and secured the co-operation of Otaheitans in

---

[216] "Mutiny on the Bounty" International Exhibition Guide. Nicholas Rodger, Assistant Keeper PRO p 17 Manorial Research plc, 1989.

[217] "The Life of Vice Admiral Bligh" G Mackaness Ch xiii 1951

his enterprise. On only one occasion on the First Breadfruit Voyage did he have an Otaheitan flogged and that was when Tinah encouraged him to put a thief to death.

Bligh has even been called a sadist, but this is plainly ridiculous because his private correspondence to Duncan Campbell shows that he took pleasure in avoiding flogging, if possible; and took no pleasure in other people's distress.

Representation of Bligh being involved in sadistic acts in the 1935 MGM film is false representation.

Some people have represented Bligh as one who flogged his seamen with more lashes and with more frequency than other Captains. However, a biographer writes [218]: "Many (in the Bounty) had suffered harder men than Bligh and several in ships where flogging took place much more frequently than in 'the Bounty'."

Professor Greg Dening [219] writes that "from 1765 when John Byron made his dash across the Pacific in the Dolphin until 1793, when George Vancouver tried to ease Spain off the North West of North America, fifteen British naval vessels came into the central Pacific for purposes of discovery or appropriation ... fifteen hundred and fifty six British sailors were aboard those fifteen vessels. Of them, 21.5 per cent were flogged. Cook flogged 20 per cent, 26 per cent and 37 per cent respectively on his three voyages. Vancouver flogged 45 per cent of his men. Bligh on the 'Bounty' flogged 19 per cent and on the 'Providence' 8 per cent. It was the least number of men punished on any ship that came into the Pacific."

No charge of injustice against Bligh really stands up, while Dr Mackaness described Bligh's treatment of William Purcell, the Carpenter, at Adventure Bay, Tasmania as showing "justice, mercy, shrewdness and discretion".

The suggestion by Richard Hough that Bligh was suffering from paranoia before the Mutiny is not supported by any paranoid symptoms exhibited by Bligh; in fact, Bligh's behaviour was not irrational or abnormal in comparison with what he usually did or with what other naval commanders did at that time.

---

[218] "Captain Bligh and Mr Christian" R Hough Ch 6 1972
[219] "Mr Bligh's Bad Language". G Dening 1992, pp62-3.

Bligh by Bligh

A recent suggestion is that Bligh had a Napoleon complex, the complex of the small man who compensates for his smallness by the size of his ambition. This will really not do, as Bligh was 5 ft 8 inches tall and though slightly less tall than Christian was nevertheless of a sufficient height not to be categorised as being liable to such a complex.

He certainly wasn't a "diehard reactionary" and is numbered as a "progressive" person by one biographer [220] and as having "versatility" by another.

Bligh is said to have been guilty of deceit and falsification in his "Narrative" as well as in the ship's log. It is true that he omits incidents in his official log which he wrote in his private log, but many of these omissions concern John Fryer, the Master, whom he did not wish to bring to trial. He also omitted references of a critical nature to Fletcher Christian in his private log at a time when, until the Mutiny, he wished to promote his interests. No biographer appears to have uncovered any falsification of his records other than omissions, although Bligh did admit to planning to keep Tinah in the dark about the death of Captain Cook. What is important too is that there is a great consistency between his logs and his "Narrative".

The biographer, M Darby, denies[220] that Bligh was either "rapacious" or "mean". He had after all given up a salary of many times what he was earning in "Bounty" and he was "out of pocket" in his pursing on "Providence". As a Lieutenant in charge of H M armed transport "Bounty", he did not have to make a profit, but he was required to do so on HM armed transport "Providence" when he was a Post Captain.

One critic spoke of Bligh's vehement animosity against his officers, but all the evidence goes to show that Bligh did not bear grudges against any of his officers. He expected them to carry out their duties efficiently and only turned on them if they failed in their duty. After sharply rebuking defaulters, he was quite prepared to resume normal relations. Another critic spoke of Bligh's contempt for his officers, but this is belied by the occasions on which Bligh thanked both his officers and his crew. It is difficult to believe that Bligh was being hypocritical when, following the

---

[220] "Who caused the Mutiny on the Bounty?" M Darby Ch 7 1965.

A preliminary assessment of Wm Bligh following the 2nd Breadfruit Voyage.

vain attempt to get round Cape Horn, he thanked all his officers and crew.

The taunt of Bligh being "parsimonious" probably derives from his reduction of the bread (biscuit) allowance to maintain a sufficient allowance spanning the whole outward journey. But this reduction of allowance of bread (biscuit) was based not on parsimony, but on sound planning of supplies to maintain a steady and sufficient diet, which was explained to the ship's company.

The charge that Bligh allowed discipline to disintegrate is not supported by the evidence. No one openly defied his orders and the incident of the coconuts was about crew members stealing behind the Commander's back, when the officers of the watch were thought by Bligh to have been negligent in preventing theft.

Bligh was not "generally bad tempered". Lieutenant Tobin tells us of "tornadoes of temper" when things were going wrong, but a "plaster to heal the wound" after "the unbridled licence of his power of speech". Otherwise Tobin thought him to be "placid and interesting".

Bligh was not a "nagger". A biographer writes [221] in answer to that charge: "Nor did Bligh overstep the norm as a nagging officer".

Particularly hurtful are charges of pettiness and inflexibility, for Bligh gave up his cabin at Cape Horn to ensure that his crew could sleep in dry conditions when their own bedding had been saturated. This was neither petty nor inflexible. It is difficult to isolate any example of where Bligh was petty, but he was certainly inflexible in his resolve to ensure that the enterprise was successful. His vision of the migration of Otaheitan people to New Holland (Australia) is a grand one – to bring "a people without land to a land without people".

Bligh has even been accused of being a bisexual. Darby mentions this as a possible component of her speculative Freudian explanation of Christian's delusions. A source counter to this hypothesis is derived from Peter Heywood's correspondence with Captain Beechey in 1830, about the last meeting Christian had with Peter Heywood and George Stewart at Otaheite. Peter Heywood wrote [222]: "At that last interview with Christian he also

---

[221] "Mutiny on the Bounty" International Exhibition Guide p 146 G Kennedy 1989 Manorial Research plc 1989.
[222] "The Mutiny of 'the Bounty'" J Barrow 1961

communicated to me for the satisfaction of his relations other circumstances connected with that unfortunate disaster which, after their deaths, may or may not be laid before the public. And although they can implicate none but himself, either living or dead, they may extenuate but will contain not a word of his in defence of the crime he committed against the laws of his county".

This secret seems to rule out a homosexual relationship of Christian with anyone else, but may well refer to Christian's mental state at having to leave Mauatua. Suggestion that this secret is about Christian's mental instability due to the effects of a previous dose of venereal disease is less convincing and is not consonant with his later behaviour.

The biographer, Richard Hough, goes on to suggest that Bligh might have had a homosexual relationship with Peter Heywood. But Bligh was a religious and moral family man; further, the penalty for homosexuality under the Article of War XXIX was death. It is inconceivable that Bligh would have risked his life, reputation or the success of the voyage for such a relationship. He claimed to have been acting as a father to Heywood, being his lover would have been out of the question. In any case, Peter Heywood had been posted to the shore camp at Otaheite.

Captain Lamb who previously sailed under Bligh in "Britannia", a merchant vessel on the West Indian run, said that Bligh was "blind to his (Christian's) faults" when Christian showed some "indifference" to his duties. Bligh may be criticised for making allowance for Christian on the basis of their friendship, but Bligh clearly planned to promote Christian to the rank of Acting Lieutenant as he had been denied a commissioned officer. It is interesting that Christian had already seen service as an Acting Lieutenant on his return from India. Bligh had already employed him as an Able Seaman and as Master's Mate, a post which was a traditional point from which an acting commissioned officer might be chosen. Masters were never promoted [223] to commissioned rank at sea. John Fryer's problems were not therefore based on disappointment or anger at Bligh not promoting him, but by his own mistakes and the rebukes which he rightly received for them.

---

[223] "Mutiny on the Bounty" International Exhibition Guide, Glyn Christian p 52 Manorial Research plc, 1989.

A preliminary assessment of Wm Bligh following the 2nd Breadfruit Voyage.

To the charge that Bligh was "fretful, impatient and seriously lacking in imagination", it is possible to counter that argument with Lt Tobin's judgement that Bligh was "placid and interesting" except when provoked. The open boat journey required incredible patience while the passage through the Torres Strait would have been disastrous under an impatient commander.

Tobin commends Bligh for "foresight" and that quality is not one likely to be present in a person seriously lacking in imagination. Bligh had anticipated that he required flexibility in his orders in case it was not possible to negotiate the passage of Cape Horn on the outward journey. His planning of supplies and the boats needed showed foresight and imagination.

Bligh is also charged with being inordinantly "conceited" and "immodest". He was not being immodest in saying "My conduct has been free from blame". But he was being less than honest in leaving himself open to the charge of conceit when he said "I never failed in anything I undertook". He did fail in the 1st Breadfruit Voyage, even if he was finally successful in the 2nd.

Bligh is most vulnerable to criticism on "the unbridled licence of his power of speech". In polite society, his language would have been unacceptable; but this was the 18th century Royal Navy and his language, even his abusive language, would not usually have been taken entirely seriously: "Lubberly rascals","vagrant",or "Damn your blood".During the coconut incident, when Bligh thought his officers were covering up for the thieves, he is said to have accused them of lying, as they were unable to account for the loss of the coconuts taken during their watch. By modern standards, Bligh should have disciplined his officers in private, but that was not the way at that time and that was certainly not the way Bligh had been trained by Captain Cook.

No one to my knowledge has criticised Bligh as a navigator, although Fryer complained that Bligh implied that he had fewer navigational aids than were available to him. Bligh was however left without tables [224] which would have enabled him to work out longitude accurately and was without accurate chronometers to confirm local and mean times by which longitude might also have

---

[224] "Mutiny on the Bounty" International Exhibition Guide, Andrew David p64, Manorial Resarch plc, 1989.

been determined. Fryer claims that he could have done as well under those circumstances, but his inefficiency in other naval matters was not reassuring.

Bligh's skills in cartography especially in the matter of "running surveys" were remarkable and were admired by Flinders as being better than Cook's for the same piece of coastline.

During the open boat voyage, Bligh has been commended [225] for "leadership of a high order".

---

[225] "Mutiny on the Bounty" International Exhibition Guide, Richard Ormond, Director of National Maritime Museum p 8 Manorial Research plc, 1989.

CHAPTER 19

Leith, Spithead and the Nore Mutinies and the Naval Victory of Camperdown
1795-1797.

To understand the context in which events in this chapter took place, it will be necessary to trace some European events from the French Revolution in 1789.

The European monarchies of Austria and Prussia were very concerned about what was happening in France. On the 27th August 1791, the declaration of Pillnitz by Leopold II of Austria and Frederick-William II of Prussia threatened intervention in support of counter-revolutionary French emigrés. In April 1792, the Revolutionary Government of France declared war on Austria. In August of that year, Prussia invaded France and was driven back at the battle of Valmy during the next month. In November, the French defeated an Austrian army at Jemappes.

However, a French decree in November 1792 declared the Scheldt estuary an international waterway and it was this measure which threatened British treaty obligations to Holland.

On the 1st February 1793, France declared war on England and Holland. A small expeditionary force under the Duke of York was sent to Holland. In March 1793, France declared war on Spain. French counter-revolutionaries were active in a number of places in France and in August 1793 a British naval force under Lord Hood was invited by counter-revolutionaries to go to the French Naval base at Toulon. A French revolutionary army under Carnot however in December 1793 besieged the base. Napoleon Bonaparte was an artillery officer in the besieging forces. The British managed to destroy thirteen ships of the line, but failed to destroy eighteen before they retired.

In 1794, the French Victory at Fleurus left their opponents in disarray and the small British expeditionary force fell back towards Holland. In December 1794 and in the following month, the French were able to cross frozen rivers to drive the British out of Holland into Northern Germany. On the 20th of January, the French proclaimed a Dutch Revolutionary Republic and gained possession of the substantial Dutch fleet.

Between the Spring and Summer of 1795, France made peace with Prussia, Sweden and Spain, but Russia joined Austria and England. At Quiberon Bay, Brittany, French royalists and British forces were worsted, while, in the West Indies, British forces lost about 80,000 men from disease.

We can now follow again the progress of the career of William Bligh. On the 29th of April 1795, Bligh's half pay ended and the next day he joined [226] "HMS Calcutta", a 24-gun armed transport as Captain. He offered Bond the post of First Lieutenant, but Bond turned it down.

In October, Bligh wrote [227] to Sir Joseph Banks telling him about a mutiny at Leith, near Edinburgh. The crew of "HMS Defiance" under Captain Sir George Home mutinied because of oppressive treatment, restrictions on shore leave and the dilution of their grog. Bligh said that he was left to secure perilously the end of the mutiny from small boats transporting troops which boarded the ship. It was then not necessary to fire on "Defiance" from other ships of the line also at Leith.

In 1795, twin sons were born to Betsy and William, but tragically the boys died within a day of their birth. Their family consisted of six daughters of whom two were twins and one daughter Ann was mentally disordered and epileptic.

On the 17th of January 1796, Bligh joined "HMS Director" [228] a 64-gun ship of the line, with a crew of 491 men. He took with him some of the crew of "Calcutta" which speaks well of his command of that vessel.

No member of the Director's crew were flogged until the 15th of March 1796 when a seaman received twelve lashes for mutinous

---

[226] PRO Admiralty log 51/1102.
[227] Bligh to Banks 19.10.1795 ML C218 p 7.
[228] PRO Admiralty log 51/1156 et al.

behaviour. Four days later, however, two of the crew in a shore party were flogged one receiving twelve lashes and the other twenty four.

This treatment might be compared with other punishment in Admiral Duncan's fleet, when four months later two seamen were sentenced to be flogged around the fleet with three hundred lashes for desertion, also seven months later when a seaman in another vessel was sentenced to a hundred lashes for racketeering. A surgeon stopped the flogging after eighty lashes, but the remaining twenty lashes were delivered eighteen days later.

Richard Humble [229], author and biographer, has calculated the average number of lashes prescribed by Bligh in 1796 was about thirteen and that "considering the seriousness of the worst crimes was extremely lenient".

The following letter shows Bligh's regard for one of his crew members:

"15th March 1796

I beg leave to represent to the Lords Commissioners of the Admiralty that on the 1st of Septr last, when His Majesty's ship Calcutta under my command .... I rated Daniel Stewart as Master at Arms and having no communication afterwards, I gave him an acting order signed by myself until we put into port with Admiral Pringle to get him fuller authority. Until our return to the Nore and quitting the Calcutta we did not recollect any more of it. From the Navy Board I find the order he needs from me is not sufficient to authorise his being paid. I therefore hope their Lordships will look over the ommission and direct the said Daniel Stewart, later of the Calcutta to be paid as Master at Arms". Daniel Stewart did receive the appropriate pay for the acting rank.

In May 1796, Bligh responded to a petition by the widow and child of a Dutch Surgeon at Samarand (Dutch East Indies) who had helped the survivors of the Open Boat Voyage. The dead man's effects had been received in Holland but without any documents. On the 10th of May, Bligh wrote to the Admiralty: "I therefore beg

---

[229] "Captain Bligh" Richard Humble p147

leave to present to their Lordships this petition on behalf of a child and mother, praying their Lordships will direct that in case any papers have been taken in Dutch ships (by the British) under the different addresses stated in the petition, they may be searched after in the Commons (place where goods were impounded) and returned to the parties concerned, to whom only they can be of any use. I hope that their Lordships will pardon the liberty I have taken to trouble them with this circumstance. I feel it in some degree my duty to show the high confidence the petitioners have that such services as their relatives rendered to us will not be forgotten".

After receiving no reply, he wrote again on the 21st of May.

In March 1796, Napoleon was appointed to the command of the French Army in Italy, where in the summer of that year he inflicted defeats on the Austrians.

In August 1796, by the Treaty of San Ildefonso, Spain entered into an alliance with France, whose forces in December 1796 made an abortive expedition from Brest to Southern Ireland, being dispersed by a gale.

On the 12th of February 1797, Bligh began work on a survey of the East Coast convoy route from the Humber to Harwich. Early that year, England faced an invasion force on the other side of the Channel with the navies of France, Spain and Holland hostile to her.

On St Valentines Day, the 14th of February 1797, Admiral Jervis severely mauled the Spanish fleet at the Battle of Cape St Vincent.

The finances of the country in the fifth year of war were strained, particularly the size of the National Debt following the War of American Independence. This was exacerbated by large financial payments to our allies, Austria and Russia during the two previous years. The size of the Navy alone had increased from a peace-time level of 16,000 to 120,000 men. In addition to the press gang to raise crews for its ships, the government in 1795 passed legislation to recruit offenders and vagrants into the Navy.

The Government however had done nothing about maintaining the value of the seaman's pay which had not been changed for more than a hundred years in spite of inflation reducing its value by about 30%. The inadequacy of the pay was evident when able seamen in the merchant service were paid four times that received in the Royal Navy. The pay of the ordinary seaman was very much less.

In February 1797, there had been expressions of discontent about wages on more than one ship of the line of the Channel Fleet. In March, a petition from representatives of the crews of thirty eight ships was sent to Admiral Lord Howe who, being unwell at Bath, sent the petition to the Admiralty, who ignored it.

The seamen's major grievances related to wages, poor supplies, absence of fresh vegetables on ships in port, inadequate treatment of the sick and their exploitation by surgeons, and corruption by pursers. Other grievances included harsh treatment, restrictive conditions on shore leave, denial of wages to wounded seamen, inhuman conditions of imprisonment on board ship, unfair shares of prize money and failure to receive prompt payment of arrears of pay.

The grievances were highlighted [230] by the flogging to death of a seaman on "HMS Malborough" under Captain Nicholls.

In mid March, "HMS Director" joined the North Sea Fleet off the Dutch coast. On the 10th of April, Bligh recalls that six members of the crew refused or neglected duty and were flogged for it; during that week, five other members of his crew were also punished.

On the 12th of April, Lord Bridport, deputy to Admiral Lord Howe, remonstrated with the Admiralty but he was ordered to take the Channel Fleet to sea next day. The ship's crews refused to sail.

By the 22nd of April, a pay increase from 6 shillings to 7 shillings a week for an able seaman, for instance, was obtained and a Royal Pardon for the mutineers.

The mutineers wanted Parliamentary recognition of their pardon, but there was delay in getting approval for such a Bill. The mutiny then spread to Plymouth involving a further twenty six ships.

"HMS Director" returned to Yarmouth from the Dutch station on the 25th of April, when Bligh was able to announce the Admiralty decision.

Before "HMS Director" was sent for a re-fit at the Nore on the 6th of May, there had been illegal musters on "HMS Venerable", the flagship of the North Sea Fleet.

---

[230] "The Great Mutiny" J Dugan Ch 8 and 9 1966

The Mutiny at Spithead, off Portsmouth, broke out again on the 7th of May, after which the Mutiny spread on the 12th of May to the Nore (Thames Estuary) starting on "HMS Sandwich".

Admiral Lord Howe was now sent to Spithead, where there were sixteen ships of the line, to negotiate with plenary powers, while the Nore Mutiny, where there were only three ships of the line, was ignored for the time being. Howe negotiated a deal on the 15th of May which confirmed the pay increase and removed one hundred and fourteen officers including thirty three commissioned officers.

The demands of the Nore mutineers were later formalised and included articles: that the terms for the Channel Fleet be available to the North Sea Fleet; that certain officers be removed; that some advance payment be paid to pressed men; that an amnesty be declared for previous deserters; and that the Articles of War be altered to encourage volunteers.

Unlike some other officers, Bligh was not immediately sent ashore by the Nore mutineers. He was asked to remove three of his officers for ill treatment and he agreed to confine them and then send them ashore. A week after the Nore Mutiny started, Bligh was put ashore by the mutineers.

On the 26th of May, Bligh was selected by the Admiralty to report on the situation of the North Sea Fleet. On the 27th of May, Admiral Duncan in command of the North Sea Fleet was instructed to proceed to the Nore. Many ships had refused to sail to the Dutch station. Two ships refused to sail from Yarmouth and two others defied the order but later changed their minds. Just after Duncan left with twelve ships on the 28th of May, Bligh reached Yarmouth, from where he reported on the 30th of May. Bligh wrote [231] "... it appeared to me very doubtful and hazardous what would be the conduct of the favourable party of seamen, if employed against the other". At one point, Duncan could only rely on his flagship "HMS Venerable" and "HMS Adamant" (74 guns). Eight of Duncan's ships joined the mutineers at the Nore.

The mutineers decided to blockade the Thames but Vice-Admiral Bruckner ordered all officers ashore, removed the marker buoys in the Thames and cut off supplies. "HMS Leopard" tried to escape, other ships decided to give up the Mutiny and "HMS Repulse" ran

---

[231] PRO Admiralty 1/524 F149.

aground and was fired on by "HMS Monmouth". By the 13th of June, the Mutiny at the Nore had collapsed. The red flag of mutiny was hauled down.

On the 13th of June, Admiral Lord Keith, Second in Command to Bruckner, asked officers in charge of all the ships involved in the Nore Mutiny to submit a list of 10 names of guilty men. Lieutenant MacTaggart in the absence of Bligh prepared a list and was soon after asked by Vice Admiral Bruckner on "HMS Sandwich" to let him have a list of malcontents including their positive as well as negative characteristics. Lt MacTaggart submitted a further list of nineteen names.

On the 16th of June, Bligh resumed his command, confirmed the list of ten names which Lt. MacTaggart had sent to Admiral Lord Keith, but promised an amnesty for other members of the crew.

However, on the 22nd of June, Admiral Lord Keith asked for further information not merely on the original ten names but also on the further nineteen names submitted by Lt. MacTaggart. Early in July, Bligh received a list excluding 29 members of his crew from pardon, but he was not at all satisfied with this and negotiated a pardon for all but the original ten named by MacTaggart on condition that promises of good conduct were obtained.

More than fifty two mutineers in the fleet were condemned to death and some mutineers were sentenced to be flogged from ship to ship.

The comments [232] of a 20th century Admiral on a later incident are instructive about these mutinies: "Fundamentally, what came to roost was the long neglect of successive British Parliaments to establish a just system of manning the navy, of rewarding the seamen, of alleviating the hardships of service and brutality of discipline. It was that long continued neglect that had caused the difficulties of manning the fleet from the time of Charles II onwards and had brought on the mutinies of Spithead and the Nore".

England's security was for a short while dependent on the good faith of the Spithead mutineers, who had agreed to put to sea, if the French fleet attacked.

The North Sea fleet however would have been at the mercy of the Dutch fleet during the mutiny if the Dutch had attacked ships in the Thames Estuary, as it had done in the previous century.

---

[232] "Statesmen and Sea Power" Admiral Sir Herbert Richmond, Appendix V 1946

Britain was in alliance with Russia, but the Russian fleet was not in the vicinity on the 11th October 1797 when a Dutch fleet of sixteen ships of the line, five frigates and four brigs were at sea.

A British fleet of similar size under Admiral Duncan namely seven 74-gun ships, seven 64-gun ships, two 50-gun ships and eight other vessels brought that enemy fleet to battle. The Dutch fleet were proceeding back to port. Duncan divided his forces into two, one of which he led personally to attack the enemy van, the other was led by Vice Admiral Onslow which was to fall on the enemy rear.

The log of "HMS Director" records that that ship under Bligh's Captaincy engaged the last ship but one in the enemy line, and that it forced a ship to surrender or "strike" its colours, before Bligh proceeded to attack unengaged ships in the van.

At five minutes past three (3.5) "HMS Director" found the "Vrijheid", the flagship of Admiral de Winter, unengaged and, after some action, "HMS Director" claimed to have dismasted "Vrijheid", but it was not until 3.55 that "Vrijheid" surrendered. Bligh was hailed by Duncan to board her to receive the surrender of the Dutch Admiral.

Duncan's report to the Admiralty read: "The action commenced about Fourty Minutes past Twelve o'clock. The Venerable soon got through the Enemy's Line, and I began a Close Action with my Division in the Van, which lasted near Two Hours and a half, when I observed all the Masts of the Dutch Admiral's Ship to go by the Board; she was however defended for some time in a most gallant Manner; but being oppressed by Numbers her Colours were struck..." Both "HMS Ardent" and "HMS Powerful" had also been engaged with the "Vrijheid", "the Ardent" taking heavy punishment.

Forty years after the victory, an anonymous critic [233] made a disingenuous attack on Bligh's role in this battle: "But the most modest of the shy ships was certainly the Director (64) because in her log book... it is recorded she got alongside of him (Admiral de Winter) at 3.5... Now in Duncan's letter... it is stated that the Venerable commenced action at half past twelve and ceased firing at three..."

---

[233] United Services Journal 1837 vol ii p 147-149

The reviewer deliberately distorted the timing in Admiral Duncan's letter to try to deny "HMS Director" its part in the action. Professor Kennedy points [234] to other errors made by the reviewer.

There was however one shy ship "HMS Agincourt" under Captain John Williamson, the same officer who was responsible for covering the return of Captain Cook from the beach at Kealakekua Bay. He was Court Martialled for disobedience to signals at Camperdown which charge was proved in part and he was barred from going to sea. The other Captains including Bligh and the Flag Officers received a Gold Medal.

Viscount Duncan wrote [235] to Bligh later: "I have mentioned to the Admiralty that if your ship is paid off, I hope they will immediately give you another as I have always observed her conducted like a Man of War".

This victory of Camperdown in 1797 substantially reduced the size of the Dutch fleet as eleven ships were either captured or destroyed. It therefore reduced the risks involved in trading in the Baltic but more crucially it considerably reduced the risk of the invasion of England for the time being. However, the Battle of Camperdown is one of the British Naval victories that has been underestimated in importance.

On the continent of Europe, French power was threatening, especially as on the 18th October, they signed the Treaty of Campo Formio with Austria, so isolating Britain further.

In December 1797, a further naval mutiny, in which Bligh was not involved, was put down ruthlessly.

---

[234] "Captain Bligh – the man and his mutinies" Gavin Kennedy Ch 32 1989.
[235] ML C218 p59.

CHAPTER 20

The Battle of Copenhagen, surveying, Courts Martial and appointment as Governor of New South Wales.
1798 – 29.4.1805

During the next two years, Bligh as Captain of "HMS Director" was mainly occupied with surveying for the Admiralty and the protection of convoys.

In May 1798, Napoleon managed to take an expeditionary force to Egypt, eluding the attention of Nelson who was left without frigates which would almost certainly have discovered so large a convoy. In July 1798, Napoleon won victories at the Battle of the Pyramids and at Aboukir against the Turks. On the 1st of August, Nelson brought the French Fleet to action at the Battle of the Nile when eleven French ships of the line were either sunk or captured, and only two French ships of the line and two frigates escaped.

In August 1798, Bligh made public a navigational model he had designed for taking bearings under emergency conditions. In September 1798, Bligh wrote to Banks that he was one of a Court Martial dealing with an Irish rebel. The man was one of sixteen Irishmen who plotted to seize "HMS Diomede" and sail her to an enemy port in Holland.

In June next year, Bligh Court Martialled the Master of "HMS Director" for impertinence. The charge was proven and the Master, Mr Ramsey, left the ship.

On the 9th of November 1799, Napoleon successfully brought about a Coup d'Etat and established the Consulate. About this time, Bligh was escorting a convoy of "East Indiamen" from St Helena to England.

On leaving "HMS Director" on the 2nd of July 1800, Bligh was back on half pay, but he was engaged to carry out a survey of

Dublin Harbour. This was a "regular survey" with adequate time for preparation and execution as opposed to a "sketch survey" or "running survey". In January 1801, he undertook a short survey of the harbour of Holyhead.

Early in 1801, Russia, Sweden and Denmark at the instigation of Napoleon revived the Northern Alliance or the Alliance of Armed Neutrality first negotiated in 1780, aimed at excluding British ships from the Baltic and improving the prospects of the merchant navies of those countries. This posed an enormous threat to supplies of timber and other materials required by the Royal Navy, and also a threat to British merchant ships, if that trade was to be carried in neutral vessels.

The British Government decided that that Alliance should be broken up by persuading Denmark by diplomacy or by force to leave the Alliance. Admiral Sir Hyde Parker was put in command of a fleet for this purpose and Vice Admiral Lord Nelson was appointed his Second in Command. Parker wished to delay the fleet leaving until after he had held a ball on the 13th of March to celebrate his wedding to a young bride, but Nelson wished to be able to prevent the Russian fleet joining that of either of its allies or part of the Russian fleet returning to its Naval base at Kronstadt from its station at Reval, once the Baltic ice melted. The First Lord of the Admiralty, Lord St Vincent, ordered Parker to leave promptly and the fleet left on the 13th of March.

Bligh was appointed [236] to 64-gun "HMS Glatton" on the 13th of March and joined the fleet, which aimed to anchor just north of the Sound where the Kattegat narrows between Sweden and the Danish Island of Zealand. A Government envoy had been sent on in a frigate to Copenhagen with a forty eight hour ultimatum. On 23rd of March the envoy, Nicholas Vansittart, returned with a rejection of the ultimatum by the Crown Prince of Denmark. Parker's original plan was to skirt the Island of Zealand on the west side and approach Copenhagen, situated on the east of the island, from the south. On the 26th of March, he changed his mind. The fleet was detained for three days by head winds, but on the 30th of March the fleet sailed largely unmolested through the Sjaelland Sound on the east of Zealand and anchored five miles south of

---

[236] PRO Admiralty log 51/1333

Copenhagen. At a Council of War on the 31st of March, Nelson proposed an attack on the Danish fleet with a small British squadron, part of the fleet of eighteen British ships of the line and thirty five smaller vessels. He asked for a squadron of ten ships of the line and was offered twelve. At a second council of War, Nelson's plan of attack was discussed and adopted.

The Danish fleet of eleven ships of the line, ten smaller vessels and six batteries lay in a very strong position. Seven ships of the line, five vessels similar to sloops and four batteries were situated south of the Trekroner Fort, two ships of the line and four brigs were situated north of this Fort and two ships of the line and one frigate elsewhere were protected by this and other Forts. The Danish ships on each side of the Fort were anchored in a waterway known as the King's Channel flanked on the west by the flats of the shore and on the east by an extensive lozenge shaped shoal known as the Middle Ground and beyond that the waters of the Outer or Holland Deep.

Nelson's plan was to enter the Outer Deep, sail around the south end of the Middle Ground into the King's Channel so that his first ship would engage the first ship at the South end of the Danish fleet, his second ship would engage the second Danish ship and so on. He proposed to ignore those Danish ships north of the Trekroner Fort, while the frigate "Amazon" under Captain Riou and other frigates were to engage the attention of the Forts. This tactic meant that his whole squadron would not have to pass the Forts in the north and he could choose to have the benefit of the current in the King's Channel. On the nights of the 30th and 31st of March, pilots surveyed the waterways. But their work was not adequate for the occasion as events proved; "HMS Agamemnon" ran aground on the Middle Ground as it was proceeding down the Outer Deep.

Nelson's squadron anchored at the South end of the King's Channel on the afternoon of the 1st of April.

Captains were given a final briefing at 8am on the morning of the 2nd of April. The squadron moved forward at 9.30am after which inadequate surveying by the pilots claimed two further casualties, "HMS Bellona" and "HMS Russell", both ships running aground.

"HMS Glatton" under Bligh faced the Danish Flagship "Dannebrog" under Admiral Fischer while "HMS Elephant",

The Battle of Copenhagen.

Nelson's temporary flagship, was next to and northward of "HMS Glatton". The log of "HMS Glatton" records that action started at 10.26am. Its fore top mast was shot away and seven upper deck guns were disabled at 11.24am. At 12am the "Dannebrog" surrendered and Admiral Fischer left for another ship, it was later learnt. At 1.15pm, Admiral Sir Hyde Parker was sufficiently worried at what was happening to signal that action should be discontinued. At which point, Nelson put his telescope to his blind eye and said "I really do not see the signal". Nelson did however arrange a truce at about 2pm to offer terms to the Crown Prince of Denmark. The action ended at 2.45pm. Admiral Graves, Second in Command of the Squadron, and Captain Bligh were hailed aboard "HMS Elephant" to be thanked by Nelson.

Five of the Danish ships of the line were put out of action, so too three of the four floating batteries. At 4pm, a fire on the "Dannebrog" caused by its engagement with "HMS Glatton" reached the magazine and the ship exploded.

Captain Riou in "Amazon" died during his encounter with the Trekroner Fort, after he obeyed Parker's signal to discontinue action.

The British lost 350 dead and 850 wounded while the Danes estimated their casualties at between 1600 and 1800 men. Bligh reported that his casualties on "HMS Glatton" were 17 killed and 34 wounded. More than 200 men on "Dannebrog" died before the explosion.

A permanent armistice was negotiated after a series of truces. The Danes agreed to leave the Northern Alliance and the British agreed not to bombard Copenhagen.

Nelson wished to proceed at once against the Russian Fleet, but Parker sent back for instructions to the Admiralty. Parker was, in fact, recalled and Nelson proceeded at once to try to prevent that half of the Russian fleet at Reval from retiring to its base at Krondstadt in the Gulf of Finland. By this time, however, he was too late and the Russian ships had left for Krondstadt. The assassination of Czar Paul by strangulation brought Czar Alexander to power and, in June 1801, a Convention between Britain and Russia was signed. The threat from the Northern alliance had been dissipated and Napleon's plan in that area had been frustrated.

Nelson wrote of the Battle of Copenhagen: "I have been in a hundred and five engagements, but that of today is the most terrible of them all".

Bligh was given command [237] of "HMS Monarch", whose Captain had been killed in the battle. It was a larger ship, being a 74-gun ship of the line. Parker had first appointed one of his own lieutenants as Captain, but that appointment drew protests from the officers and crew of "HMS Monarch" whereupon Parker changed his mind and appointed Bligh on the 12th of April.

Nelson himself criticised the work of the pilots which had resulted in the grounding of three ships of the line and which could have seriously affected the outcome of the enterprise. Bligh was so annoyed with the pilots with whom he was involved that he refused to have dealings with them and characteristically upbraided them.

Bligh asked Lord Nelson for a testimonial and in return was prevailed upon to take some Danish porcelain to Sir William and Lady Hamilton. Lord Nelson wrote: "to Admiral, the Earl of St Vincent 14th April 1801.

Captain Bligh – of the Glatton, who had commanded the Director at Camperdown – has desired my testimony to his good conduct, which, although perfectly unnecessary, I cannot refuse; his behaviour on this occasion can reap no additional credit from my testimony. He was my second, and the moment the action ceased, I sent for him on board the Elephant, to thank him for his support.

> I am &
>
> Nelson and Bronte".

"HMS Monarch" was away next day. It reached the Nore on the 7th of May via Yarmouth. Bligh was criticised for landing wounded sailors at night at Yarmouth and for not allowing the crew ashore there. It is probable that Bligh wished wounded sailors to be treated on shore as soon as possible and that celebrations should be delayed until the ship safely reached the Nore.

The day the crew reached the Nore, they and their Captain were paid off. If the crew had celebrated at Yarmouth, it is certain that some of the crew would have been left behind and would have missed the paying off.

---

[237] PRO Admiralty log 51/1333.

On the next day, Bligh took [238] over command of "HMS Irresistible", Nelson's flagship at the Battle of St Vincent, a 74-gun ship of the line.

On the 25th of May, Bligh was made a Fellow of the Royal Society for services to navigation, botany, etc. Sir Joseph Banks had been the President of the Society since 1778.

Later in 1801, hostilities with France ended under the Peace of Amiens. But in December 1801, Napoleon sent an armed force escorted by thirty five ships of the line to recover the island of Haiti. Britain later declared war on France as a result of this and of France's failure to give up occupation of Holland. The French Expedition was decimated by fever and Napoleon saw fit to sell off Louisiana to the United States at 4 cents an acre, because Louisiana could not have been held by France against a British blockade and against the unfriendly attentions of the United States.

Early in 1802, the Blighs' eldest daughter Harriet had married and late in the year a son was born.

On the 28th of May 1802, "HMS Irresistible's" crew were paid off and Bligh was back on half pay.

In March 1803, Bligh wrote [239] to the Admiralty offering his services, particularly in regard to surveying. This was rewarded later that year by three important surveying commissions. The first between September and October 1803 was to survey [240] Dungeness and its approaches. The second was to report [241] on the coast around Flushing in November, and the third was to report [241] on the Cornish port of Fowey in November and December.

It was probably at this time that an amusing incident [242] occurred when Bligh was arrested in the Cornish harbour of Helford in the belief that he was a French spy.

Since his disasters in the West Indies and in America, Napoleon had been building up French naval forces and had prepared a large expeditionary force in preparation for an invasion of England. It is

---

[238] PRO Admiralty log 51/1407
[239] PRO Admiralty 1/529
[240] PRO Admiralty 1/529 Cap B 382, 383
[241] PRO Admiralty 1/529 Cap B 385
[242] "History of Cornwall" R Polwhele 1816

*Portrait of Wm Bligh by John Smart circa 1803
by courtsey of the National Portrait Library, London*

not surprising that British naval resources therefore should have been maintained at numbers greater than the combined forces of Spain, France and Holland.

On the 2nd of May 1804, Bligh was appointed [243] to "HMS Warrior", a 74-gun ship of the line. Later that year, Britain intercepted and sank a Spanish treasure ship, anticipating a declaration of war by Spain, as that country had been subsidising Napoleon's war effort.

On the 11th of October, Admiral Keith was ordered by the Admiralty to: "send Bligh in 'HMS Warrior' with two of the best Flushing pilots to survey the entrance to the Scheldt and to report on the best placing for a squadron there". This order was clearly linked to the threat of a possible invasion from that quarter.

However, "HMS Warrior" was then at sea having left port in July and was due back in November.

As early as July or August of that year, there had been difficulties between Bligh and his Second Lieutenant John Frazier. Mr Knowles, a Midshipman, said later at a Court Martial that during Lt Frazier's watch he had been called with Frazier on two occasions to appear before Bligh to report on fog signals. Bligh, who had apparently been monitoring the signals, told Knowles on the second occasion he did not believe him and accused him of telling lies but took the matter no further. Mr Cocks, Master's Mate, told [9] of an incident which occurred after 8pm at night on the 9th of October, the ship's Corporal complained to Lt Frazier, who was officer of the watch, that although he had taken one pack of cards away from the wardroom steward, he found him still playing with another pack. Bligh came out of his cabin and asked Frazier why "he spoke so loud" for by doing so he was neglecting the ship's duty. Frazier contradicted Bligh who warned him "...take care, Sir, I am looking out for you". Mr Cocks continued: "Sometime after Mr Frazier was going to set the main stay sail; Captain Bligh told him upon his peril, if he ever set a sail or gave an order while he was on deck, he would confine him or make him rue it". Bligh clearly thought it an act of insubordination for a junior officer to ignore the presence of a senior officer when ship's orders were being implemented.

---

[243] PRO Admiralty log 51/1407

John Honeybone, an AB gave evidence [244] that he had seen Lt Frazier jostle Bligh when he was using a sextant.

On the 18th of October, Lt Frazier had a fresh accident to his leg which he had previously injured and he asked Bligh to obtain a "medical" survey of his condition. The ship's Surgeon, Mr Cinnamon, said that between the accident on the 18th and the day he put Frazier on the sick list (the 20th), Frazier's leg was swollen and he was not fit for duty. First Lieutenant Johnston gave evidence that Lt Frazier came on deck on the 19th of October, sat down on the arms chest and gave orders. Bligh had already given orders to the Surgeon that he should not place or keep any person on the sick list unless he could give him medical help. The sick list for the 20th of October was seen by Bligh and he wrote on it that Frazier's name should be taken off. The Surgeon took Frazier's name off the sick list on the 21st of October, on which date Bligh wrote to Vice Admiral Collingwood. Frazier was ordered to take a watch on the 22nd of October and he was told that he was permitted to sit whilst on duty. Frazier came on deck on the 22nd of October, but refused the order to take a watch sitting down. The same thing happened on the 23rd of October, after which Bligh put him under arrest.

Bligh wrote to Vice Admiral Collingwood again on the 27th October:

Warrior off Rochfort

Sir,

Lt John Frazier from his application as being fit to serve ... was appointed 2nd Lieut of the Warrior under my Command.

On his joining the ship he had an habitual lameness in his ancle, which had been occasioned by the bones being broken by accident in the Merchant Service, with which he however asserted he was capable of doing his duty, and did so to the 18th inst. when by our shortness of water and provisions & being out nearly 14 weeks, it was to be expected we were soon to return to port. On this evening he wrote to me requesting I would apply to you for a survey on him, which I

---

[244] PRO Admiralty 1/5368

did on the 21st by enclosing his letter and remarking I thought he was the same as he had hitherto been. In consequence you directed that as he, Lt Frazier, was represented to be very much in the same state as he had been for some time past, it would be an accommodation to him to wait until then, but Lt Frazier conceiving this application of his exempted him from further service and that keeping watch would militate against his being discharged by survey on his arrival in port & thereby he would be obliged to return and experience a winter's cruizing, did refuse to do any further duty, altho' he had my assurance of every indulgence. The Surgeon put him one day the 20th inst., in his sick list, but the next day finding no inflammation in his ancle, and that the appearances were no other than it must at all times have been subject to, he no longer continued him under his care & in consequence I ordered him to keep watch, but he refused. On the 22nd I directed Lt Johnson – 1st Lieut – to tell him it was my orders he was to take his watch.

He came on deck in consequence, but on Lieut Boyack asking him if he was come to relieve him, he replied "no, I am only come up to take the air" – would not relieve him and went below soon after – at 8 next morning, the 23rd, he was again called on to relieve Lt Russell and I sent him word by Mr Cosnaham, midshipman, it was my orders he should relieve him, to which he returned me an answer he was too lame. I again sent and repeated the orders to him and gave him till 9 o'clock to comply, but he refused to obey me inasmuch that he would not come on deck to keep his watch. And for which contumacy and disobedience on the 22nd and 23rd, I ordered him under arrest and request he may be tried by Court Martial.

    I am, Sir, etc

    Wm Bligh

On the 13th of November, Frazier wrote requesting a counter Court Martial of Bligh:

His Majesty's Ship Warrior

Sir,

I beg to state to you that William Bligh Esq Captain of His Majesty's Ship Warrior did on 9 Oct last publicly on the quarter deck of his Majesty's Ship Warrior grossly insult and ill treat me being in execution of my office by calling me rascal, scoundrel and shaking his fist in my face and that at various other times between the ninth of July and the thirtieth Day of October 1804 he behaved himself toward me and other commissioned warrant and petty officers in the said ship in a tyrannical and oppressive and unofficerlike behaviour contrary to the rules and discipline of the Navy and in open violation of the Articles of War. I have therefore to request that you will be pleased to order a Court Martial to be assembled to try William Bligh Esq, Captain of His Majesty's Ship Warrior.

I am, etc
John Frazier Lieutenant

Frazier's Court Martial took place on the 23rd of November. A key excerpt from the minutes of that Court Martial reads [245]: "... as owing to his having hurt his leg afresh on 18 Oct on the occasion of his having gone to the Dreadnought for water and fallen between two casks... the Surgeon said that after the accident in the launch Lt Frazier's leg was very much swelled and prior to the 20 Oct had told Lt Frazier that he should lay past for duty at that time as he was not fit to do it. Up to the 18th he had agreed with Captain Bligh, but never after that date and he removed Lt Frazier from the sick list because of the order written on the sick book and signed by Captain Bligh". Frazier was acquitted by the Court.

On two occasions, on the 19th of October and again on the 22nd of October, Frazier had voluntarily demonstrated that he was able to come on deck and as early as the 19th of October had voluntarily sat down on an arms chest and given orders, as Bligh asked him to do on the 21st of October. From a common sense point of view, it would appear that Bligh had the edge and that Frazier was swinging the lead; but Bligh had set unsatisfactory conditions on

---

[245] PRO Admiralty 1/5367

the scope of the Surgeon's work and Frazier was able to use that to secure his acquittal. It was now Bligh that was to be under attack. His Court Martial was held on the 25th and 26th of February 1805. It was generally accepted that Bligh's language was abusive, but there was contradictory evidence [246] given as to whether this constituted tyrannical, oppressive or unofficerlike behaviour: Mr Cocks, the Master's Mate, had been asked by Lt Frazier to make a record of the incident in which Bligh said that Frazier "spoke so loud" at night. Bligh said Frazier had neglected his duty, but Frazier contradicted this and Cocks confirmed that Bligh had called Frazier a rascal and scoundrel and had shaken his fist in his face. He also spoke of the occasion on which Frazier gave orders on deck without acknowledging the presence of his senior officer. Cocks said he had never sailed with a better Captain than Bligh.

Mr Knowles, Midshipman, spoke of the two occasions one night when Bligh spoke to him and Lt Frazier about fog signals. Bligh called Knowles a liar and said that he and Lt Frazier were "a parcel of villains and scoundrels..." but Knowles did not believe that Bligh acted in a tyrannical or oppressive way.

Lt Boyack confirmed that Bligh had used abusive words and he felt that such words lessened their dignity as officers and was degrading in the extreme. At the end of July, Boyack said that he heard Bligh say that I "rule with a rod of iron", and that he said to Mr Jewell, the Boatswain, that "if he had him in a dark corner, he would do for him'.

Mr Cinnamon, the Surgeon, said that Bligh called Lt Frazier "an imposition on the service or an imposter". When Cinnamon said Frazier couldn't do his duty, Bligh is said to have stated in violent language that Cinnamon was wrong. Cinnamon was so agitated at the time of those events that he couldn't remember what Bligh had said. He did remember that Bligh used abusive words to Mr Keltie, the Master.

Mr Queade, the Surgeon's assistant, agreed with the Surgeon and added that Bligh had used verbal and physical abuse towards Mr Jewell, the Boatswain.

Captain Mortimer, a Marine officer in the Warrior, said that Bligh had verbally abused Mr Jewell and Mr Waller, the Carpenter. He

---

[246] PRO Admiralty 1/5368

said that Bligh had used tyrannous, oppressive and unofficerlike behaviour to Naval Officers, but that he had been "polite and attentive" to the Marines. Lt Russell said that Bligh had verbally abused Lt Johnston, Mr Keltie and Mr Jewell.

Mr Jewell acknowledged the abuse, but said it was not serious and he would sail with Captain Bligh again.

Lt Pascoe said that Bligh had called Mr Keltie "a Jesuit" and the Gunner "a damned long pelt of a bitch". He did not believe that such verbal abuse constituted tyrannous, oppressive or unofficerlike behaviour.

Mr Keltie, the Master, confirmed that he had been called a "Jesuit" and other abusive names. He said that Bligh had been "cruel" to order Frazier on duty in his condition and that he had also been cruel in summoning Mr Waller, the Carpenter, to supervise a "fishing of the yard", a carpentry operation to strengthen a sail support, when the Carpenter was unwell below.

Mr Cinnamon, the Surgeon, was asked to give further evidence and said that it was not cruel, nor even severe, to ask the Carpenter to supervise the operation; in fact, Mr Meggs, the Carpenter's assistant, said that the Carpenter had actually volunteered for the task.

Lt Johnston, the First Lieutenant, said Bligh had no intention of harming his officers with his language. When the service was being neglected, Bligh did react strongly and did move his arms in a way characteristic of him. Mr Mills, Midshipman, supported what Lt Johnston said. Mr Simmons, the Gunner, denied that Bligh had called him "a damned long pelt of a bitch" and said that he would as soon sail with Bligh as anyone.

At his Court Martial, Bligh spoke of himself in the following way: "I candidly and without reserve avow that I am not a tame and indifferent observor of the manner in which officers placed under my orders conducted themselves in the performance of their several duties; a signal or any communication from a commanding officer have ever been to me an indication for exertion and alacrity...".

Bligh spoke tellingly of the relationship between discipline and mutual support: "... and not with a premeditated view of any personal insult to my Prosecutor or reducing the rank which he holds in it, concerning an incumbent duty in our relative situations to render that rank mutual support, which its dignity indispensably requires, as, without such impressions, discipline would not ensure obedience in ships of war".

Although, some officers did not take Bligh's language too seriously, others did find it offensive and, in their cases, Bligh's language did distract in some degree from mutual support. Frazier was however only concerned with devising his own discharge on medical grounds without concern for mutual support.

The Court were of the opinion that the charges were in part proved and did therefore adjudge Captain William Bligh of "HMS Warrior" to be "reprimanded and to be admonished to be in future more correct in his language".

On the 7th of March, Bligh wrote [247] to Sir Joseph Banks: ".... I defy the world to produce one act of malevolence or injustice.. all but four officers in the ship and the whole ship's company declare the late charges infamous...". I suppose Bligh refers to the four commissioned officers Captain Mortimer, Lt Frazier, Lt Boyack and Lt Russell. He should have added Mr Cinnamon, and Mr Keltie, but he did have the support of Lt Johnston, Lt Pascoe, Mr Mills (Midshipman), Mr Ranwell (Master's Mate) and Mr Simmons (Gunner).

Within a very short time of sending this letter, Bligh was to receive a very special surprise.

Sir Joseph Banks wrote [248]:

My Dear Sir

An opportunity has occurred this day which seems to me to lay open an opportunity of being of service to you; as I hope I never omit any chance of being useful to a friend whom I esteem, as I do you, I lose not a minute in apprising you of it.

I have always since the first institution of the new colony at New South Wales taken a deep interest in its success, and have been constantly consulted by His Majesty's Ministers through all the changes that there have been in the

---

[247] Bligh to Banks 7.3.1805 Alexander Turnbull Library Wellington NZ
[248] Banks to Bligh 15.3.1805
Part of letter between brackets – sets out Lord Camden's criteria
HR NSW Vol 6 p 35.

department which directs it, relative to the more important concerns of the colonists.

At present, King, the Governor, is tired of his station; and well he may be so. He has carried into effect a reform of great extent, which militated much with the interests of the soldiers and settlers there. He is consequently disliked and much opposed and has asked leave to return.

In conversation, I was this day asked if I knew a man proper to be sent out in his stead – one who had integrity unimpeached, a mind capable of providing its own resources in difficulties without leaning on others for advice, firm in discipline, civil in deportment and not subject to whimper and whine when severity of discipline is wanted to meet emergencies-. I immediately answered: As this man must be chosen from among the post Captains, I know of no one but Captain Bligh who will suit, but whether it will meet his views is another question.

I can therefore, if you chuse it, place you in the government of the new colony with an income of £2000 p.a. and with the whole of the Government power and stores at your disposal, so that I do not see how it is possible for you to spend £1000; in truth King who is now there receives only £1000 with some deductions and yet lives like a prince and, I believe, saves some money; but I could not undertake to recommend anyone unless £2000 clear was given, as I think that a man who undertakes so great a trust as the management of an important colony should be certain of living well and laying up a provision for his family.

I apprehend that you are about 55 years old; if so, you have by the tables an expectation of 15 years life and in a climate like that, which is the best I know, a still better expectation; but in 15 years, £1000 a year will at compound interest of 5% have produced more than £30,000 and in case you should not like to spend your life there, you will have a fair claim on your return to a pension of £1000 a year.

Besides, if your family goes out with you, as I conclude they will, your daughters will have a better chance of marrying suitably there than they can have here; for as the colony grows richer every year, and something of trade seems to improve, I can have no doubt but that in a few years there will be men there capable of supporting wives in a creditable manner, and very desirous of taking them from a respectable and good family.

Tell me, my dear Sir, when you have consulted your pillow, what you think of this. To me, I confess, it appears a promising place for man who has entered late into the status of a post-captain, and the more so as your rank will go on, for Phillip, the first Governor, is now an Admiral, holding a pension for his services in the country.

I have &
Joseph Banks.

William and Betsy Bligh had to take some hard decisions. Betsy was a very poor sailor and couldn't face the journey. Of their six daughters, Harriet alone was married and Ann suffered from epilepsy with a severe mental handicap. They decided that the offer be accepted and their daughter Mary should accompany William. It is not hard to imagine that they planned that William should only stay about four years or less in New South Wales, the time that Governor Phillip stayed before he returned in poor health to promotion and a pension. After all, William had promised Betsy not to take part in another naval expedition, but he could reasonably claim that this was not such an expedition and it was hardly an opportunity they could miss, but he clearly wanted to get back to his wife and family as soon as possible.

He was officially appointed Governor of New South Wales on the 29th of April.

In August 1805, the British sent a force to capture the Cape of Good Hope as the Dutch were now held subject to Napoleon. This annexation secured the route to India and to New South Wales.

On the 5th of October, Harriet's son died when only three years old. William and Betsy had lost their first grandson. Because William had been appointed Governor of New South Wales, he was not available to be selected by Nelson as a Captain of a ship of the line in the fleet he gathered, although there is no doubt that Nelson would have clearly chosen him if he had been available. The news of the Victory at Trafalgar on the 21st of October was however tempered with the news of the death of Nelson.

Bligh left England for Australia in February 1806.

CHAPTER 21

Background to Bligh's Governorship of New South Wales

1787 – Spring 1806

It is easier to understand the problems facing Governor Bligh in 1806, if some salient facts about earlier Governors are first considered.

Captain Phillip was the first Governor of New South Wales and he left England with the "First Fleet", transporting largely convicts and their marine guards and arriving in 1788.

In 1789, the British Government decided to raise a Corps for special purposes to replace the marines and supplement their armed forces there. Major Grose (or Grosse) of the 90th Regiment contracted with the Government initially to raise three hundred rank and file at a price of 3 guineas per recruit, and later a further two hundred rank and file. The first company left with the "Second Fleet". Grose was allowed to recruit for other ranks at a lower price and kept the difference. The new Corps was called the New South Wales Corps and was placed under the command of Captain Lieutenant George Johnston; when the Corps arrived in New South Wales, the marines who had guarded the convicts were either demobilised with an offer of 25 acres of ground or encouraged to enlist in one of the companies of the new Corps with the offer of a bounty of £3 and a land grant of 50 acres on later demobilisation.

In 1790, Phillip, after being wounded by an aboriginal, applied for a year's leave and offered to resign subject to certain conditions. In 1792, Phillip returned to England due to ill-health, but expecting to return. Phillip left a memorandum which specified an area of

Sydney to be known as the "domain" which was not to be leased but reserved for Government.

During Phillip's Governorship, John McArthur [249] arrived in the Colony, with the "Second Fleet". McArthur was born near Plymouth, Devon in 1767, the son of a Scot who was said to have been an army agent or supplier. As a youth, McArthur was signed on as an Army "ensign", but on peace being declared at the end of the War of American Independence in 1783 he was discharged. He was first apprenticed as a stay maker from which he derived his nickname of "Jack Bodice". He then became a farmer in the West Country and married the daughter of a country gentleman in Devon. He gave up farming to buy an ensigncy in the New South Wales Corps and arrived when only twenty three years old in New South Wales in 1790 with a debt of £500 [250]. Governor King, a decade later, spoke of McArthur then: "Many and many instances of his diabolical spirit has shown itself before Governor Phillip left this colony, and since, although in many instances he has been the master worker of the puppetts he has set in motion".

There were however two sides to John McArthur. He is an Australian folk-hero and villain not merely because he was a pioneer of the wool industry and experimented with the cross breeding of sheep for wool, but because he made other people the tools of his greed.

When Governor Phillip left the colony in November 1792, Grose became Acting Lieutenant Governor, although he had only been in the colony since February of that year. In fact, Grose delegated widely to Lt McArthur. However, Grose himself introduced martial law and appointed some military officers as magistrates and jurors and replaced some civilian constables with soldiers. It was from this time that officers of the New South Wales Corps, British officers, began to develop a trade including an alcohol monopoly at the expense of non-commissioned officers and privates of the NSW Corps and at the expense of free settlers, emancipated convicts and the convicts.

---

[249] Variously spelt McArthur, MacArthur, Macarthur. John, unlike his wife and family, usually used the spelling "McArthur", while they used the spelling "Macarthur".

[250] HR NSW Vol 4 p216.

Two decades after their landing in New South Wales, it was written [251] that "the officers of the NSW Corps sojourning here for the long period of twenty years have effectively aggrandised themselves by the acquirement and accumulation of considerable landed and personal property and having at their disposal the force that has been destined to uphold the necessary obedience to the laws... they have arrogated to themselves the most unlimited authority, as it is now but too fully evinced by their having rendered themselves paramount to the civil power, changed not only the very forms of justice in the commencement of the revolutionary career, but have annihilated her very existence in the territory".

A large part of the responsibility for this state of affairs must rest with the British Government; a later Governor wrote [252]: "It is well known that from the inadequacy of the pay to support them, all the officers of the NSW Corps were compelled to become traders and farmers, which cannot be tolerated in a regiment of the line without the most pernicious consequences to its discipline, subordination and respectability".

The free settlers later described [253] the actions of the NSW officers as follows:

(a) the officers had been (and still continue), merchants, traders and dealers; they employ convicts as their agents; and that fact gave then "a dangerous influence"; they kept up expensive establishments which nothing but a continuance of abuses could support.

(b) the officers monopolised the whole of the spirits brought into the Colony, which they purchased at 10 shillings per gallon and retailed at £2 – £6 per gallon.

(c) the officers participated in "land jobbing". They were interested in impeding agriculture, knowing that the more settlers were ruined, the cheaper could they purchase their estates and the less grain grown by the settlers, the better price they could get for their own.

---

[251] HR NSW vol 6 p605 Wm Gore to Lord Castlereagh
[252] HR NSW vol 3 p77 Governor Macquarie
[253] HRA Series 1 vol 7 p149. Hawkesbury Free Settlers.

Background to Bligh's Governorship of New South Wales

(d) the officers paid for their goods in promissory notes which they redeemed with property in some instances...

The effect of the officers' action on non-commissioned officers and privates by paying in kind was disastrous, being described [254] by a contemporary of those times as follows: "This system of monopoly and extortion compelled the soldier to serve his Majesty for half his nominal pay".

The same author, a transported Irishman, wrote: "Every soldier got 25 acres of land. Many of them when intoxicated sold their tickets for rum. Mr MacArthur used to supply them with goods, and so obtained from these improvident and foolish men their tickets by which he acquired enormous landed property."

The officers of the NSW Corps, led in their trading activities by John McArthur, not only monopolised alcohol but tried to corner the market in imported goods and to develop a grain as well as a meat monopoly.

By encouraging rum as the medium of exchange, they tried to establish control of all trading.

Colonel Grose left the Colony in December 1794 and was replaced by Acting Lieutenant Governor Paterson, who earlier had bought a Captaincy in the NSW Corps, arrived in New South Wales in 1791 and later took over command of the Corps.

In September 1795, Governor Hunter arrived to take over from Paterson. Next year, Hunter found it necessary to rebuke Paterson, who was in charge of the NSW Corps for the conduct of the Corps:

"I must declare to you, Sir, that the conduct of this part of the NSW Corps has been in my opinion the most violent and outrageous that ever was heard of by any British regiment whatever".

John McArthur resigned in 1796 from the post of Inspector of Public Works, a situation he had held since 1793. The resignation arose from a disagreement between McArthur and Governor Hunter. McArthur wrote to the Secretary of State, the Duke of Portland, criticising Hunter.

---

[254] The Memoirs of Joseph Holt vol ii p293

In the same year, 1796, Richard Atkins was appointed Acting Judge Advocate. He had arrived in the colony in 1792 and became a Justice of the Peace. In 1798, Atkins, a JP at Parramatta, and McArthur, a commandant at Parramatta, were in dispute. During the time of Governor Hunter, the two most senior New South Wales Corps officers, Paterson and Johnston, quarrelled and this resulted in Johnston being sent back to England under arrest.

In 1798, Governor Hunter wrote [255] "There are people here who would most readily prepair for his sacred head another crown of thorns and erect another cross for his second crucifixion; and none I am persuaded more so than the person (McArthur) of whom I have complained".

In the summer of 1798, Governor Hunter tried to limit the activities of the Officer Cartel by opening up the market for imported goods to all comers, but within nine days, the officers challenged this Government Order and Hunter gave in, making a further order, specifying officers as agents for these goods.

By the Autumn of 1798, the effects of the Officer Trade Cartel on the settlers were dire. It was said that people were nearly naked, being unable to obtain or afford clothes.

The next year, Hunter had to reply to anonymous charges against him made to the British Government, who did in fact recall him, and surprisingly McArthur claimed the credit for Hunter's recall. Governor Hunter left in 1800 and was replaced by Governor King.

Soon after taking up the Governorship, Governor King sent a despatch to the Secretary of State setting out in great detail criticisms of John McArthur. This despatch never arrived at its intended destination and it is conjectured that it was the object of theft, probably connived at by John McArthur.

Governor King wrote [256] of John McArthur in 1801: "The points I have brought home to him are such that if properly investigated must certainly occasion his quitting the NSW Corps and the Army". In that year, Paterson and McArthur were involved in a duel in which Paterson received a bullet in the shoulder, after which McArthur was sent under arrest to England. McArthur took

---

[255] HR NSW vol 3 p429
[256] HR NSW vol 4 p611

with him samples of wool to interest the Government. As Napoleon had interfered with supplies of Spanish wool, the British Government was very interested. The charges against McArthur were dismissed, McArthur resigned from the army and was promised land for sheep farming.

In the next year, Governor King brought about a reconciliation between Paterson and Johnston, but afterwards quarrelled with Paterson about the NSW Corps. In the same year, 1802, John McArthur made approaches in England to Sir Joseph Banks but, because Banks knew of unfavourable comments about McArthur, no encouragement was given. In that same year, Joseph Foveaux was made a Lieutenant Colonel in the NSW Corps originally having bought a Lieutenancy in the NSW Corps in 1789. He had been Lieutenant Governor of Norfolk Island, a dependency of New South Wales.

At that time, Foveaux was the richest person in the colony with more than 2000 acres of land and more than 1200 sheep, not far behind was John McArthur with more than 1900 acres and more than 900 sheep. It is interesting that McArthur had only 500 acres four years earlier.

In 1803, Governor King was instructed by Lord Hobart to develop a new settlement, Port Dalrymple, in Tasmania. Paterson's first attempt at establishing a settlement was unsuccessful, but succeeded in the next year.

Late in the year 1803, it was decided to recall Governor King, who had intimated that he would want to be recalled, if McArthur returned to New South Wales.

At a sale of a flock of King George III's sheep at Kew in 1804, Sir Joseph Banks offered to collaborate with John McArthur, but was given the same treatment which he himself had given McArthur two years earlier. Sir Joseph was sufficiently affronted to prevail on Lord Camden to reduce an offer of 10,000 acres of land being given to McArthur to one of 5,000 acres.

In the same year, Lieutenant Colonel Foveaux returned to England due to ill health.

Governor King gave an early pardon to George Crossley, a lawyer who had been transported in 1800 with a seven year sentence for being convicted of perjury and consequently permanently debarred from practising as a lawyer. King pardoned him to make him personally responsible for his debts.

Irish State prisoners in New South Wales brought about a revolt in 1804 which was put down by George Johnston, commanding the New South Wales Corps. For this action, Governor King awarded George Johnston a considerable land grant.

Early in 1806, King made [257] several leases of land in Sydney, at least one of which was in the "domain" as designated by Governor Phillip. King had, however, established port regulations which improved the security of the colony by discouraging convicts from escaping. King however failed to break the Officer's connection with trade, particularly of rum, a connection which London wanted to see broken.

Governor King, of all previous Governors and those acting in that capacity, made the largest land grants [258]:

Phillip	3,389 acres
Grose	10,674
Paterson	4,965 (1794/5 only)
Hunter	28,650
King	60,411

The 5,000 acres sanctioned by Lord Camden for John McArthur would have been included in the land grant figure for Governor King.

John McArthur arrived back in New South Wales in 1805, giving up the army to concentrate on political and pastoral matters. Bligh had been appointed in the spring of 1805 to succeed King.

---

[257] HR NSW vol 6 p359
[258] HR NSW vol 3 p808

CHAPTER 22

Journey to New South Wales and Governorship
2.1.1806 – 26.1.1808

In late January 1806, William Bligh and his daughter Mary left for New South Wales. Mary was married to Lieutenant Putland, an officer in HMS Porpoise which was escorting the convoy that included the Transport "Lady Madeline Sinclair" in which Bligh and his daughter were sailing.

Bligh was the senior officer in the convoy but Captain Joseph Short received instructions to command "the Porpoise on all occasions in the absence of Captain Bligh". However Bligh had been appointed Captain of "Porpoise" from the 14th of November 1805. Joseph Short was able to use the courtesy title of Captain under the convention of the times, but he was not then of Post Captain rank.

The convoy initially consisted of one convoy bound for the Caribbean Islands and another bound for Australia. On the 26th of February, Bligh did issue an order to the Transport "Fortune" before the convoy for the Caribbean parted company with that for Australia. On the 27th of February, Short was able to open Admiralty secret orders, which reserved the right of Bligh to determine the convoy's course. Short issued a copy of this to Bligh.

Short had been asked by Bligh if he would transfer Lieutenant Putland to "Porpoise" from the Transport "Lady Madeline Sinclair" as Bligh's aide-de-camp, but Short was not prepared to tell Bligh when a decision might be expected. On the 28th of February, Bligh gave Short an order that Lieutenant Putland should be his aide-de-camp. Short threatened Bligh with recall as Governor General of New South Wales to appear as a witness, if Bligh should court martial him.

189

One can only presume that by the 3rd of April, relationships between Bligh and Short had deteriorated to the point where Bligh found it necessary to exercise his rights, namely his direction of the course, by causing the "Lady Madeline Sinclair" to alter course. Captain Short proceeded to fire a shot both ahead and astern of the transport and then outrageously ordered his officers to prepare a shot to hit the transport.

Short apologised to Bligh at the Cape of Good Hope but there was to be further trouble when they reached New South Wales.

On arrival there, Bligh set up a Court of Enquiry to examine what had happened. Short was criticised by the court and his charges against two of his Officers were not substantiated. However, Short continued to press charges against these officers, so Bligh asked him to return to face a Court Martial in England. When he refused to return, he was arrested and sent back with his family. Tragically on the voyage back, Short's wife and one of his seven children died. This bereavement as well as other rivalries against Bligh must be taken into account in Short's acquittal. The President of the Court [259] Admiral Sir Isaac Coffin made representations to the Admiralty to replace Bligh as Governor with his preferred nomination Captain Kent, while Captain Short later plotted [260] with Captain Kent and ex-Governors or ex-Lieutenant Governors Grose, Hunter and King against Bligh.

In February and March of 1806, there had been disastrous floods of the Hawkesbury river in New South Wales resulting in the devastation of much of the wheat crop which was then grown predominantly in that area. This had caused much distress and added to the miseries brought about by the monopolies of the NSW Corps.

Governor Bligh arrived in New South Wales early in August 1806 and the official landing took place on the 8th of August. Governor King made certain land grants to Bligh on the 10th of August: 240 acres near Sydney which Bligh called "Camperdown", 105 acres near Parramatta which he called "Mount Betham" and 1000 acres between Sydney and Hawkesbury which he called "Copenhagen". On the 13th of August, Bligh assumed the governorship and King returned to his property in Parramatta. Bligh received an address

---

[259] HR NSW vol 6 p388

[260] Bligh family correspondence ML Safe 1/45 p123-5

of congratulations signed by George Johnston for the military, Richard Atkins for the civil power and John McArthur for the free inhabitants. An address of welcome by these three men was published in the Sydney Gazette on the 24th of August.

The Reverend Henry Fulton, an ex-convict Irish Priest, spoke [261] of conditions in New South Wales at this time: "On Governor Bligh's arrival in August 1806, the colony was in a very distressed situation... the settlers were involved in debt, chiefly by their lust of spirituous liquors and the great quantity of that noxious beverage that had been imported, as it was disposed of then chiefly by barter... Some people got spirits by permission of former Governors and in such quantities as those Governors chose, at from 8 – 10 shillings per gallon, and paid it away at 2,3 or 4 pounds per gallon in barter to workmen, settlers, shopkeepers..."

Due to the effect of the Hawkesbury floods on the supply of cereals, a Government and General Order of the 23rd of August reduced the allocation of cereals but increased that of meat to those eligible to receive Government stores. On the 25th of August, a public notice indicated relief for cereal producers, while a Government and General Order of the 8th of September gave relief specifically to the Hawkesbury flood area.

The first meeting between Bligh and McArthur on about the 13th of September has been differently reported. McArthur claimed later that Bligh showed his animus against him by threatening to take away the 5,000 acres given by Governor King. It is however unlikely that Bligh would have said any such thing, as he knew that Sir Joseph Banks and Lord Camden had struck a deal whereby McArthur would have 5,000 acres. McArthur would have known that Sir Joseph Banks had reduced Lord Camden's original proposal to give McArthur 10,000 acres outright. For a time, McArthur continued to visit Government House.

On the 22nd of September 1806, Governor Bligh received [262] an address signed by 135 free inhabitants of Sydney disclaiming McArthur as a person able to speak on their behalf and claiming that he was responsible for a rise in the price of mutton by his withholding supplies from the market.

---

[261] HR NSW vol 6 p696
[262] HR NSW vol 6 p188

During September 1806, Bligh sent food, clothing, barter articles and medical supplies to the new settlement on the Derwent River in van Diemen's Land (now Tasmania).

On the 4th of October 1806, new Port Regulations were issued to organise ports more efficiently and to ensure that penalties were imposed on ships attempting to take convicts out of the country.

About this time, Governor Bligh made a tour of the Hawkesbury River district. He received [263] an address from 224 settlers of that district, who also objected to McArthur signing on behalf of the free inhabitants. In addition to the problems caused by the floods in their district, the settlers complained of ships being sent away without being able to unload their cargoes so that the NSW officers could force up prices for their own benefit. They also complained of low grain and agricultural prices, as well as a depreciating currency.

It is particularly interesting that the settlers drew up a Bill of Rights and it is against these criteria that Bligh's Governorship should be judged: Freedom of trade; fair open market to prevent the monopolies and extortion practised; to protect the merchant and trader in their properties and the people in general in their rights, privileges and liberties; to suffer the laws of the realm to take their due course without control in matters of property; to see that justice was administered by the courts, according to the known laws of the land; and to cause payment to be made in such money or government orders as would pass current in the purchase of every article of merchandise without drawback or discount.

Bligh responded quickly to the distress caused by the Hawkesbury floods. He used cattle from the Government herds to provide beef to prevent starvation and he offered incentives to farmers by forward price guarantees for grain in the following year. His action was appreciated [264] by Lord Castlereagh on behalf of the British Government.

The Reverend Samuel Marsden, principal chaplain to the Colony, wrote [265] of events at that time: "When Governor Bligh took the command, many serious evils existed and which had been

---

[263] HR NSW vol 6 p191
[264] HR NSW vol 6 p398
[265] Marsden to Banks 28.9.1808 ML Series 43.03/CY 3007/863-868

gradually maturing for the whole 13 years I lived in the settlement. The greatest of these was the Barter of Spirits, all others were only Branches that sprung from and were connected with this. Governor Bligh soon saw the unhappy situation in which he was placed. He was convinced that if he allowed the Barter of Spirits, the labouring class would continue in ruin and distress, and the general welfare of the Colony would be sacrificed; and to attempt to prohibit this Barter would be dangerous. I had frequent conversations with him on this subject and told him it would be a dangerous attempt, tho' the time would arrive when the distresses of the Colony would compel those in Authority to adopt this measure."

"After I left the Settlement, Governor Bligh dared to issue an order, prohibiting the barter of Spirits. From the moment I saw the order, I was convinced that he would not carry it into execution; and was very apprehensive of the consequences. I knew well that, by doing this, he had risqued his Government, Character and all that could be dear to him..."

A week before the 1st of November 1806, the day on which he made a General Order prohibiting the barter of spirits, Bligh wrote [266] to London: "that prohibiting the barter of spirit will meet with the marked opposition of those few who have so materially enriched themselves by it".

Bligh went ahead with his plans and Lord Castlereagh expressed [267] full approval, giving him full authority to make regulations for control of the liquor trade and asked hm not to fail in rigorously levying penalties for breaches of his regulations.

Bligh's proclamation on the 1st of November 1806 dealt not only with the barter of spirits but also tackled the problems of a depreciating currency and the uncertain value of private bills. "All checks (cheques) and promissory notes... shall be payable in sterling money". So ran part of a General Order [268].

On the 5th of November, Bligh wrote to the Secretary of State that he would be touring the Colony of New South Wales to make himself conversant with the problems of the settlers.

---

[266] HR NSW vol 6 p249
[267] HR NSW vol 6 p399 and following
[268] HR NSW vol 6 p198

On the 15th of November, an officer on board HMS Porpoise by name of Tetley complained formally about Captain Short and a week later the Acting Master, Daniel Lye, made a further complaint about his Captain. Six days later, Lye was arrested by Short. This news was brought to Bligh who set up an Enquiry on the 10th of December, led by ex-Governor General King. Tetley and Lye were exonerated, and the charges against Short were proved. When Tetley's leave was stopped and Lye arrested again by Short on the 25th of December, Bligh set up an Enquiry specifically about Short the next day. As a result of which, Short was ordered home on the 1st of January 1807 to be court martialled there.

At the beginning of 1807, Bligh made a land purchase of 170 acres and later a further 110 acres, proposing to develop a model farm and dairy within his property. On the 17th of January, he made a land grant [269] of 790 acres to Mrs King, wife of ex-Governor King. It was surely an embarrassment to Bligh that she called the property "Thanks". He also made a land grant of 600 acres to his daughter and son-in-law for them to establish a residence and farm. It is less than satisfactory that Governors used land grants as a form of patronage and they gave land to their successors on the understanding that a substantial land grant would be provided as a "quid pro quo". However, the land grant to his daughter was unwarranted and brought legal difficulties [270] in 1841, when the unrecorded Crown Grants to Governor Bligh were also reviewed. Land at Parramatta was surrendered as a settlement of that dispute.

It is of considerable interest that Bligh carried out a census called a General Muster in 1807. The results pointed up social problems which would require attention: Married women 395; concubines 1035; legitimate children 807; illegitimate children 1025; free men who had never been convicts 166. It will be noticed that the married women were then having an average of two children, while the concubines were averaging one, but the larger number of concubines meant that a larger number of illegitimate children were being born. Bligh was to attempt to influence problems arising from transportation later.

---

[269] HRA Series 1 vol 4 p15
[270] HRA Series 1 vol 6 Introduction p xiii

On the 8th of March, a ship called "Dart" part owned by John McArthur arrived in New South Wales. Among its cargo were liquor stills, some ordered by Captain Abbott and some consigned to but not ordered by John McArthur. The naval officer, Dr Harris, confiscated the key working parts of the stills but allowed the other parts of the stills to be delivered. Repercussions from that decision were to surface later in the year.

In May 1807, a trial of eight Irish prisoners was held at the Criminal Court of Jurisdiction concerning a conspiracy to prison mutiny. Six prisoners were acquitted of these charges of conspiracy and two found guilty [271] for which they were sentenced to be flogged and to transportation to Norfolk Island. However, Lieutenant Minchin, a New South Wales officer, some years later [272] testified that the Criminal Court of which he was at that time a member had acquitted the prisoners and that they had been brought before magistrates a little later and condemned on the same charge. This statement, at odds with the press report at the time of the Criminal Court hearing, was presumably designed to imply that Bligh had interfered in the legal process.

In June 1807, a ship called "Parramatta" also part owned by John McArthur, left New South Wales. A bond of £900 was pledged to be forfeited in the event of a convict staying away. A life convict was soon after found to be missing. Evidence that a convict had escaped in "Parramatta" was later found when missionaries in Tahiti complained about the activities of that life convict who had landed there from "Parramatta". When that vessel returned to New South Wales later, there would be trouble.

In July 1807, John McArthur took Andrew Thompson, Bligh's Bailiff, to Court over a promissory note expressed in bushels of wheat given by Thompson to McArthur. The Magistrates Court, taking into consideration Bligh's General Order on currency, ruled against McArthur, who appealed then to Bligh. That appeal failed and McArthur complained [273] to London. From this time, McArthur discontinued his visits to Government House, although Bligh called to visit him when he was sick.

---

[271] Sydney Gazette 7.6.1807 quoted by Mackaness '51
[272] "Proceedings... Trial of Lt Col Johnston" Bartrum p395 1811.
[273] HRA Series 1 vol 6, p323 following

Bligh by Bligh

In July, Bligh issued a General Order about leases. He was particularly concerned to enforce the lease conditions relating to that part of Sydney designated by Governor Phillip as "the domain" as well as the conditions specified in the leases issued by Governor King. The General Order in fact only affected one lease in the domain, but it did involve the demolition of a small number of properties where building had taken place despite conditions in the lease for properties outside the domain. The order required that this work should be completed by November that year. Some speculators, who had ignored lease conditions, did suffer.

Earlier in the year D'Arcy Wentworth took over as Assistant Surgeon the control of Parramatta Hospital. Bligh had heard from settlers that workmen frequently malingered by pleading sickness and being employed by the Assistant Surgeon at Parramatta on his own farming and domestic activities. Bligh therefore denied him two servants supported by the Government stores which to his predecessor had been granted. It came to Bligh's notice that four convicts at Parramatta Hospital, who were thought fit for work had been working personally for D'Arcy Wentworth. Bligh ordered Oakes, the Chief Constable of Parramatta, to arrest these four men with a view to returning them to their masters. The senior Corps officer at Parramatta was Abbott and he presumed to be able to give orders to the Assistant Surgeon who refused the order to return them to the hospital, because it conflicted with the instructions which the Governor General Bligh had given. D'Arcy Wentworth, the Assistant Surgeon, was arrested by Abbott and publicly reprimanded. Wentworth continued in trouble with Bligh because of his misuse of labour at the hospital, being suspended as Assistant Surgeon while his case was being referred back to London. Early in August, Wentworth's request to leave the colony was for some while under consideration. At the end of August, Wentworth asked the Chief Surgeon Jamison, with what was he being charged. No answer was given to this question by Bligh, probably because it was obvious what the charge involved. Bligh was later rightly criticised by the Secretary of State for not specifying the nature of the charge, however obvious.

In September, D'Arcy Wentworth was denied his request to return to Britain. It would appear that Macarthur and the officers of the New South Wales Corps orchestrated the saga about Wentworth, to be an embarrassment to Bligh.

Secretary of the Commander in Chief, the Duke of York, about the Governor's "glaring acts of indecorous and oppressive conduct":

(a) Interference in the interior management of the Corps by selecting and ordering both officers and men on various duties without the Commandant's consent.

(b) Abusing and confining the soldiers without the smallest provocation and without consulting their commanding officer.

(c) Casting the most undeserved and opprobrious censure on the Corps in company at Government House.

Johnston referred specifically to two instances of interference: on one occasion, Bligh sent for three named soldiers to strengthen his bodyguard and, on another occasion, he selected five officers to sit as members of a Criminal Court out of their proper turn.

Bligh was not likely to be popular with the NSW Corps as he had taken away their "spirit monopoly". His concern to ensure his own safety by being sure of his own bodyguards is understandable. Johnston later made it [278] plain that he was not prepared to surrender his own rights of choice in these matters. He insisted "he was to be umpire of those persons who should be on the roster". In addition to being Governor of New South Wales, Bligh was also Captain General of the NSW Corps. He must have felt justified in acting in a way which he believed was in the best interests of the Colony, particularly where this involved minimal interference with the NSW Corps.

In this same month of October 1807, Lieutenant Minchin complained to Ex-Governor King, alleging "tyranny" and "oppression",but not specifying what was involved.

On the 10th of October, Bligh wrote [279] to Sir Joseph Banks about what needed to be done in New South Wales: "The most material thing to be done is to make everyone confident he will enjoy a just and upright Government – remove without delay the very unfit and very disgraceful Judge Advocate – change the NSW Corps and send them to India. Whatever soldiers are to be here, let them be soldiers and not those who are without exception ingrafted with

---

[278] "Proceedings ... trial of Lt Col Johnston" Bartrum p60 1811
[279] Bligh to Banks 10.10.1807 ML Series 40.072/CY 3007/240-246

Convicts. I found two officers Magistrates, but there never shall be another under my Government... The officers are so connected by property and intercourse with the emancipated convicts, both of Men and Women, their influence affects public Justice. The Judge Advocate is a disgrace to human Jurisprudence. The Criminal and Civil Courts should be changed and regulated by Rules approximating to those of England – the Officers of the Crown should be honourable Men and at least we should have an Attorney General as well as a Judge besides some respectable Lawyer or Solliciter. Let this be done and all will be well – at present, justice is not duly administered in its first stages and my decision in the last does not relieve the subject altogether for what he has suffered in the course of the trial ..."

"If Government supports my Dignity and determinations, things will go on right, and let them be aware of this, as I am not here for my ease or comfort, but to do justice and relieve the oppressed poor Settlers who must be the support of the Country and are honester Men than those who wish to keep them under".

Between the 10th and 25th of October 1807, a number of people friendly to McArthur wrote letters to influential people in Britain critical of Bligh. On about the 10th of October, Dr Jamison, the Chief Surgeon, wrote to the Secretary of State Windham; on the 15th of October, Blaxland wrote to the Under Secretary Chapman, while Fitz, a deputy Commissary, also wrote to Chapman. On the 17th of October, D'Arcy Wentworth an Assistant Surgeon, wrote to Castlereagh, the previous Secretary of State, while Jamison wrote to Castlereagh the next day. On the 22nd of October, Blaxland wrote this time to Castlereagh. On the 25th of October, Harris the ex naval officer sacked by Bligh, wrote critically to ex Governor General King.

Mr Justice Evatt wrote in his book "the Rum Rebellion" that he believed these letters to have a common source, namely McArthur himself.

On the 11th of October, McArthur wrote [280] to Captain Piper, commandant of Norfolk Island; "The Corps is galloping into a state of warfare with the Governor..."

---

[280] Piper Papers ML A 256 p481-3

On the 31st of October, Gore, the Provost Marshal, wrote a letter to Castlereagh complimenting Bligh.

On the 31st of October also, Bligh wrote [281] a long official despatch to London, excerpts from the despatch include: "As to the military, about seventy of the privates were originally convicts... and is to be feared may lead to serious consequences... Considering this to be the case, there is no remedy but by the change of military duty, a circumstance which can only prevent a fixed corps becoming a dangerous militia; while, by the removal of both officers and men, it would be a valuable corps for immediate service... with respect to Mr Atkins, more particularly he has been accustomed to inebriety; he has been the ridicule of the community; sentences of death have been pronounced in moments of intoxication; his determination is weak; his opinion floating and infirm; his knowledge of the law insignificant and subservient to private inclinations; and confidential cases of the Crown, where due secrecy is required, he is not to be trusted with ... the floating paper money of an undefined value, besides an unsafe medium, is now obliged to be drawn payable in sterling".

In that month, an anonymous satirist wrote: "O tempora! O Mores! Is there no CHRISTIAN in New South Wales to put a stop to the tyranny of Governor Bligh".

In a letter to Sir Joseph Banks on the 5th of November, Bligh reveals a wry sense of humour in describing a request to him by John Blaxland, who "was so indiscreet as to .... write to me for permission to carry on a distillery and offered me a part of the firm, as he was pleased to call it".

On the 25th of November 1807, an NSW Corps officer named Kemp who had had a disagreement earlier in the month with George Johnston, the officer commanding the Corps, told Bligh that a subscription was being organised whereby McArthur would be the agent to represent to London grievances against Bligh. Bligh had already that month told his patron Sir Joseph Banks that he was deferring going to visit the settlements outside Sydney due to difficulties with the military officers.

On the 30th of November, Bligh received the welcome news that he had been promoted to the rank of Commodore, as from the 27th

---

[281] HR NSW vol 6 p355

of February 1807 and that as a result he could fly a broad pendant on a vessel in which he might embark.

In the same month, the ship "Parramatta" returned to New South Wales from Tahiti (Otaheite). McArthur had broken port regulations by permitting a convict to be taken out of the colony in this ship and so forfeited his bond of £900.

The Court confirmed the forfeiture and McArthur appealed to Bligh, but he refused to override the findings of the Court. McArthur refused to pay and attempted to disclaim responsibility by abandoning the vessel on the 7th of December. The Judge Advocate Richard Atkins a little later wrote to McArthur asking him to come to Sydney the next morning to explain why the crew of "Parramatta" had broken the port regulations "by coming unauthorised on shore". The Judge Advocate used the words in his letter "in command from His Excellency the Governor". As a result of this, the Judge Advocate received a letter from McArthur declining to attend, whereupon the Judge Advocate issued a warrant [282] to arrest McArthur and bring him before the Magistrates on the following day. It is a measure of Richard Atkins' incompetence as a Judge Advocate that he did not issue an official summons in the first place as it allowed McArthur to complain that the warrant was illegal. McArthur deflected the Chief Constable of Parramatta, Mr Oakes, sent to arrest him, by giving him his written response [283] to the warrant:

> "Mr Oakes,
>
> You will inform the persons who sent you here with the warrant you have now shown me and given me a copy of, that I will never submit to the horrid tyranny that is attempted, until I am forced; that I consider it with scorn and contempt, as I do the persons who have directed it to be executed."

This letter was considered by a Bench of Magistrates including Major George Johnston and they decided on the basis of a defiance of the judicial process by McArthur that a second warrant should be made for McArthur's arrest. On the basis of this warrant,

---

[282] HRA Series 1 vol 6 p310
[283] HR NSW vol 6 p475

McArthur was arrested [284]. Yet McArthur claimed that this warrant and his subsequent arrest was also illegal.

On the day after his arrest on the 16th of December, McArthur was brought before a bench of Magistrates including the Judge Advocate, Major Johnston and Captain Abbott and committed for trial at the Court of Criminal Jurisdiction to be held on the 25th of January 1808. McArthur was given bail. Bligh followed these matters and during these last proceedings sent a communication to the Judge Advocate, questioning an objection made by McArthur to the presence on the Bench of Robert Campbell, Naval Officer, whom he was suing perversely for the worth of "Parramatta".

It is important to be aware that the charge [285] against McArthur, emanating from the first warrant, was that he had illegally stopped the provisions of the master, mates and crew of the schooner "Parramatta" thus compelling them to violate the Colonial Regulations by coming unauthorised on shore. He had also refused to pay the £900 forfeited under his bond. The charge, emanating from the second warrant, involved defiance of the judicial process as well.

On the 19th of December, Andrew Thompson, Bligh's one-time bailiff, wrote to Bligh reminding him that "... the grand design of showing what great improvements and progress could be made on farming and colonial estates here, season by season, under strict attention and industry, proper plans, and good management... has had its desired effects to convince and excite all descriptions of people to that spirit of adventure and persevering industry which ultimately give a people happiness, plenty and independence."

It would appear that Thompson's services to the Governor had been dispensed with following Thompson's conviction for distilling alcohol illegally. In possibly forged correspondence purporting to have been written earlier in the year, Thompson admitted to indulging in sharp practices by exchanging cows for cows in calf and sows for sows in pig. Bligh's instructions to Thompson were clearly that he should indulge in no impropriety and that animals received from the Government herds should be paid for.[286]

---

[284] HR NSW vol 6 p476
[285] HRA Series 1 vol 6 p310
[286] HRNSW vol 6 p451

Bligh by Bligh

On the 21st of December, four days after his case had been committed to the Criminal Court, McArthur demanded repayment of a fourteen year old debt owed to him by Richard Atkins, the Judge Advocate. Atkins had issued a promissory note in the name of his brother which had been dishonoured. Atkins said he would repay the debt with interest in spite of the Statute of Limitations which absolved him from the need to pay. McArthur and Atkins however disputed the amount of the interest.

On the 29th of December, McArthur wrote a memorial [287] to the Governor: "... in the most earnest manner entreating the Governor to appoint a Judge Advocate who should be disinterested in the event of the trial."

Next day, the Governor replied that "a Court of Civil Jurisdiction is open to take cognizance of all civil actions". On the 1st of January 1808, McArthur attempted to press his case by ridicule: he would have "to call upon Mr Atkins to issue a writ to bring himself before himself".

The English Judge Advocate General, the Right Honourable Charles Manners Sutton spoke [288] of this problem later by stating: "it was perfectly incompetent to any person brought before that Court to offer a challenge against the Judge Advocate sitting upon it; he might as well offer a challenge against the Judge in this country sitting at the Assizes. The Governor has no more right to change the Judge Advocate who sits upon that Court than he has to change a Judge in England or anywhere else."

It is particularly relevant that McArthur brought the case against the Judge Advocate after his committal to the Criminal Court.

The Judge Advocate, Richard Atkins, answered that as McArthur was under committal for trial before him, he could not communicate with him about this "at present".

In a despatch, dated the 30th of December 1807, Lord Castlereagh, once again the Secretary of State, wrote to Bligh of his displeasure over the failure by Bligh to specify charges against the Assistant Surgeon D'Arcy Wentworth. However, a despatch dated the next day expressed Castlereagh's approval of Bligh's policies concerning the challenging of the military officers' monopolistic

---

[287] HR NSW vol 6 p395
[288] "Proceedings... Trial of Lt Col Johnston" Bartrum London 1811

practices at the expense of the settlers, adding that the King's approbation was also to be communicated.

On the 1st of January, Thompson wrote again to Bligh saying: "I took the liberty of properly putting forward with the greatest energy among the respectable people here and other parts of the country this enclosed address". This address referred to the peoples' "fullest and unfeigned sense of gratitude" to Governor General Bligh and to their hope that "a law might be administered by trial by jury of the people".

On the 11th of January 1808, Bligh discovered [289] that plans known to Major Johnston were made to bring Captain Abbott, a magistrate, to Sydney in place of Captain Kemp to bring about "a preponderancy" of magistrates in favour of McArthur.

Bligh insisted that the plans could only be effected after the 27th of January, that is after the trial.

About this time, the funeral of Lieutenant Putland, husband of Mary, Bligh's daughter, took place. Major Johnston was the chief official mourner, certainly a hypocritical position to take up in his case, but he probably thought the occasion offered some sort of camouflage for what he had in mind.

McArthur made a further appeal to Bligh to take Atkins off the case and on the 12th of January threatened to write to Downing Street to complain about the matter. Bligh now tried to anticipate trouble which McArthur might raise. He was concerned that McArthur might try to inconvenience the public and upset worshippers by building on lot 77, Church Hill, (Bligh's plan of Sydney 1807), which had been leased by Governor King to McArthur for fourteen years, "not withstanding it belonged [290] to the church which was too much confined". Lot 77 also contained a public well.

On the 13th of January, the Surveyor General, Mr Grimes, wrote on behalf of Bligh that the Governor had "particular orders respecting the ground contiguous to the Church; that he cannot allow any person to build near it; that he is sorry to inconvenience Mr Macarthur, but that any situation he may fix on to an equal extent the Governor will allow him to occupy it".

---

[289] HRA Series 1 vol 6 p424
[290] HR NSW vol 6 p359

McArthur put three sites forward which were unacceptable to Bligh due to prior Government commitment; Bligh put forward a site which was unacceptable to McArthur. On the 14th of January, Bligh passed a note to the Surveyor General for McArthur, setting out the impasse and confirming that McArthur should not build or "make any erections" until Bligh had consulted London, in the meantime Bligh would consider correspondence on this matter to be at an end. McArthur had other ideas and these directly challenged the Governor's wishes. He made use [291] of some soldiers from the NSW Corps to begin to erect a fence around lot 77. When Bligh found out what was happening, the fence was taken down.

McArthur, of course, knew of the charges which he might face, but he had found out that George Crossley had an alternative indictment, based on 36 George III c7, which the Governor and Judge Advocate had evidently asked to be kept up to date in case it was needed. Papers belonging to Crossley had some while ago been dropped during his carousing and were taken to McArthur.

It has not been appreciated that 36 George III c7 had a general heading of treason and it concerns the safety and preservation of His Majesty's person and government against treasonable and seditious practices and attempts.

The alternative indictment was an amalgam of the charge based on what was used in the first warrant and a charge of treason: that [292] McArthur had (il)legally imported or caused to be imported two stills; that in defiance of the Governor's order he had removed or caused the bodies of the stills to be removed to his own house; that by the false and libellous words he had uttered in the court when prosecuting Robert Campbell Junior he had endeavoured to bring the Governor into "disrespect, hatred and contempt"; he desired "to raise dissatisfaction and discontent... against the Constitutional Government"; that he wrote a "false and libellous defamatory letter ... with intent to raise dissatisfaction in the master, mates and crew... of 'the Parramatta'" in consequence of which they abandoned the vessel; that he "refused or neglected to attend when summoned"; that he used "false, libellous, wrongful, seditious and unlawful words" to the Chief Constable of Parramatta and finally

---

[291] "Proceedings... Trial of Lt Col Johnston" Bartrum p183 London 1811
[292] HR NSW vol 6 p465

that "being a malicious and seditious man, ... he had been deceitfully, wickedly and maliciously contriving against William Bligh Esq".

The British Government later took legal counsel about this matter. Counsel said [293] that McArthur's conduct was such as properly rendered him the object of a criminal prosecution for seditious libel against the Government.

McArthur asked to know the nature of the indictment on the 20th of January and was told by Atkins that the charge was "not treason", so presumably Bligh and Atkins were not going to advance the alternative indictment at the trial on the 25th of January. However, McArthur claimed that he could not obtain a copy of the indictment. Atkins informed him that he was not legally entitled to a copy of the indictment until he was informed of it at the trial.

At some time after his committal for trial, McArthur took steps [294] to try to influence the NSW Corps in his favour by promising large quantities of wine at a very low price. On the 22nd of January after the nomination of the Criminal Court was known, McArthur continued his demands on the Governor to take the Judge Advocate off his case, claiming that he was about to take him to Court for false imprisonment.

Dr Mackaness thinks [295] Bligh should have superseded Atkins with someone else in this case but it would have been illegal for him to have done so and would have only made matters worse by bringing the law into disrepute.

Also on the 22nd of January, Major George Johnston asked Bligh, if the NSW Corps could hold a monthly dinner on the 24th of each month. Bligh agreed to this and sent a gift of wine for the first occasion.

A sworn statement by Robert Campbell, the naval officer, indicated that about this time NSW officers acting with the authority of Major Johnston contrived to smuggle spirits from a ship in port. This statement was corroborated by a sworn statement by Captain Don of the American Barque "Jenny".

---

[293] HR NSW vol 7 p209 and 229
[294] HRA Series 1 vol 6 p242
[295] "The Life of Vice Admiral Bligh RN" G Mackaness ch XL 1951

Bligh was not apparently invited to the New South Wales Corps dinner on the 24th of January and McArthur did not attend, but it is significant that two of McArthur's partners, and McArthur's son and nephew attended. A more sinister connotation must be put on the evidence of Private Gillard who later swore [296] that the elevating screws of two field guns at Government House were taken away about this time on the order of Lieutenant Minchin of the New South Wales Corps.

The Provost Marshal, Mr Gore, later wrote to Mrs Bligh about an incident which happened about this time: John McArthur apparently made a deal with three non-commissioned officers for them to take his part in anticipated trouble to come for which they would receive specified properties. McArthur later, after the rebellion, seems to have reneged on the deal and had the men committed to prison for debt on the properties.

The Court of Criminal Jurisdiction met on the 25th of January to try McArthur. The six military officers were sworn in but McArthur interrupted at this stage to object [297] to the Judge Advocate hearing the case and he insulted the Judge Advocate by saying he had been involved "in the propagation of malignant falsehoods" and by claiming that the Judge Advocate was in a conspiracy with George Crossley "to deprive me of my property, liberty, honor and life". At this point, he produced a copy of the alternative indictment prepared by George Crossley. These insults were clearly designed to provoke in the Judge Advocate a charge of contempt of Court and this is exactly what happened. The Judge Advocate announced that he was going to commit McArthur to jail for such contempt, but Captain Fenn Kemp announced his objection and said he would commit the Judge Advocate to jail. The Judge Advocate now adjourned the Court. Captain Fenn Kemp however determined that the six officers constituted a Court, although this was contrary to the Letters Patent constituting the Court of Criminal Jurisdiction.

This sequence of events indicated [298] that McArthur had "deliberately attempted to upset the administration of the colony,

---

[296] "Proceedings ... trial of Lt Col Johnston" Bartrum p112 1811
[297] HR NSW vol 6 p422
[298] HRA Series 1 vol 6 pxxv

to force an immediate issue with Bligh, and to implicate openly, the members of the Court in an illegal procedure."

The interpretation is confirmed by other evidence: McArthur is said [299] by his son to have known of the alternative indictment prepared by Crossley before the issuing of the first warrant for his arrest and it was this which dictated his reaction to the Chief Constable of Parramatta, Mr Oakes. His object was to drive the Governor into violent and precipitate measures.

We must presume then that the alternative indictment was added to after McArthur's refusal to recognise the first warrant as there is a reference to "false, libellous, wrongful, seditious and unlawful words" to the Chief Constable of Parramatta.

In the presence of the six officers, McArthur asked for and received a military escort. McArthur had therefore removed himself from the oversight of the civil power and the Provost Marshal, William Gore, asked him to give bail but he refused.

Gore obtained a warrant for the arrest of McArthur from a bench of four magistrates including the Judge Advocate. The six officers informed [300] Bligh that they had agreed a person other than Atkins should prosecute McArthur. Bligh demanded the return of the Judge Advocate's documents taken by the six officers. They said [301] they would return attested copies or they would be prepared to give the original documents to a new Judge Advocate. These conditions were unacceptable to Bligh. Before the six officers adjourned their illegal Court, they admitted McArthur to bail.

Bligh now sent a message to Major Johnston at his home about four miles outside Sydney asking him to come to Government House without delay due to "particular public circumstances which have occurred". Johnston merely sent a verbal message that "he was too ill to come, having that evening before fallen out of his chaise on his return from the public dinner". This message was, of course, rightly interpreted by Bligh as Johnston having withdrawn support from him.

---

[299] "Some early records of the Macarthurs..." S M (Macarthur) Onslow (ed) p147 footnote, Sydney 1914
[300] HRA Series 1 vol 6 p 221
[301] HR NSW vol 6 p426

Bligh claimed later that further tampering with the two field guns at Government House occurred that evening with the removal of screws to the gun breeches.

On the 26th of January, the Provost Marshal arrested McArthur on the warrant signed the previous day. Dr Mackaness criticises Bligh for agreeing to this warrant as McArthur had been given bail. But McArthur had only been given bail by an illegal Court which Bligh did not recognise. McArthur had also taken himself out of the hands of the Civil Power and the Provost Marshal rightly asked for a warrant from the Magistrate's Court.

The six officers let Bligh have a copy of McArthur's address to the Court and requested McArthur's release, but Bligh had no intention of agreeing to their requests.

The Judge Advocate with the help of George Crossley drew up and signed a memorial [302] for the Governor detailing what had happened and saying "that the crimes so committed amount to a usurpation of His Majesty's Government and tend to incite or create rebellion or other outrageous treason" and then asking the Governor to "take such measures in this case as the nature thereof... may require".

Bligh had legally been given emergency powers which only the present Judge Advocate could give him.

Each of the six officers was issued with a summons to appear before the Governor at 9am the following morning to answer charges about actions which constituted grounds for a Court Martial for "treasonable practices".

Johnston claimed that Dr Harris at 4pm that day brought information to him that an insurrection of the inhabitants was anticipated. Apart from a small number of conspirators, that was just not true. Bligh wrote again to Johnston briefing him on the situation and proposing that, as Johnston was not able to be in Sydney, the command of the NSW Corps might be given to Abbott. Johnston sent a verbal message [303] that he would get a written message to the Governor in the evening.

---

[302] HRA Series 1 vol 7 p224
[303] HR NSW vol 6 p578

Robert Campbell, the naval officer, later stated [304] what he believed to be the Governor's plans at this stage: "he understood if they (the six officers) did not comply with the Governor's requisition, that the commanding officer was to be directed to put them under military arrest; that the magistrates, with the Governor, were to be assembled for the purpose of investigating the accusation made against the officers of the Court by the Judge Advocate; and if proved that they had acted treasonably, they were to be committed to jail".

Despite being "too ill to come to Sydney", Johnston arrived back that day at 5pm. He said [305] later he was asked to arrest the Governor and if he did not, "an insurrection and massacre would certainly take place". He did however assume the title of Lieutenant Governor, immediately signing a warrant for the release of McArthur.

A Lieutenant Governor could however only be appointed [306] by commission from the King and the Letters Patent appointing a Governor directed that the officer highest in rank within the territory and its dependencies became administrator in the event of the death or absence of the Governor or Lieutenant Governor.

Johnston was therefore clearly a usurper, particularly as he was not even the officer highest in rank and did not even bother to talk to the Governor, when requested to do so.

McArthur returned for a quick discussion with Johnston in a side room and then wrote [307] a petition to Johnston resting it on a gun in the barrack square: "the present alarming state of the colony in which every man's property, liberty and life is endangered induces us most earnestly to implore you instantly to place Governor Bligh under arrest..." Professor Kennedy writes (1989): "No objective reading of the events can conclude otherwise than that the only person whose property and liberty were at risk was McArthur..." When the petition was written, there were only four ordinary civilians present [308] : Badgery, Lord, Blaxcell and Bayly, of whom

---

[304] HR NSW vol 6 p 439
[305] "Proceedings ... trial of Lt Col Johnston" Bartrum p151 1811
[306] HRA Series 1 vol 6 p7
[307] HR NSW vol 6 p434
[308] "The Life of Vice Admiral Bligh" G Mackaness ch XLI 1951

the last two mentioned were ex-officers. There were also eight officers on duty, two surgeons who were civil officials and one surgeon under suspension. Grimes, the Surveyor General, signed the petition in tenth place and said [309] he signed after Bligh's arrest. After this, further signatures of about a hundred other inhabitants were obtained but only when it was clear that the usurpation had been successful.

The petition or requisition has been misrepresented therefore as a free expression of popular opinion when it was, in fact, a product of McArthur and signed by only a few of his acquaintances, before the document was biased by the arrest of the Governor.

Captain Fenn Kemp and three officers were deputed [310] to go to Bligh to demand his resignation. At 6.30pm, Major Johnston at the head of more than 300 officers and men of the NSW Corps marched on Government House.

Bligh could not at first be found. He had changed into his uniform and asked for horses to be made ready. He collected important papers and went upstairs. He says he thought of escape to the Hawkesbury District where he had strong support, but he decided that he must secure some important papers on his person and tear up documents which might compromise those people who had helped him, but who would be in great danger if the NSW Corps took over.

In order to have time to sort these documents, he decided to conceal himself behind a bed when a search for him was imminent. By such means, he evaded the first search, so giving himself more time to secure some papers pertinent to the defence of his administration.

In fact, Bligh was prepared to jeopardise his own reputation and risk taunts of cowardice by concealing himself behind a bed while he worked to secure information to convict his enemies and to protect his friends.

He did, in fact, manage [311] to secure on his person important papers relating to McArthur's trial on the 25th of January as well as

---

[309] "Proceedings ... Trial of Lt Col Johnston" Bartrum p285 1811
[310] HRA Series 1 vol 6 p213
[311] HR NSW vol 6 p619

to tear up papers which were disposed of by his staff and did not fall into the hands of his enemies.

Bligh has been accused of "completely losing his head", being "in a state of panic" and of "hiding ingloriously". His actions however belie those charges.

Sergeant Sutherland and Lance Corporal Marlborough who arrested Bligh, gave conflicting evidence relating to the arrest. Lance Corporal Marlborough in an affidavit made about three months after the event said that he caught Governor Bligh by the collar and dragged him out from under a bed, while Sergeant Sutherland at the court martial of Lieutenant Colonel Johnston over three years later said that he had helped Bligh over the bed.

At the same court martial, Bligh, while giving his evidence for the prosecution, said that he thought "how I could possibly get clear of the troops that had surrounded the house and get to the Hawkesbury", where "I know the whole body of the people would flock to my standard". He also said: "...with my papers about on the floor, I was discovered by the soldiers on the other side of the bed"... "An honourable mind will look for some other motive for my retirement and will find it in my anxiety for those papers which during this enquiry have occasionally been produced to the confusion of those witnesses who thought they had no longer existed".

This incident was not so much "hiding ingloriously" as "hiding to a good purpose".

On the basis of this incident, Bligh has been accused of cowardice. Dr Mackaness notes [312] that after a critical examination of all the evidence by a number of competent and impartial investigators (Owen Rutter, H S Montgomery, Lt Commander Geoffrey Rawson and Dr H V Evatt), all these writers agree in exonerating Bligh from the charge of cowardice and in asserting that the chief motives in hiding, as was proved at the trial of Lt Col Johnston were to enable him to effect his escape to the Hawkesbury, to destroy certain important papers and to secure and conceal certain others which were vital to his administration.

Bligh was arrested at Government House and Johnston proclaimed Martial Law.

---

[312] "The Life of Vice Admiral Bligh" G Mackaness, Ch XLII '51

There is evidence [313] that a conspiracy to depose Governor Bligh took place before the day of his arrest. A letter from Captain Abbott, Second in Command of the NSW Corps, to Ex Governor King has the words: "I think it is likely several of us will be sent for, and particularly Johnston, who had he followed the advice I gave him previous to his taking the step, that in that case – meaning of arresting Ye Governor – to send for Colonel Paterson immediately afterwards".

By advising Johnston to send for Paterson in Tasmania immediately after the arrest, Abbott was suggesting a less brazen method of usurpation, but it was still usurpation nevertheless. Captain Abbott claimed [314] that he was at Parramatta on the day of Bligh's arrest, so the conspiracy involving Johnston took place before that.

---

[313] HR NSW vol 6 Appendix A p 832
[314] HR NSW vol 6 Appendix A p831

CHAPTER 23

The rebellious Interregnum and Bligh's return
27.1.1808 – 25.10.1810.

The day following Governor Bligh's deposition on the 26th of January, Major Johnston revoked Martial Law which he had imposed the day before.

On the same day, he made a General Order [315] dismissing most of Bligh's civil officials. The replacement of these officials had probably been given his attention much earlier. However, far from encouraging the smuggling of liquor, he had now to consider its control. He had the American ship "Jenny" escorted from port and arranged for its seizure when it returned without authorization.

On the 30th of January, his second General Order was concerned with attending divine service to give thanks. It is ironic that Johnston should have made such an order, especially involving the new church of St Philip, to which Bligh had given so much attention.

On the 1st of February Bligh's wife, Elizabeth, wrote to Sir Joseph Banks and to an Under Secretary of State drawing attention to false representations to the Admiralty being made about Governor General Bligh and to a letter injurious to him which was circulating in Portsmouth and London.

On the 2nd of February, the Court of Criminal Jurisdiction was convened to try McArthur.

The Surveyor General, Charles Grimes, had been illegally appointed Judge Advocate and so he was illegally presiding over that Court. It was decided against the usual convention that there should not be a prosecutor and it is unsurprising that McArthur was acquitted on the original charge. Captain Abbott was so

---

[315] HR NSW vol 6 p454

dismayed at the irregularities which occurred that he protested [316] to Johnston that it was a parody of a trial.

Also on the 2nd of February, Johnston wrote to Paterson his senior, in what is now Tasmania but unfortunately that letter has not survived.

On the 8th of February, a meeting at the new church resolved[317] that an address of thanks be presented to the new administration, in particular to John McArthur "as having been chiefly instrumental in bringing about the happy change". It was also resolved to present a sword to Johnston for "the wise and salutary measures he had adopted to suppress the tyranny which ruled this country". The meeting also discussed who should go to London as the delegate of their case. It was decided that this person should be McArthur and that subscriptions should be made to cover expenses. It was claimed that £1000 was raised, but some promised subscriptions never materialised and the resulting recriminations led to quarrels, after which McArthur decided that he would go to London only as a witness for Johnston. On the 12th of February 1808, Johnston appointed McArthur, Colonial Secretary of the Colony.

On the 15th of February 1808, Mrs Bligh, not yet of course knowing of her husband's deposition, wrote to him about plots which had been made in England against him by Ex Governors Hunter and King and by Ex Lieutenant Governor Grose, Admiral Coffin and Captain Short. She obtained confidential information about this from the Secretary of the Admiralty, Mr Marsden, and she maintained private communications with Sir Joseph Banks.

On the 6th of March 1808, Arndell, a magistrate dismissed by the new rebel administration, wrote to Bligh of his grief at the Governor General's deposition. He believed that McArthur, Johnston and the military officers had acted purely for "private advantage" to themselves, but at the expense of the settlers. He pointed out that signatures for the requisition on behalf of Johnston were extorted by threats following the deposition of Bligh.

The new administration was soon finding itself in trouble. Johnston wrote [318] to Lord Castlereagh: "the unanimity in which I

---

[316] HR NSW vol 6 Appendix p832
[317] HR NSW vol 6 p513
[318] HR NSW vol 6 p584

felt so much pleasure I quickly discovered was not to be preserved without a sacrifice of His Majesty's interests and a departure from the regulations that have been made to check the importation of spirituous liquors into the colony".

John and Gregory Blaxland had been causing Johnston much trouble by their attempt to remove Captain Russell from the command of the vessel "The Brothers", which they part owned. The case against the Captain failed through lack of evidence, but when the Captain was assaulted on board ship, Gregory Blaxland was convicted of assault. Captain Russell then proceeded to bring a case against the Blaxlands. At this trial, the court without an indictment against Captain Russell brought in a verdict against him. On the 3rd of April 1808, Johnston issued a proclamation declaring the sentence against Captain Russell invalid. The Judge Advocate Grimes resigned and McArthur procured the dismissal of the magistrates Harris and Symons.

On the 11th of April, the free settlers petitioned [319] Johnston charging McArthur with "monopoly and extortion". Another memorial [320] to Johnston also said that the Colonial Secretary of the Colony, McArthur, was "the scourge of the Colony by fermenting quarrels between His Majesty's officers, servants and subjects". The settlers also wrote in that month to Lieutenant Colonel Paterson in Tasmania saying [321]: "the whole government appears to be put in the hands of John McArthur Esq who seems a very improper person ... and we believe him to be the principal agitator and promoter of the present alarming and calamitious (sic) state of the colony".

On the 24th of May, McArthur wrote to Captain Piper on Norfolk Island that, apart from three people "there is not a man that affords Johnston the least support, and most of them oppose everything..."

Although Lieutenant Colonel Paterson had been summoned to Sydney soon after Johnston had illegally taken the title of Lieutenant Governor, he declined to come until he had received orders from London. On the 30th of July 1808, Lieutenant Colonel

---

[319] HRA Series 1 vol 6 p572/3
[320] HR NSW vol 6 p597
[321] HR NSW vol 7 p596

Foveaux arrived in Sydney. As he was senior in rank to Johnston and because Johnston was ready to step aside, Foveaux took over as Lieutenant Governor. He had left England in January when, of course, the news of the deposition of the Governor was not known; in fact, he was coming out to be a Lieutenant Governor under Bligh.

Because he decided to maintain Bligh under arrest and to prevail upon him to go back to England, Foveaux soon fell out with Bligh.

On the 8th of August, Bligh wrote [322] to Paterson demanding that the mutiny be put down and that the deposition be reversed. On the 31st of August, Bligh wrote [323] to Lord Castlereagh explaining how Foveaux was mishandling the situation. Foveaux unconvincingly explained [324] why he acted as he did. In extenuation of his position, it might be said that he faced a militia in revolt and that he did not have forces to confront it. He did however have the option of either joining Paterson or of returning to England rather than colluding with the rebellion, but, as we have seen, he was a leading beneficiary of the monopolies and extortion practised by the officers of the New South Wales Corps.

During this same month of August, settlers wrote to Bligh saying that the ills of barter have returned under the rebels. His administration they approved of, they wished to emphasize that they had no foreknowledge of the rebellion, neither did they act nor take part in it.

Paterson replied to Bligh on the 29th of September that he was not returning until he had received instructions from London.

Edward, son of John McArthur, reached England in September when news of Bligh's deposition was first known. He wrote [325] to his father: "Our late affairs make little impression on the public mind and excite still less attention at the offices, for Spain and Portugal attract all their attentions..."

Following the treaty of Tilsit on the 7th of July 1807, Portugal was the only European ally left to Britain, although Spain was not really favourably disposed towards Napoleon. On the 30th of November 1807, the French took Lisbon after Portuguese royalty left for Brazil.

---

[322] HR NSW vol 6 p701
[323] HRA Series 1 vol 6 p588 following
[324] HRA Series 1 vol 6 p623 following
[325] "Some early records of the Macarthurs..." SM Onslow (ed) p167

The rebellious Interregnum and Bligh's return

In February 1808, France began the occupation of Spain, but in May of that year the Spanish rose up against the French in Madrid and in a number of other places. On the 30th of May 1808, the Spanish people appealed to London for help. Arthur Wellesley, later the Duke of Wellington, was sent to Portugal at the end of June. The Spanish defeated a small French force at Baylen during the summer, while Wellesley won a victory at Vimiero.

British fortunes in Spain were less happy a short while later. On the 17th of January 1809, British forces had to be evacuated from Corunna and their Commander, Sir John Moore, was killed.

Wellesley was among those evacuated, but he returned to Portugal in April 1809, leading to the defeat of some of the French forces at Talavera in Spain. In October 1810, Wellington had to retreat to Torres Vedras, an area he had fortified to defend Lisbon. In March 1811, the French had to raise the siege of Lisbon enabling Wellesley to begin a series of campaigns, finally leading to the invasion of France from Spain.

During the illegal administration of Foveaux, the free settlers wrote [326] a memorial dated the 4th of November 1808 to Lord Castlereagh in London: noticing the assistance Bligh gave to the settlers following the flood, also his General order which stopped the barter of spirits. The settlers particularly rejected Johnston's claim that the change of Government was at their request. They asked for the reinstatement of Governor Bligh.

Foveaux had issued a General Order for the muster or census of landowners. George Suttor, a free settler, declined to attend, as he did not recognise the illegal administration. He was arrested and brought [327] before an illegal court where he was fined and sentenced to six months imprisonment.

On the 1st of January 1809, Captain Porteous under Bligh's orders took command of HMS Porpoise and arrested [328] Lieutenant Kent who had been in command. Kent was charged with sailing from Port Jackson without orders, also with having hauled down Bligh's broad pendant on board HMS Porpoise and again proceeded to sea without his orders or any person duly authorised

---

[326] HRA Series 1 vol 7 p137
[327] HR NSW vol 7 p1
[328] HR NSW vol 7 p74

to give the same and finally with having permitted Lt James Symons to quit His Majesty's service and carry home dispatches from the persons who had usurped the Government, and not having apprehended him and brought him to punishment. Kent was to be sent for Court Martial in England.

On the 9th of January 1809, Lieutenant Colonel Paterson took over the command from Foveaux, who had warned him that Bligh would try to have him arrested. Paterson was senior to Foveaux who was only too ready to hand over the responsibility for the rebellious state of affairs.

Paterson used Foveaux and Abbott as his advisers and kept Johnston in the dark about what he was doing. However, he did use Johnston and Abbott to try to threaten Bligh either to leave Australia and release HMS Porpoise for duty at Norfolk Island or to be forcibly removed from Government House.

Bligh wrote [329] to Lord Castlereagh with grim humour: "They suffered me to remain quiet... only very much annoyed by the sentinels, who, constantly heated with liquor, seemed to have been directed to bellow 'All's well' with peculiar tones of hellish composition"; and again he wrote [330] with the same grim humour: "... in my drawing room before the portraits of our beloved Majesties, which were veiled, I observed that it was a fortunate circumstance His Majesty saw nothing of the transaction... I refused to comply with their requisition" (Johnston and Abbott's requisition of written threats).

On the 30th of January 1809, Bligh and his daughter were forcibly removed from Government House and given two rooms in the barracks. Bligh immediately appealed to Paterson and began negotiations on a deal. About this time, he was anxious about the safety of his daughter and himself, thinking [331] that his enemies might take the opportunity of doing away with him by poisoning his food. His predicament was real and the punishment meted out to his friends by the illegal administration was harsh.

Bligh has been accused of reacting with paranoia on this occasion, but his thoughts of self preservation were hardly paranoid.

---

[329] HR NSW vol 7 p172
[330] HR NSW vol 7 p173
[331] HR NSW vol 7 p175

On the 4th of February, Bligh and Paterson signed an agreement: Bligh would embark with his daughter on HMS Porpoise on the 20th of February; he would proceed to England with utmost despatch; he would neither touch at nor return to any part of the territory with His Majesty's orders; he would not in any manner interfere with the government of the colony or place any impediment in the way of the outfitting of the Porpoise. Paterson would remove the additional restraints recently placed upon Bligh; he would permit Bligh to return to Government House where he could communicate with his friends; Paterson would allow such persons to accompany Bligh to England, as Bligh thought proper to name.

"To the strict and unequivocal observance" of this agreement, Bligh solemnly pledged [332] "his honor as an officer and a gentleman".

The agreement between Paterson and Bligh was first broken [333] by Johnston who refused to allow Palmer to accompany Bligh to England, giving the excuse that Palmer had to adjust certain claims made against the Crown prior to his suspension.

Once Paterson allowed the agreement to be broken, Bligh could quite reasonably consider the agreement to be at an end without compromising his dignity. Professor Kennedy said [334] that Bligh reneged on the agreement, but there was no agreement once Paterson had allowed it to be broken.

Bligh said [335] "I have at last by finesse got possession of my ship". He had planned an agreement with Paterson which he did not believe Paterson would keep. Paterson with the highest cards made the agreement. Palmer was nominated to accompany Bligh to England and Johnston couldn't support Paterson in the agreement. It really was a finesse which safeguarded Bligh's honour as an officer and a gentleman.

On 17th of February 1809, a memorial letter was sent by 14 free settlers to Viscount Castlereagh, Secretary of State for the Colonies: "that your memorialists.. were every way fully satisfied and content under His Excellency's (Governor Bligh's) administration.

---

[332] HR NSW vol 7 p17
[333] HR NSW vol 7 p45 and 73
[334] "Bligh" G Kennedy Ch 29 1978
[335] HR NSW vol 7 p67

His Excellency was doing all that public virtue or private worth could accomplish to correct abuses, re-establish discipline, protect and encourage sobriety and industry".

"That your memorialists believe the following causes principally led to the rebellion: that the officers had been – and still continue – merchants, traders and dealers, which was carried on by employing convicts as their agents in different parts of the colony, by which means a great number of the inhabitants are in debt to them as their agents which gave them a dangerous influence; and they had entered upon expensive establishments, which nothing but a continuance of abuses could support...".

On the next day, six civil officers wrote to Bligh "..These feelings are still rendered more pungent and intense when we behold your Excellency thus confined, harassed, and variously insulted and so long a period of suffering, forced out of the colony on account of your courage, determination, integrity and fidelity to your Sovereign in promoting the general good, in opposing smuggling and monopoly, in repressing seditious practices, in causing the laws to be executed with impartiality and rendering the rich as well as the poor amenable to them. We see with sorrow and alarm that John McArthur, Esq, is so far above control as to be able to subvert the Government in order to rescue himself from justice; and we therefore fear for our lives, liberties and properties when an individual settler possesses so much power. As he has done this by his influence over the officers of the New South Wales Corps...".

Bligh later issued a proclamation stating that the NSW Corps was mutinous and ordering ships captains not to take any person supposed to be connected with the rebellion out of the Colony.

On the 12th of March, Paterson wrote to Lord Castlereagh complaining about Bligh. In one of his letters to London, Paterson said that Bligh was involved with "concubines". This has been described [336] by Professor Kennedy as an "outrageous suggestion" in the light of his family circumstances and past conduct. It must surely be considered as fabricated abuse without any evidence to support it.

---

[336] "Bligh" G Kennedy Ch 29 1978

Bligh sailed finally on the 17th of March from New South Wales to the Derwent River, Tasmania. Paterson purported to claim on the 19th of March that Bligh had reneged on the agreement and ordered that no one should communicate or correspond with Bligh, his family or persons on HMS Porpoise. He threatened those who flouted this order "as abettors of sedition and enemies to the peace and prosperity of the Colony".

Two people, Palmer and Hook, who publicised Bligh's proclamation were brought before a Court. Refusing to recognise the jurisdiction of the illegal Court, they were fined and imprisoned.

Johnston, McArthur and some other dissidents sailed on the 29th of March for England. Paterson had not discussed these arrangements with Johnston and so Johnston had had no choice. It however suited McArthur that it would be Johnston rather than himself who would be tried and as long as the New South Wales Corps dominated the Criminal Court in New South Wales, McArthur was safe.

On the 1st of April, appropriately All Fool's Day, Paterson issued a General Order commending the exemplary good conduct of the NSW Corps.

It had been decided in London that Bligh's advice on the recall of the NSW Corps and the replacement of the Judge Advocate should be taken, but it was also decided that Bligh should be relieved. Lord Castlereagh wrote to Bligh that he was being recalled but this involved "no loss of the King's confidence", Brigadier General Nightingall of the 73rd Regiment was first chosen to succeed Bligh, but he later withdrew due to illness. Colonel Lachlan Macquarie, the Second in Command of the 73rd Regiment, received his commission as Governor General on the 8th of May 1809. Lord Castlereagh on the 14th of May gave him instructions [337] in a letter: "take immediate measures for placing Major Johnston in close arrest and for sending him Home in order that he may be tried for his conduct on his return to England; and as Govr Bligh has represented that Mr McArthur has been the leading promoter and instigator of the mutinous measures which have been taken against His Majesty's Governor, you will, if examinations be sworn against him, charging him with criminal acts against the Governor and his

---

[337] HR NSW vol 7 p143/4

authority, have him arrested thereupon and brought to trial before the Criminal Court of the settlement". Other instructions were given to Macquarie to annul official appointments following the deposition; to restore deposed officials, except Atkins who was to be recalled; to cancel any land grant made after Bligh's arrest; to send back the NSW Corps to England; to restore all Bligh's papers to him and to restore him as Governor for 24 hours; thereafter to take up the Governorship.

It will be observed that McArthur was only to be tried in New South Wales when the officers of the NSW Corps, who provided a majority on the Criminal Court, had been recalled.

In May 1809, settlers in the Derwent area sent Bligh an address of loyalty and sympathy. Lieutenant Governor David Collins in Tasmania had welcomed Bligh in March, giving his daughter rooms in Government House there and made his own house available to Bligh, but following Paterson's orders [338] not to revictual HMS Porpoise, Collins found himself in a dilemma which he resolved by siding with Paterson. The settlers in Tasmania clearly had other sympathies.

The Reverend Henry Fulton wrote [339] to Lord Castlereagh about Paterson; he described him as "almost a paralytic from a former intemperance" due to alcohol.

During his Governorship, Bligh had only made land grants of 2180 acres, but during the rebellious interregnum, Johnston had made [340] land grants of 5660 acres, Foveaux of 8325 acres, and Paterson a massive 68101 acres. It is important to realise that some naval officers of "HMS Porpoise" including Captain Porteous, Lieutenant Kent and Lieutenant Oxley accepted land grants from the rebels before Bligh recovered his ship. This fact clearly soured relations between Bligh and the officers of "HMS Porpoise" so much so that Surgeon Macmillan of "HMS Porpoise" wrote of Bligh on the 9th of June 1809 as a "vain, weak, selfish tyrant". Maintaining the dignity of his rank as Governor General as well as that of a senior naval officer of the rank of Commodore was presumably interpreted as vanity; being deposed from the position

---

[338] HR NSW vol 7 p101
[339] HR NSW vol 7 p58
[340] HR NSW vol 7 p808

of being a Governor General was interpreted as weakness; and recovering his post as First Captain of "HMS Porpoise" over that of Captain Porteous was interpreted as selfish tyranny. The remarks of the Surgeon of "HMS Porpoise" can be branded as exaggerated sarcasm, influenced by those who had received gifts from the rebels.

In addition to such land grants, the rebels gave away [341] cattle from the Government herd and free pardons and emancipations. William Gore, the Provost Marshal under Bligh, wrote of people benefitting from the rebellious interregnum being expected to support the rebels. "An expectation they entertain at the testimony of the persons, who accept leases, grants or pardons from them should they be called on as evidence by the Court hereafter, will appear at least inconsistent and doubtful..."

Relations between Collins in Hobart and Bligh in "HMS Porpoise" were now hostile. Collins ordered punishment for anybody in van Diemen's Land (Tasmania) communicating with Bligh, while Bligh ordered Captain Porteous to fire on boats ignoring instructions from "HMS Porpoise". Collins then wrote to Captain Porteous saying that the small boats of "HMS Porpoise" would be fired on if they approached the land. In July 1809 Bligh wrote to Lord Castlereagh that Collins was now mutinous; while Collins wrote to Castlereagh that Bligh was seizing supplies sent to Hobart.

Late in July, John McArthur wrote to his wife Elizabeth from Rio de Janeiro: "... Colonel Johnston is at my elbow complaining of the rheumatism and the ravages of old age...".

In August 1809, the Government and General Order declared that the NSW Corps is to be numbered in the 102nd Regiment; on the same day, a detachment of the 73rd Regiment arrived, declaring who would succeed Bligh as Governor General. Also in August 1809, Atkins, the Judge Advocate again, received a free grant of 500 acres from the rebel leader Paterson.

In September 1809, Lord Castlereagh received legal advice from J G Harris: that on the 1st of January 1808 the administration of Governor General Bligh was just and vigorous; that Bligh's restrictions on the barter of spirits was obnoxious to officers of the NSW Corps; that McArthur was involved in trade barter and that he brought about breach of the Colonial Regulations by causing the

---

[341] Wm Gore to Mrs Bligh ML Series 42.11/CY3007/830-857

master and crew of the ship "Parramatta" to come illegally on shore; that McArthur's written response to Oakes'warrant was libellous; and that the Judge Advocate's memorial to the Governor General on the 26th of January 1808 referred to "treasonable practices".

In November 1809, the Earl of Liverpool, then Secretary of State for the Colonies, received legal advice from V Gibbs and T Plumer: "We think Major Johnston, Mr McArthur, and the persons concerned with them, were guilty of a conspiracy and high misdemeanour in the arrest and imprisonment of Governor Bligh and in the assumption of the Government of the colony of New South Wales on themselves... as he (Johnston) certainly may be tried for mutiny by Court Martial under the Mutiny Act, we think the proper step, as to him would be to bring him to a Court Martial".

"That Lieut-Col'l Foveaux is also liable to be tried by a Court Martial on a similar charge of mutiny in continuing the arrest and imprisonment of Governor Bligh on his taking the command in the settlement".

"That as these offences were committed out of the Kingdom, there is no jurisdiction here to try Mr McArthur and the civil persons concerned with him; and therefore, he should be sent back to New South Wales".

"That the evidence to be collected from the correspondence, principally affects John McArthur, Nicholas Bayly, Doctor Townson, John Blaxland, Garnham Blaxcell and Thomas Jamieson, as having previously concerted together with Major Johnston the arrest and imprisonment of Governor Bligh, and having afterwards borne a part in the assumed Government."

Colonel Lachlan Macquarie arrived in New South Wales on the 28th of December 1809 with an official landing three days later. He assumed the Governorship next day, the 1st of January 1810, proclaiming His Majesty's "utmost regret and displeasure on account of the late tumultuous proceedings – and mutinous conduct of certain persons towards his late representative William Bligh Esquire". Macquarie [342] went on to regret Bligh's absence from the Colony and his own need to take immediate control,

---

[342] HR NSW vol 7 p252

which prevented him from reinstating his predecessor for 24 hours according to his written orders.

Macquarie had brought with him the 73rd Regiment of Foot under Lieutenant Colonel Maurice O'Connell and this enabled the new Governor to replace in its entirety the NSW Corps, with its majority hold on the Criminal Court.

A Government and General Order (GGO) on the 2nd of January 1810 demanded the return of documents taken by the rebels, but most of the documents which Bligh had had taken away from him were largely taken to England by McArthur and Johnston and were never returned, but a few documents recovered by Bligh in New South Wales proved very useful in showing that perjury was committed among witnesses for Johnston.

Two further proclamations [343] were made on the 4th of January: All appointments and land grants made since Bligh's deposition were cancelled subject to the discretion of the New Governor. All trial verdicts were annulled during that period but to prevent malicious litigation, all civil officials were granted indemnity for their actions and legal proceedings against them were prohibited.

Macquarie wrote to Bligh in Tasmania. On the 17th of January, Bligh arrived back in Sydney to a thirteen gun salute. Next day, he landed to inspect a guard of honour of the 73rd Regiment and received a complimentary message to "Commodore Bligh" from the new Governor.

Bligh declined an opportunity to dine at Government House because he had first accepted an invitation from Lieutenant Colonel O'Connell.

Bligh remained in New South Wales to collect evidence, having now a copy of Johnston's statement of justification.

Bligh wrote [344] to his wife on the 8th of March 1810:

Macquarie "has taken Foveaux as his friend... this mark of favour to Foveaux has astonished and depressed the loyal people very much..."

Macquarie seems also to have listened more carefully to the rebels than to those people loyal to Bligh, or to Bligh himself. Bligh

---

[343] HR NSW vol 6 p252

[344] William Bligh to Betsy ML 8.3.1810, Safe 1/45

wrote: [344] Macquarie has "not taken my opinion in any case whatever". He tried not to be provoked; "all we do is to act with mildness and avoid any altercation or appearance of displeasure".

Macquarie seems to have believed the rebels when they said Bligh had reneged on his agreement with Paterson. The new Governor wrote [345] to his brother in March: "... Governor Bligh certainly is a most disagreeable Person to have any dealings or publick business to transact with; having no regard whatever to his promises or engagements however sacred and his natural temper is uncommonly harsh and tyrannical in the extreme ... It is an undoubted fact that he is a very improper Person to be employed in any situation of trust or Command, and he is certainly very generally detested by high, low, rich and poor, but more especially by the Higher Classes of People".

Bligh's continual refusal to dine at Government House was probably as a protest that he had not been reinstated for the 24 hours prescribed by London, that his advice was ignored and that Macquarie had given preferment to rebels like Foveaux.

Macquarie wrote [346] to Lord Castlereagh:

"... in justice to Governor Bligh, I must say that I have not been able to discover any act of his which could in any degree form an excuse for, or in any way warrant the violent and mutinous proceedings pursued against him on that occasion, very few complaints have been made to me against him and even those few are of a trifling nature".

In April, free settlers supporting Bligh in both Sydney and the Hawkesbury district were given permission by Governor Macquarie to hold public meetings to vote addresses of condolence and congratulations to Bligh and "to refute in the most public manner the false and infamous charges exhibited against the inhabitants of the colony by Lieutenant Colonel George Johnston".

The Chairman of the Sydney meeting was Provost Marshal Gore who after accepting motions favourable to Bligh rejected other amendments. Governor Macquarie permitted a new meeting to be held that afternoon, by which time most of Bligh's supporters had

---

[345] Journal of the Australian Historical Society vol XVI part 1 p27 quoted by Mackaness 1931
[346] HR NSW vol 7 p378

dispersed. Amendments unfavourable to Bligh were passed at that meeting. However Governor Macquarie decided against publication of the addresses and amendment. An address [347] of thanks signed by 460 inhabitants was however presented to Bligh "... so far from their being an imminent necessity for it (a rebellion against the Governor), the administration of justice and the whole conduct of the Governor was such as to call for the gratitude and thanks of the people of the colony".

What happened just before Bligh sailed for England is best described in a sensitive letter [348] he wrote to his wife:

"The Hindostan" Rio

My dearest Love,

Happily, I am thus far advanced to meet you and my Dear Children. I am now well, as is our Dear Mary, altho I have suffered beyond what I can at present describe to you. Providence has ordained certain things which we cannot account for; so it has happened with us – my perfect reliance that everything which occurs is for the best is my great consolation. In the highest feelings of comfort and pride of bringing her to England, although I thought she could be under no guidance but my own – my heart devoted to her – in the midst of most parental affections and conflicting passions of adoration for so good and admired child, I at the last found what I had the least expected Lieut Col^r O'Connel commanding the 73 Reg^t had unknown to me won her affections. Nothing can exceed the esteem and high character he has. He is likewise Lt Govr of the Territory – A few days before I sailed, when everything was prepared for her reception and we had even embarked, he then opened the circumstance to me – I gave him a flat denial for I could not believe it – I retired with her, when I found she had approved of his Addresses and given her Word to him. What will you not my Dear Betsy feel for my situation at the time, when you know that nothing I could say had any effect: at last overwhelmed with a loss I could not retrieve, I

---

[347] HRA Series 1 vol 7 p146, et al
[348] Bligh to Mrs Bligh Rio 11.8.1810 ML Safe 1/45

had only to make the best of it – My consent could only be extorted for it was not a free gift. However, on many proofs of the Honor, Goodness and high Character of Colonel O'Connel and his good sense which had passed under my own trial, I did, like having no alternative, consent to her marriage and gave her away at the ceremony consumated at Government House, under the most public tokens of respect and veneration..."

Governor Macquarie gave the couple a farm called Riverstone.

On the 12th of May 1810, after a farewell banquet the night before, Bligh left Australia with some of his supporters and with him sailed also the remnants of the infamous NSW Corps now to be called the 102nd Regiment of Foot. Foveaux had sailed earlier in March.

John McArthur wrote [349] of the NSW Corps "...what a bustle their removal must have created. It is a happy event for the colony, for a more improper set of men could not be collected together than they have lately become".

Paterson died on the 21st of June 1810 at Cape Horn returning to England.

Bligh reached England on the 25th of October 1810.

---

[349] "Some early records of the Macarthurs..." S M Onslow (ed) p195

CHAPTER 24

The Courts Martial of Lieutenant Colonel George Johnston and Lieutenant Kent RN
25.10.1810 – 31.7.1811.

Soon after Bligh arrived back in England, John McArthur now also in England wrote to his wife on the 11th of November 1810 that he was about to sue Bligh for damages amounting to £20,000. McArthur and Foveaux had come to an accommodation [350], working on behalf of Johnston.

On the 16th of November, Johnston wrote [351] to the Earl of Liverpool saying he could "produce incontestable evidence of his (Governor Bligh's) tyranny and oppression of the people he was sent to govern; of gross frauds and shameful robberies committed upon the public property entrusted to his care; and lastly I will prove that he has been guilty of heretofore unheard of and disgraceful cowardice".

The forthcoming trial of Lieutenant Colonel Johnston was to examine all this evidence making this a virtual trial of Governor General Bligh as well as a trial of Lieutenant Colonel Johnston.

Among those who returned to England with Bligh was Palmer, the official Commissary under Bligh's Governorship. The Comptroller's office examined his accounts at the request of the British Government, because the Treasury had received various insinuations of irregularities concerning these accounts. The Comptroller's office reported that accusations arose from "personal pique" and were too vague to justify a formal inquiry.

---

[350] "Some early records of the Macarthurs..." SM Onslow (ed) p206
[351] Ibid p208-210

Major Johnston had been promoted to Lieutenant Colonel of the 102 Regiment of Foot, previously the NSW Corps. On the 13th of December 1810, Bligh wrote to the Admiralty requesting promotion to flag rank. However the Admiralty clearly wanted to see the outcome of the trial of Lieutenant Colonel Johnston and to see that Bligh himself was not embroiled in litigation before they acted. The Court Martial of Lieutenant Kent RN was held on the 8th of January 1811 and this meant that this officer had been under arrest for just over two years, which must have been a mitigating circumstance in the trial. The Court was of the opinion that Lt Kent was trying to do his duty and that the third charge against him was not proven. He was acquitted on a technicality.

Bligh was among those people meeting the Prince Regent on the 27th of February at his first levée.

The Court Martial of Lieutenant Colonel George Johnston began [352] at Chelsea Hospital on the 7th of May 1811 – continued by adjournment to the 5th of June – on a charge of Mutiny for deposing William Bligh Esq FRS. Bligh had arranged with the permission of the Court for a Mr Bartrum of Clement's Inn to take a short-hand transcription of the trial.

The British Government in September and November of 1809 had received independent [353] legal advice on the papers of Bligh, Johnston and Foveaux.

T G Harris one of these lawyers, counselled that the overthrow of the Governor originated "in a preconcerted plan between the officers of the NSW Corps and some discontented inhabitants of the settlement" and "the whole detail combines a degree of preparation and a regularity in the execution of the measure which are very striking". The free settlers – as a consideration of importance- were shown not to have been a significant influence behind the insurrection. "Some few of them appear as advisers, the rest as spectators prepared to witness the act of the military ..." Of charges against Bligh, Harris writes [354] "No instance of arbitrary power exercised towards any person whatever is produced",but he speaks out on the guilt of Johnston, of his supporters and

---

[352] "Proceedings... Trial of Lt Col Johnston" Bartrum (ed) 1811
[353] HR NSW vol 7 p209
[354] HR NSW vol 7 p212

particularly of McArthur. Two other independent lawyers Mr Gibbs and Sir Thomas Plumer gave similar opinions to T G Harris, but added [355] that there was a case for bringing Foveaux to trial for mutiny in continuing the arrest and imprisonment of the Governor.

At the Court Martial of Lt Col Johnston, the defendant and his supporters were unable "to produce incontestable evidence of his (Bligh's) tyranny and oppression of the people he was sent to govern" or of the other charges he made against Bligh.

The Prosecutor, Charles Manners Sutton, the Judge Advocate General, described [356] the speciousness of John McArthur's reasons for bringing about a rebellion: "It seems the first cause of grievance was the detention of that ship of yours and the forfeiture of the bond for £900; the next is about a post that was taken away from your ground; and these seem to have been the principal part of all the causes of the revolution".

At Johnston's Court Martial, the charge was that "Johnston ... did ... begin, excite, cause and join in a mutiny... causing to be seized ... causing to be imprisoned... Wm Bligh, Captain General and Governor in Chief".

Bligh opened the prosecution recalling "the wretched condition" of the colony when he arrived in Sydney in August 1806 confirmed by his visits to different parts of the colony that year, seeing "habitations and public store houses falling into decay". His Government Order of the 14th of February 1807 banned the barter of spirits, a practice which was debilitating the colony.

The address of Sydney inhabitants (460 signatures) to Bligh on the 4th of May 1810 was quoted to disavow Johnston's claims that there was no alternative to the deposition of the Governor, that an insurrection prior to massacre was about to take place, and that the multitude was incensed. The address went on to point to Bligh's "wisdom, zeal and important services", as well as his "meritorious administration", and stating that the name of Bligh merited "veneration and esteem".

The witnesses for the prosecution of Johnston followed. John Palmer, who had been in the colony since 1790 and was Commissary under Bligh, said that "the settlers" ... were "best

---

[355] HR NSW vol 7 p229
[356] "Proceedings.... Trial of Lt Col Johnston" Bartrum (ed) p213

satisfied in Governor Bligh's time; more so, I think, than in any other Governor's"... "His conduct in general gave satisfaction to the settlers... except a few... He always administered justice, according to my ideas, impartially to everybody and to all ranks of people"... "Before the 26th of January 1808" (the day of Bligh's deposition) ... "I never saw the colony in a more thriving state, or people in general better satisfied".

Francis Oakes, the Chief Constable of Parramatta under Bligh, indicated that "...there was no danger of insurrection if the military had supported the Governor... I saw Sydney in no way of confusion till such time as the drum and fife beat to arms, then I saw the regular inhabitants run towards Government House."

William Gore, the Provost Marshal under Bligh, told the Court that "prior to the 26th of January 1808, colonists generally ... were extremely well disposed towards Governor Bligh and the colony was extremely tranquil."

"Barter of spirits and private notes (for the settlement of financial transactions) were ended, also imprisonment without a warrant, corporal punishment to obtain confessions was stopped ... also discharge from prison without prior notification to the Provost Marshal". Gore himself was imprisoned without a warrant by order of John McArthur and was sent to the coal mines for four months.

The Reverend Henry Fulton, a Sydney Chaplain, spoke of "impartial justice" under Bligh's Governorship. As a result of Fulton continuing to support Bligh after the deposition, this chaplain lost his accommodation in Sydney under the rebels.

Edmund Griffin, Bligh's Secretary, attested to "the improved state since Bligh arrived" and he went on to declare the Governor "humane and very impartial".

The prosecution case against Johnston drew attention to the pre-planning of the rebellion, noting that "elevating screws of the two guns (were) taken off a few days before by Lieutenant Minchin's order", but that these were "pointed at Government House at about 6 or 7 o'clock on the 26th of January 1808",... "while the regiment was on the march".

George Sutter, a settler, who arrived in the colony in 1800, enthused over Bligh "a very excellent Governor, conducive to the improvement of agriculture".

Martin Mason, a doctor in private practice, who arrived in the colony in 1798, noted that "Settlers were universally contented on the 1st of January 1808", as evidenced by the Address to Governor General Bligh of that date. There was then "abundance of grain". Speaking about the Governor, Dr Mason said Bligh was "a strict disciplinarian, impartial in the administration of justice". Bligh's arrest brought about "greatest regret among cultivators and every sober and industrious inhabitant".

After the deposition of Bligh, Mason said that "the Address to Johnston was unpopular" and that "there was a threat of jail, if he did not sign" and that "there was the threat of loss of indented servants".

It is significant that the Address to Johnston after the deposition was put together by a small group at the house of Andrew Thompson. It certainly appears that Andrew Thompson, previously Bligh's farm manager, was quick to change sides on Bligh's deposition and this must call into question some of the documents purporting to be letters of Thompson to Bligh before the deposition. It is not unremarkable that these letters were not produced at Johnston's trial, although they featured in the phoney trial of John McArthur in February 1808 under the rebels.

Nicholas Divine, appointed Principal Superintendent of the convicts in 1789, said of Bligh's deposition that the convicts "expressed their sorrow very much".

Charles Walker, Commander of a brig belonging to John McArthur, gave witness that not more than five civilians knew of the conspiracy, excepting, of course, "military officers in the know".

Lieutenant Colonel Johnston relied on a written defence. His actions purported to "prevent a massacre and the plunder and ruin of an infant colony". He was "goaded into frenzy by the injustice, tyranny and oppression of Captain Bligh". He was required as "Saviour" to stop "violation of public justice and private property", to confront "tyranny"... "Caprice" ... "perpetual violence"... "real injury and gross verbal abuse" and to challenge the Governor's "intention to imprison and prosecute for treason" the six officers nominated for the Criminal Court. He claimed there was "frantic indignation that every calamity must have ensued".

Johnston's first despatch to the Secretary of State Lord Castlereagh, which was incidentally written by John McArthur, was quoted: there was no alternative to the deposition of Bligh, that an insurrection leading to massacre was inevitable without intervention and that the multitude was incensed. The defence of Johnston went on to say that "His Majesty's Government was dishonoured by cruelties and merciless executions". The Governor he said had "betrayed high trust" of His Majesty, and by "a pre-determined plan to subvert the laws, to terrify and influence the courts, ... bereaved ... those obnoxious to him... of fortune, their liberty and their lives".

The Defence of Johnston wrote of oppression, following a progressive course, producing alarm and terror. The Governor's administration was said to be "hated and detested, as well as feared".

The pre-planning of John McArthur's trial beginning on the 25th of January 1808 was objected to, particularly as Crossley, a transported convict but freed under Governor King, described as infamous, was involved in that planning.

Johnston's defence claimed that there would have been despair if the six officers nominated for the Criminal Court had been arrested, leaving only two officers to carry out military duties, leading to terror and consternation, insurrection and massacre. The specious motive of the Officer Commanding was said to be the preservation of the colony and the safety of Governor Bligh.

The Defence then called witnesses: Richard Atkins, a magistrate since 1792 and Judge Advocate from the 13th of December 1800, was the first to be called. He admitted that Bligh did not influence him before he made a legal decision, but dread of Bligh's reaction to that decision did influence him. He remonstrated with Bligh over the suspension of the surgeon D'Arcy Wentworth which he termed as illegal. Bligh however insisted that this was not a legal matter and is purported to have said "Damn the law" – which is unlikely as Bligh had the right after all to suspend without explanation D'Arcy Wentworth, as being a servant of the Crown and Government employed medical officer.

Atkins also admitted that there was no address to the Governor complaining about any matter, yet he supported Johnston in saying that the population was driven to frenzy by oppression.

It must be remembered that Atkins had been shown by Bayly, Johnston's secretary, the despatch Bligh has sent in October 1807 to the Secretary of State, in which Bligh spelt out various reasons why Atkins should be replaced, mentioning problems with drink as well as having a poor grasp of the law. Yet in spite of being biased against Bligh, Atkins did not agree that an insurrection of the settlers was in prospect, in fact, he spoke of Bligh as "an honourable honest man".

John McArthur was next called for the defence of Johnston. The meeting in 1806 between Governor Bligh and John McArthur at Parramatta Government House was recalled, where McArthur purported to say that Bligh damned the Privy Council as well as the Secretary of State. McArthur may have been given a 14 year lease on Lot 77 in Sydney by Governor King with a condition that he should build on it, but McArthur provokingly began to erect a fence which interfered with access to the Church and to a well. When Bligh stopped this fencing, McArthur interpreted this speciously as "dispossessing me of my land". It was admitted in the defence case that no leaseholders were dispossessed, but that many were prevented from building. Bligh said that where land was required for future public purposes, such restrictions were imposed.

McArthur claimed the arrest was occasioned by the dread that six officers nominated for the Court were about to be sent to gaol, that there was dread of an insurrection if this happened.

Captain Kemp, previously of the NSW Corps, was questioned on a number of topics by Johnston. He informed the Court that Blaxcell, McArthur's partner, and Bayly, Johnston's secretary-to-be, had assured Johnston that an insurrection was on the eve of breaking out, before McArthur was freed from gaol. He also told the Court that Governor King had a letter from the Commander-in-Chief, the Duke of York, giving him power to nominate any officer for a particular duty, without reference to the Commanding Officer.

Captain Kemp said that "Bligh had behaved in so handsome a manner towards me that I trust I shall ever entertain a grateful remembrance". When Kemp returned from van Diemen's Land (Tasmania) in September 1807, he was involved in a bitter dispute with Johnston which was only resolved through the mediation of Governor Bligh. Kemp's conduct during the deposition of Bligh hardly tallied with entertaining a grateful remembrance.

Lieutenant Minchin was the next witness who accused Bligh of two cases of double jeopardy. One case concerned O'Dwyer, an

Irish state prisoner, the other case concerned Prosser and some convicts who absconded.

In the case of O'Dwyer, he was acquitted on a charge of conspiracy, but on representations that O'Dwyer was a danger to the colony, Bligh agreed that the Irish state prisoner should be held on Norfolk Island. Captain Abbott was asked: "do you not in your conscious believe ... that had not O'Dwyer and the other prisoners been secured, a insurrection would have taken place" to which the answer from Captain Abbott was "I have no doubt of it".

The answer by John McArthur to the same question was: "I certainly do believe, from the bustle and activity among the Irish prisoners, that an insurrection was intended, and that nothing but the apprehension of the prisoners prevented it".

In the case of Thomas Prosser and others, the Sydney Gazette of the 22nd of February 1807 reported that Prossor and others "were indicted for stealing a boat... and being all acquitted were desired to be held in custody as prisoners that had attempted to escape from the colony until His Excellency's pleasure concerning them should be known".

The Sydney Gazette for the 1st of March 1807 continued "... before a bench of magistrates, the persons concerned in taking away a boat, etc, with intent to escape from the colony were sentenced to severe corporal punishment".

The first charge therefore related to the supposed theft of the boat for which the defendents were acquitted. The second charge related to the intent to escape from the colony for which punishment was prescribed. There was therefore no double jeopardy of being tried twice for the same offence. However it is relevant to point out that Lieutenant Minchin was a member of the Court both on the occasion of the acquittal and on the occasion when punishment was handed out for a different offence, yet he clearly had not expected the prosecution to find evidence to refute his accusation.

Charles Grimes, Principal Surveyor since 1796, provided a signature on McArthur's requisition to arrest Bligh, admitting he signed after the arrest of Bligh. There were therefore as few as eight or nine signatures on that requisition, possibly even fewer made before Bligh's arrest.

John Harris, Bligh's dismissed Naval officer did say houses were pulled down in the domain at Sydney, but that , in the case of Redman's house, only an addition was pulled down.

Captain Abbott, previously of the NSW Corps, admitted that Bligh had repaired the barracks and that only eight people had signed McArthur's requisition to arrest Bligh before Grimes signed, and he had admitted to signing after Bligh's arrest.

The Court heard read a letter dated the 6th of March 1808 from Mr Thomas Arndell, a magistrate under Bligh and a retired medical man:

"Sir – it has been a matter of grief and disappointment to me, as well as the majority of the inhabitants of this colony, that your Excellency has been deprived of your authority, and placed in confinement and restraint under a military guard by a body of ambitious and discontented men, who wish to govern this territory in a manner that will suit their own private advantage, and gratify their avarice and lust of power; without any respect to the English nation or Government, to common honesty, morality, religion, or justice. They have said that they deprived you of your command because you were charged with crimes which rendered you unfit to govern one single moment longer in this colony".

"But what were these crimes? You wanted to bring to justice John McArthur, who, in the most contemptuous manner, had bid defiance to His Majesty's Government in this colony; and when six officers of the New South Wales Corps, excited by a private conversation and a seditious speech of the said McArthur, had asked in an unlawful manner, you were determined to resist such proceedings in a lawful way. These were the immediate crimes which caused your confinement; but as they dare not openly avow these as the crimes they alleged after the deed was done, they proceeded, by the terror of military execution, to extort from your friends something on which they might found more plausible charges to palliate the enormity of their wickedness – by the same terror I was, through weakness, induced to sign a paper which my heart and better judgement abhorred. Your salutary regulations, in preventing the barter of spirits, an iniquitous traffic, which raised one order of men on the ruins of another, and on the general injury of the colony at large; and the prohibition which you issued to a certain species of Colonial currency by which monopoly, extortion and forestalling were greatly restrained, were the true causes of their rage and discontent. In order to enforce these regulations better, you endeavoured to have the Court of Justice formed according to the Patent and you showed your pointed disapprobation to partiality and delay in their proceedings; you endeavoured to subject the rich as well as the poor to the laws of the colony: – and these measures they have styled a settled plan of subverting the laws, terrifying and influencing the Courts of Justice, and depriving everyone who had the misfortune to be obnoxious to you of their property, liberties and lives...

(signed) Thomas Arndell."

Mr Arndell signed the Address to Johnston on the 30th of January 1808. Johnston's Defence wrongly attributed Arndell's signature to the Address to Johnston of the 8th of March 1808.

One of Johnston's Defence witnesses, D. D. Mann said that he had to surrender his leasehold in the Domain at Sydney, but he was offered compensation.

One item of the Defence particularly interested the Court. It was that two serjeants were issued orders to keep soldiers in the guard house sometime after 4.30pm on the 26th of January 1808, the day of the deposition, but before 5pm when Johnston arrived. One member of the Court noted aloud that this indicated a prior plan.

Another serjeant by name R Mason had been one of Bligh's bodyguard, who had requested his Commanding Officer to remove him. He gave as his reason: "ill treatment and bad language... in calling me 'tremendous buggers' 'wretches' and 'villains'". The first of these insults is not one which Bligh used in other contexts and it would be surprising if he actually used it. It is, of course, possible that Johnston proposed that the serjeant should ask him to be removed from the bodyguard.

Johnston's defence ended with reference to Bligh's purported boast that there was "no law but his own", purported references to insulting and vilifying ministers as well as threats, ill treatment and bad language.

The Judge Advocate General, the Right Honourable Charles Manners Sutton, read Bligh's reply to the Defence of Johnston.

Bligh had still not been able to recover all his papers to protect his name.

The first consideration was to deal with the imputation of cowardice. On the approach of the rebels, Bligh put on his uniform and collected papers with which he would deal in an upper room behind a bed to give him more time for a more detailed selection before an inevitable arrest. He selected private and confidential documents from the Secretary of State as well as documents which might compromise people who would support him against the rebels. Some correspondence he tore up and a few documents he concealed about his person. There was conflicting evidence given about his arrest, whether Bligh was under or behind the bed. Bligh confirmed that he was behind the bed and this supported the evidence of Serjeant Sutherland "I put my hand across the bed to help him over it".

Bligh acknowledged that there were six private homes built in the Domain in Sydney, an area set aside by Governor Phillip not to be built on by private persons. Governor King had in some cases allowed leases to be bought for periods up to fourteen years. Bligh in early 1807 issued a Government Order confirming Governor Phillip's plan and in July 1807 extended the deadline till November 1807. Two houses were removed, but the owners were satisfied with the financial outcome; only D.D. Mann complained, but he was offered compensation. Some leases outside the Domain were subject to removal, where the land was required for public purposes, but again the leaseholders were compensated.

The Courts of Jurisdiction were the sentencing bodies, while the Governor General was a Court of Appeal. In the case of a teacher sentenced for seduction, the Criminal Court sentenced the offender to the pillory and 200 lashes. The Governor reduced the sentence to 100 lashes on appeal.

In replying to the accusation by Lt Minchin that Bligh had subjected two offenders to double jeopardy, Bligh reported that in the first case a man called O'Dwyer was acquitted, but that on representation by Captain Abbott and John McArthur that O'Dwyer, a convict, was dangerous, Bligh agreed to his transportation to Norfolk Island. Governor King had set a precedent for convicts, who were deemed to be dangerous, to be transported.

In the second case, Prosser and others were acquitted of the charge of theft of a boat but Prosser was convicted of "aiding and abetting" convicts escaping from the colony.

The verbal message which Lt Kent purported to have received from Bligh was inconsistent with the written message which Bligh sent to Norfolk Island.

The summons to the six officers nominated to the Criminal Court to appear on the 27th January 1808 was to seek an explanation for their conduct. The presumption that they would be immediately arrested was false, as the legal situation that there was no court without the Judge Advocate would have confronted them again. The report that the six officers would be arrested was circulated for seditious purposes.

That Bligh was unpopular was a falsity. Addresses to him from the Hawkesbury and from Sydney emphasized contentment with his administration. Campbell, Bligh's naval officer, confirmed this, as well as saying that there was a "more general and equitable distribution of spirits".

Fulton and Griffin spoke of "quiet and satisfaction". Oakes and Divine spoke of general tranquillity and good disposition to Bligh's government.

The rebels were viewed with surprise, alarm and regret. On the 26th of January 1808, Harris found himself amid two hundred people. None of whom could guess the cause of the apparent alarm.

The rebels misused public stores for their own advantage, while John McArthur escaped paying £900 for a bond forfeited, in addition to other benefits they gained by the deposition of the Governor General.

Bligh stopped irregular committal to prison and contracted the limits of arbitrary punishment. His reputation was dearer to him than his life. His actions were a vindication of his honour: the barter of spirits was confined and the distribution of private notes of exchange in kind was replaced by notes in sterling... For this, he was considered by the rebels unfit to govern.

The Court took one hour for the consideration of a verdict and recommended sentence. The Court had assembled on the 7th of

May 1811 and finished its proceedings on the 5th of June 1811. The decision following consideration by the Prince Regent was announced on the 2nd of July 1811.

> "The Court having duly and maturely weighed and considered the whole of the evidence adduced on the Prosecution as well as what has been offered in defence, are of opinion that Lieut-Col Johnston is Guilty of the act of Mutiny as described in the Charge and do therefore sentence him to be cashiered".

His Royal Highness, the Prince Regent, in the name and on behalf of His Majesty, was pleased, under all the circumstances of this case to acquiesce in the sentence of the Court:

> "The Court in passing a sentence so inadequate to the enormity of the crime of which the prisoner has been found guilty, have apparently been actuated by a consideration of the novel and extraordinary circumstances, which, by the evidence on the face of the proceedings, may have appeared to them to have existed during the administration of Governor Bligh, both as affecting the tranquillity of the colony and calling for some immediate decision. But although the Prince Regent admits the principle under which the Court have allowed this consideration to act in mitigation of the punishment which the crime of mutiny would otherwise have suggested, yet no circumstances whatever can be received by His Royal Highness in full extenuation of an assumption of power, so subversive of every principle of good order and discipline as that under which Lieut-Col Johnston has been convicted".

"The Commander in Chief directs that the Charge preferred against Lieut-Col Johnston, together with the sentence of the Court, and His Royal Highness the Prince Regent's pleasure thereon, shall be read at the head of every regiment, and entered in the Regimental orderly book".

By command of His Royal Highness, the Commander in Chief.

Harry Calvert Adj-Gen

The President of the Court was Lieutenant General Keppel. The Court consisted of five other Lieutenant Generals, two Major Generals, five Colonels and two Lieutenant Colonels.

The sentence on Johnston did however have a dramatic effect on the fortunes of John McArthur. If he returned to Australia, he would have been brought before the Criminal Court now composed of officers of the 73rd Regiment and not the NSW Corps. It took McArthur more than five years to negotiate an indemnity with the British Government before he could return to Australia.

The Judge Advocate General wrote [357] to Lord Liverpool on the 4th of July that there was no necessity for any further proceedings to be taken against other officers involved in the rebellion, as no such officer was returning to Australia in an official capacity.

Professor Kennedy wrote [358] : "that the court martial of Johnston was turned into a trial of Bligh, which on the evidence vindicates him convincingly, is perhaps the most positive defence of Bligh's Governorship".

If Johnston had been found not guilty of mutiny, then Bligh would have found himself on trial. Arrangements for bringing Bligh to Court Martial were suspended on the 9th of July on the technicality that the composition of its military and naval membership could not be resolved.

In fact, Bligh received his promotion to flag rank, being gazetted as Rear Admiral of the Blue Squadron on the 31st of July 1811, being backdated to the 31st of July 1810.

---

[357] HR NSW vol 7 p553
[358] "Captain Bligh, the man and his mutinies" Gavin Kennedy Ch 38 1989.

CHAPTER 25

The causes of the Rum Rebellion
26.1.1808 – 31.12.1809

George Johnston claimed [359] that "an enraged and indignant population", urgently, almost clamorously called upon him for relief while Lieutenant Colonel Paterson claimed [360] that "universal terror had been created among all classes of people and that no alternative was left but to put the Governor under arrest as the only means of preventing insurrection with all its attendant horrors and saving him and the persons he confided in from falling victims to the fury of the incensed populace".

This wild rhetoric does not accord with facts about the feelings of the free settlers.

John McArthur's statement about the causes of the rebellion also misrepresents the viewpoint of the free settlers. McArthur said [361] that the sole cause of the rebellion lay in "the dread that was entertained of the six officers being sent to gaol, and of the resentment that would have been excited among the soldiers and the inhabitants, the dread that was entertained of an insurrection; such were my own motives".

The insurrection of the officers leading the soldiers was real enough, but the claim to a threat of an insurrection by the free settlers was unfounded. A memorial of free settlers to Lord Castlereagh is a good example [362] of their denial of support for the insurrection, "artifice and cunning was the cause of the change of

---

[359] HR NSW vol 7 p461
[360] HR NSW vol 7 p152
[361] "Proceedings... Trial of Lt Col Johnston" Bartrum (ed) p212/3 1811
[362] HRA Series 1 vol 7 p137 (4.11.1808)

Government and not the request of the inhabitants, as stated by Major Johnston".

Meetings of free settlers in April 1810 had been planned to vote addresses of condolence and congratulations to Bligh and "to refute in the most public manner the false and infamous charges exhibited against the inhabitants of the Colony by Lieutenant Colonel George Johnston". Officers of what had been the NSW Corps and their supporters interfered with the meeting in Sydney as previously described.

It is interesting to consider the view of the British Judge Advocate General, prosecutor at the trial of Lt Col Johnston, when he considered the free settlers address of gratitude to Bligh, an address signed by 460 inhabitants. He said [363] : "two years after it (the Governor's arrest) upon cool reflection and when they could have no personal views towards Governor Bligh, in as much as he was then superseded and was returning to England and therefore no advantage was to be derived from complimenting him, that they ... still continued of opinion that ... so far from their being an imminent necessity for it (the Governor's arrest), the administration of justice and the whole conduct of the Governor was such as to call for the gratitude and thanks of the people of the colony".

The claim that McArthur's requisition for the arrest of Governor Bligh constituted a "Declaration of Independence" has been rightly characterised by Dr Mackaness [364] as "a fraud". The claim that an "immense number" of people were there at the time to endorse the signing has been shown to be fraudulent. Out of about fifteen people present, only four were ordinary citizens. Of those four ordinary citizens, two were ex-officers. The author of the requisition for the arrest of the Governor, the so-called "Declaration of Independence" was, of course, McArthur. A memorial [365] of the free settlers to Johnston had said, after all, that McArthur was "the scourge of this colony" and that "his monopoly and extortion had been highly injurious to the inhabitants generally".

---

[363] "Proceedings ... Trial of Lt Col Johnston" Bartrum (ed) p42 1811
[364] "A Life of Vice Admiral Bligh" G Mackaness ch XLI 1951
[365] HR NSW vol 6 p597

The free settlers had complained [366], it must be remembered, to Paterson that "the whole government appears to be put in the hands of John McArthur Esq who seems a very improper person... and we believe him to be the principal agitator and promoter of the present alarming and calamitous state of the colony".

Various memorials [367] of the free settlers sent to Lord Castlereagh mentioned the fear and hatred in which McArthur was held. The free settlers had, after all, dissociated themselves from McArthur from the time of the second address [368] to Bligh and had no wish for McArthur to represent their interests.

The same memorials of the free settlers sent to Lord Castlereagh referred to Governor Bligh's popularity among the farming classes. Robert Campbell, shipowner and trader, swore on oath that Governor Bligh was always impartial in his administration of justice and that the colonists in general and the settlers in particular approved of his Government. This was corroborated [369] by Captain Charles Walker who said "... I have always heard the settlers say that Governor Bligh was the only Governor that ever studied the interests of the colony...". During Foveaux's administration, the Reverend Rowland Hassell wrote [370] : "I am told that if the inhabitants was asked the question at this day how they approved of the measures that have taken place, there would not be one in twenty that would approve of them".

One group of free settlers [371] is quite specific about their understanding of the cause of the rebellion: Bligh's interference with the liquor monopolists and their trading ventures was the chief cause of his deposition.

The free settlers also had some harsh words to say about the liquor monopolists and the officers of the NSW Corps, they wrote [372] to Bligh: "the settlers .... are to a man decidedly in your favour and highly approve of your administration and most earnestly wish for

---

[366] HR NSW vol 7 p596
[367] HRA Series 1 vol 7 p137
[368] HR NSW vol 6 p188
[369] "Proceedings ... the Trial of Lt Col Johnston" Bartrum (ed) p136 1811
[370] HR NSW vol 6 p708 (August 1808)
[371] HRA Series 1 vol 7 p140 (Baulkham Hills Settlers)
[372] "Who caused the Mutiny on the Bounty" M Darby Ch 15 1965

an opportunity to express their loyalty and gratitude. It has been proposed by the settlers to send home two persons as their agents to state to HM Ministers the situation the colony was in at your arrival, the advantage it has experienced under your Government and the flattering prospect that every prudent and industrious man had of becoming independent of a set of locusts".

As many of the insurrectionists said that Bligh himself was the primary cause of the rebellion, it is necessary to look at the serious charges to see how valid or invalid they are.

Bligh was widely charged by those taking part in the rebellion with tyranny or despotism. T G Harris, the independent lawyer who was retained by the British Government to examine the papers of Bligh, Johnston and Foveaux, advised: [373] "No instance of arbitrary power (by Bligh) exercised towards any person whatsoever is produced". This statement clearly rules out tyranny or despotism, if the Governor was functioning within his statutory powers.

It clearly rules out arbitrary power to take away personal property, liberty and life, – charges which were made against Bligh. The insurrectionists also accused Bligh of "oppression"; T G Harris, the independent lawyer, writes [373] : "Nor has the confidence reposed in him in his official character in any instance been minimally betrayed".Confidence in the good administration of Governor Bligh was therefore recorded by an independent review and this clearly ruled out oppression.

T G Harris made it quite clear [374] that "under Bligh's rule the state of the Colony was satisfactory, and his administration just and vigorous".

One of the most serious charges against Bligh was made by the insurrectionists and later by Lt Col Paterson to the effect that Bligh planned to subvert the laws of the land. T G Harris continues: "there was no evidence of Bligh's determination to subvert the established laws of the colony".

Bligh was also accused of interference in the legal process. On this matter, it has been shown that Bligh claimed a privilege in the

---

[373] HR NSW vol 7 p212.
[374] HR NSW vol 7 p209

method of choosing members of the Court of Criminal Jurisdiction, but only the composition of the Court was determined by the Letters Patent of that Court, so Bligh was not exercising arbitrary or illegal powers.

In fact, Dr Harris, who supported Johnston, admitted [375] that Bligh's claim [376] that he did not interfere in the Courts of Justice was correct. While Atkins, the Judge Advocate during Bligh's Governorship, who supported Johnston at his trial, swore [377] that Bligh had never tried to influence him in legal cases.

It has already been noted that Lieutenant Minchin misrepresented his case against Bligh on "the Irish State prisoners".Minchin also misrepresented his case against Bligh over some escaped convicts. He claimed that Bligh had acted illegally and brought these men before a bench of magistrates on the same charge after they had been acquitted by the Criminal Court of which Minchin was a member. Evidence shows [378] that the convicts were charged before the Criminal Court for stealing a boat for which they were acquitted. They were however brought before a Bench of Magistrates on a different charge. Seven convicts were charged [379] with absconding and one freedman for being an accessory to this crime. This charge against Bligh for acting illegally therefore falls.

Bligh was also accused [380] of acting illegally by suspending Wentworth on the same charge for which he had already been reprimanded, but the records show that the suspension was for a different misdemeanour. Lord Castlereagh said that Bligh's action in suspending Wentworth was not approved though not illegal, but it seems that Lord Castlereagh at that time was in possession only of a number of memorials inimical to Bligh. Governor Bligh was also accused of legal threats to members of the Court of Criminal Jurisdiction, including threats of High Treason. It is important on this matter to realise that when the Judge Advocate

---

[375] "Proceedings... Trial of Lt Col Johnston" Bartrum (ed) p332 1811
[376] HRA Series 1 vol 6 p522
[377] "Proceedings... Trial of Lt Col Johnston" Bartrum (ed) p160 1811
[378] Ibid p239
[379] Ibid p332
[380] HR NSW vol 6 p522

adjourned the Criminal Court at the trial of John McArthur, it was necessary for the Judge Advocate to preside over the Court when it resumed, for there to be a properly constituted Court. The resumption of proceedings under Captain Fenn Kemp meant that those proceedings were not properly constituted and the Judge Advocate's claim of "No Court" in terms of those proceedings was correct. Bligh was therefore quite correct in threatening officers with a Court Martial when they presumed to hold illegal proceedings and their claim to be holding a Criminal Court was unfounded.

Bligh was acting within the law and Johnston's claim [381] that he was "threatening the magistrates with vengeance if they presumed to acknowledge any law, but his will" is ridiculous. All such charges then against Bligh relating to the law are not substantiated.

Johnston made general accusations of "gross fraud and shameful robberies" against Bligh claiming that he would bring "incontestable evidence" of these to light. He failed to do so and the independent legal inquiry undertaken for the British Government also failed to identify any specific charges of this nature and found "no Government lease appears to have been cancelled by Governor Bligh".

James, son of John McArthur, later accused [382] Bligh of corruption and rapacity, while others accused him of "peculations". Although there is no evidence that Bligh himself was personally involved in any corruption, rapacity or peculation, there is questionable evidence that Andrew Thompson, his farm bailiff, was so involved, possibly to ingratiate himself with the rebel leaders and provide means for the rebels to denigrate his previous employer, who had dismissed him and had not reinstated him.

Correspondence purporting to be from Thompson to Bligh in 1807 points to some sharp practices by Thompson without Bligh's promotings. Later in 1807, it appears that Thompson was dismissed following his conviction for distilling alcohol illegally. After Bligh's deposition, Thompson "confessed" to a number of corrupt practices: He used public supplies to support twenty to thirty farm employees on Bligh's model farm. He increased Bligh's

---

[381] HR NSW vol 7 p461

[382] "Some early records of the Macarthurs...." S M Onslow (ed) p221/2

stock by transferring newly born animals from the Government herds while John Jamison, the Superintendent of stock, exchanged good animals in the Government herds for poor animals in Bligh's stock. Thompson admitted that he was under orders from Bligh to pay for all stock and articles drawn from the Government stores and "everything to be fair and honourable". He also confirmed that Bligh's "grand design" of the model farm was to demonstrate methods of improvement.

There is no evidence to support the charge by Lieutenant Colonel Paterson that Bligh sacrificed the interests of Government to improve his own fortune by a wasteful expenditure of the public stores. Bligh did use the public stores to help relieve distress after the Hawkesbury floods, but otherwise he used the public stores only as a means of maintaining as free a market as possible for the free settlers and as security against monopoly tendencies. Bligh was accused by Foveaux of encouraging a state monopoly, but the free settlers seemed to have been satisfied that Bligh intervened only to remove aberrations in the market or to provide emergency relief.

Bligh has also been accused of interference in military and medical matters. We have already seen that Bligh did intervene minimally in military matters when he hand picked and increased his own bodyguard and when he claimed a privilege in nominating members of the Criminal Court of Justice to ensure a fairer trial for the Provost Marshal. In each of these cases, Bligh knew that Major Johnston was not prepared to give up his discretion voluntarily. It was easier for both parties if Bligh claimed privilege as Captain General of the NSW Corps; but Johnston still resented this.

Bligh sacked Dr Harris as Government Naval Officer and appointed Robert Campbell in his stead. Harris seems to have been deeply hurt by what happened to him and he was prominent in opposition to Bligh. Some other surgeons were subordinate to the more senior NSW Corps officers.

It was to be expected that Bligh would be criticised for his use of language. As Governor, he would have spoken his mind and would have been articulate in so doing. In the circumstances, it is likely that his enemies would have invented abuse and attributed it to him. John Blaxland said [383] Bligh "openly damned the law and

---

[383] HR NSW vol 7 p235

said there should be no law but his will ...." This is certainly blunt speaking but it is out of character with what Bligh was trying to do, namely to govern within the law. It is interesting to see what T G Harris, the independent lawyer, said [384] about this: that, though Governor Bligh had sometimes used improper and unguarded expressions respecting his authority in the courts of law, he had never improperly exercised any such authority; and that though Governor Bligh used great intemperance of language, "no act is alleged to have been committed in pursuance of the threats".

Johnston's charges against Bligh of him being a "monster of depravity" are hollow. The accusation of Bligh being involved with concubines is ridiculous and entirely without a shred of evidence.

The insurrectionists made much of the use of George Crossley, the disbarred lawyer, by Bligh and by the Judge Advocate, Richard Atkins. Bligh had used Crossley informally and so had Atkins, but Bligh refused to allow the formal use of Crossley by William Gore, the Provost Marshal. Crossley was the only reliable source of legal opinion available to the Governor and it is understandable that Bligh used him. Bligh knew all about the shortcomings of Richard Atkins, but until the British Government sent a replacement, he had to persevere with this Judge Advocate and he could not legally replace him under the terms of the Letters Patent for that post, which was a Crown appointment.

James, the son of John McArthur, admitted [385] that "nothing but extreme necessity could excuse it (the deposition of the Governor)",but he added "There is no doubt in my mind that the necessity had arisen". He justified this conclusion by citing George Crossley being called in as a legal adviser of the Government. It is useful to compare James Macarthur's comments with those of the independent lawyer, T G Harris. Harris wrote: Though Crossley was consulted by Bligh, he (Harris) did not discover that any corrupt practices were ever advised or resorted to.

It has previously been shown that the charge of cowardice against Bligh has been refuted by five independent unbiased sources.

Johnston's defence at the Court Martial rested primarily on his lack of motive. He said he was not interested personally in spirit

---

[384] HR NSW vol 7 p209 following
[385] "Some early records of the Macarthurs..." S M Onslow (ed) p221

trafficking and that he was not involved in private notes of financial settlement. However, Johnston had a convict woman as the mother of his children and he must have wanted to remain in New South Wales with his family and to develop the land which Governor King gave him following the putting down of the Irish rebellion of 1804.

Johnston must have predicted correctly as it turned out or obtained private information (Bligh's secretary was a tenant of one of the New South Wales Corps officers) that Bligh was advising the Secretary of State to recall the New South Wales Corps and replace these troops. Bligh's criticism of the agricultural and business interests of the New South Wales Corps must have convinced Johnston that he must remove Bligh to protect the largely military cartel and his own position in it, a cartel which was impoverishing the settlers. John McArthur, a leading member of the cartel, also wished to remove Bligh, so that he could extend his landholding for the development of sheep farming on his own account. Each in fact had a strong personal motive for the deposition of the Governor. John McArthur claimed to have removed both Governor Hunter and Governor King already.

In an extraordinary and effective use of irony which shows the versatility of his humour, Bligh listed [386] "the offences which rendered him unfit to govern": "The barter of spirits, a source of emolument to other Governors I prohibited; the confined distribution, an advantage to myself in common with all the officers, I extended. The former practice of irregular committal to prison I abolished. The limits of arbitrary punishment I contracted. I consulted the general good of the Colony, instead of allowing myself to be guided by the selfish policy of a few individuals; and I determined that all ranks alike should be respectful and obedient to the law. These were the offences which rendered me unfit to govern. In other words, it was no longer convenient to them, or suited to their purposes, that I should; and accordingly a scheme was devised to remove me which, after all that has been heard, the Court will perhaps think took longer to digest than the short time Colonel Johnston retired into the next room with Mr McArthur".

---

[386] "Proceedings... Trial of Lt Col Johnston" Bartrum (ed) p406 1811

CHAPTER 26

Further promotion, retirement, and death
31.7.1811 – 7.12.1817.

On the 5th of March 1812, Matthew Flinders wrote [387] to Mr Wiles, a botanist in "Providence" on the 2nd Breadfruit Voyage: "Our old friend Bligh introduced me with my charts the other day to the Duke of Clarence. He is remarkably obliging and attentive to me; yet I have been very far from courting his friendship; but I believe he is proud to have had me for his disciple in surveying and nautical astronomy". It is clear that Bligh was holding no grudges against a man who had been used to report secretly on him. During his captivity in France, Flinders had written to Sir Joseph Banks with friendly messages for Bligh and it seems that Bligh had been prepared for a reconciliation.

Tragedy was to strike Bligh next month. On the 15th of April, Betsy died. They had only been together for eighteen months since Bligh returned from Australia, but that time had been very precious as they had been parted so often and for so long previously. Betsy had been a wonderful wife for William and a good mother to their six daughters, especially to Ann who was epileptic with a severe mental handicap. Both William and Betsy had been shattered by the loss of their twin sons, William and Henry, when only a day old. The whole responsibility for looking after the family now fell on William.

In June of that year, Bligh gave evidence to a Select Committee of the House of Commons on the problems arising from the transportation of convicts. Bligh's evidence arising from his General Muster or Census was of particular use to the Committee.

---

[387] Flinders Papers, Public Library of Victoria quoted by Mackaness 1951

Further promotion, retirement, and death

In 1812, Bligh was promoted Rear Admiral of the White Squadron.

The news in October 1812 that Lieutenant Colonel Johnston was returning as a private citizen to New South Wales must have been received by Bligh with a thought that another mutineer had escaped the ultimate penalty.

Next year, on the 19th of April 1813, Bligh wrote a memorial to the Admiralty asking for pensionable retirement. He still wished to make his services available and next month he was being consulted on fees in Vice Admiralty Courts.

In 1813, he is said [388] to have been promoted Rear Admiral of the Red Squadron.

In August of that year, Bligh responded to a series of technical questions which Lord Stanhope put to him on a new design of 74-gun ships of the line. Next month, he wrote to Sir Joseph Banks stating his general approval of the initiative.

Sometime late in 1813, Bligh moved from 3 Durham Place, Lambeth, taking a lease on the Manor House at Farningham in Kent. Sir Joseph Banks put him in touch with his cousin near Maidstone. Bligh was able to maintain a social life in addition to his family commitments. At a soirée at the home of Sir Joseph Banks, Bligh asked Flinders [389] if he would dedicate his publication "Voyage to Terra Australis" to him, but his request was not accommodated.

Bligh was further promoted when he was gazetted on the 4th of June 1814 as Vice Admiral of the Blue Squadron.

After a few years of contentment within his family, Bligh must have been shocked to hear in February 1817 that the threat by the British Government to put John McArthur on trial if he returned to New South Wales was lifted. The decision could not have been really welcome to Governor Macquarie and the words [390] of Governor Darling in 1826 are not unsurprising: "He (McArthur) is equally ardent in his exertions to serve as he is to injure... It will be seen from this that the want of harmony in this society is to be ascribed solely to one individual (McArthur)".

---

[388] ML
[389] "Life of Captain Matthew Flinders RN" E Scott p392 following, Sydney 1914
[390] HRA Series 1 Vol 12 p254 following

In December 1817, Bligh's daughter Elizabeth married her cousin Richard Bligh, a lawyer.

In the same month on the 7th of December, William Bligh died in London.

It is interesting that Bligh had a signet ring and seal described [391] by the Library Council of New South Wales for an exhibition on Bligh in 1977 as having the "design of a griffin and quartermoon on crest surrounded by a mailed arm holding an axe. Motto on ring below crest is 'Linem(sic) Respice'". On the crest of another branch of the Bligh family there is above the Griffin a Knight's helmet surrounded by a mailed arm holding an axe ready to strike. The motto is "In caelo quies". (Rest in Heaven). William Bligh, a restless man, was clearly not happy with his branch motto and assumed, because there is no restriction on the assumption of English family mottos by the College of Arms, that of his kinsman, John Bligh, Earl of Darnley, "Finem Respice" (Look back at the end). At the time of assuming the Governorship of New South Wales, Bligh looked forward to being able to look back at an end of some consequence.

In fact, John Bligh, Earl of Darnley, renounced his executorship of Bligh's will. He may have been annoyed that Bligh had assumed his motto or that he believed the falsehoods propagated about William Bligh.

When we look back at the end, we see that Bligh acted honourably and that though a reputation of infamy has been infamously fabricated, he deserved, as his God will ensure, "rest in heaven". There will however be more than rest in such a place:

"Wherein the just shall dwell
And after their tribulations long
See golden days, fruitful of golden deeds,
With Joy and Love triumphing, and fair Truth".
    John Milton.

He was buried at St Mary-at-Lambeth [392] with Betsy, their two baby twin boys, and one grandson.

---

[391] DR 188

[392] Now "the Museum of Garden History".

On his tomb, the epitaph reads:

Sacred to the Memory of William Bligh
Esquire FRS Vice Admiral
of the Blue, the celebrated navigator
who first transplanted the Breadfruit tree
from Otaheite to the West Indies
bravely fought the battles of his country
and died beloved, respected and lamented
on the 7th day of December 1817
        aged 64

(Postscript: Anyone who fails to recognise the heroism of Wm Bligh is out of date and out of touch. A bit of respect is required.)

CHAPTER 27

Conclusion

Bligh was above average height at 5ft 8ins tall. He had an exceptionally fair skin, described as "of an ivory or marble whiteness". He had dark eyes and, as a young man, he had black hair according to a painting attributed to John Webber showing Bligh as a Midshipman in about 1776.

According to a painting by John Russell in 1791, William Bligh then 37 years old was prematurely grey-haired. That was only two years after the mutiny in "Bounty".

Bligh was a dutiful family man and said he assumed the role of father to Peter Heywood, a young Midshipman. His morals were above reproach and even among "the allurements of dissipation" on Otaheite, he was steadfast in his diplomacy without compromising the purposes of the Voyage.

With "integrity unimpeached", Bligh worked productively with Sir Joseph Banks, President of the Royal Society.

Bligh has been shown not to have been sadistic, tyrannical, reactionary, ruthless or cruel. He was essentially a civilised and versatile man. His skills were exemplary in navigation, cartography (map making), coastal surveying and hydrography. He was a scientist in his time with interests in anthropology, nautical astronomy, botany, ethnology and zoology. He was a competent and occasionally a brilliant writer, particularly of the writing of letters, although his spelling left much to be desired. He had some talent as an artist. His drawings and water colours of birds and animals are sensitive, although problems of perspective sometimes got the better of him.

His emotions were possibly those of a Celt, derived from his Cornish origins. He showed a full spectrum of emotions from placidity to temporary tornadoes of temper.

He was a proud man, but saved from arrogance by his religious faith. The biographer Richard Hough suggested that Bligh showed a lack of confidence when things were going well, but I see no evidence for this. His confidence in adversity was particularly marked.

His generosity was particularly well illustrated when he gave up his cabin to sailors whose bedding had been soaked by storms at Cape Horn.

Bligh was jealous of his own reputation and was sometimes unjustly abusive of others in defending it. There is some truth in Flinders criticism that he monopolised credit.

There can be no doubt that Bligh should be criticised for his abusive language. Harsh language was sometimes required in disciplining, but some excessively abusive language, although not meant, did demean others. It was particularly unfortunate that he sometimes used sectarian abuse, such as the use of "Jesuit" as an object of reproach. The painting of Bligh when he was a Midshipman shows him wearing a Masonic badge. There is however no clear case of him having given or received favours due to the membership of that organisation.

This book makes the case that Fletcher Christian was suffering from "pathological grieving" for Mauatua at the time of the mutiny. It was this rather than any misdemeanour on the part of Bligh which was the primary cause of the mutiny. Fletcher Christian was desperate to get back to Mauatua. His first attempt at returning to her consisted of putting together a semblance of a raft, but this was so insubstantial that the attempt was potentially suicidal in shark infested waters. It was only when the folly of this plan was emphasised to him that he decided to take the ship by armed force.

The contrast between 18th century and recent 20th century navigational technology is stark. There is now use of electronic position finding equipment, satellite communication systems, deck and below deck computers, infrared and colour picture representation of the weather as well as autopilot. Bligh's use of the navigational equipment available to him was however masterly. There is no doubt that he ensured in the epic open boat voyage the survival of eighteen people who in other circumstances had a very poor prospect of survival. It is apposite to compare the fate of the

Luxborough Galley in 1727 lost in the Atlantic as a result of a fire. Twenty three of the crew took to a launch, but sixteen of them died from cannibalism and only seven were finally rescued.

Bligh's leadership and seamanship were the vital factors which turned a potential disaster into an epic.

The success of the 2nd Breadfruit Voyage was ensured by quiet diplomacy in Otaheite, fine seamanship in the Torres Straits and careful management of both crew and the breadfruit plants. Following the Mutiny at the Nore, Bligh gave an amnesty to all but 10 members of the crew of HMS Director, but he had to negotiate with persistence to save the lives of a further 19 members of the crew to whom he had offered an amnesty, but whose lives were in jeopardy on the insistence of a higher command.

At the Victory of Camperdown, it must be remembered that HMS Director under Bligh's Captaincy first secured the surrender of a Dutch ship before it proceeded to other tasks including the final assault on the Dutch flagship.

At the Battle of Copenhagen, HMS Glatton under Bligh's Captaincy was in the small squadron under Nelson which secured victory. Nelson's special summons of Bligh immediately after the battle to receive his thanks is a measure of Bligh's stature and recognition of his courage in that terrible battle.

There is no doubt that those people of whom Bligh disapproved such as Governor Macquarie, who used rebels in official positions, found him a "very disagreeable person". In Australia, Bligh had to make an early decision as to whether to take on the rum monopolists or not, knowing full well that he risked his reputation and possible failure if he did the right thing; nevertheless he knew that, even if he personally failed, he could bring about a more just and better society in Australia by bringing the dangerous "militia" to justice and by reforming the administration of law there.

By taking the decision to take on the monopolists, he has been called "imprudent". The prudent course, if such it could be called, would have involved protracted negotiations with London to recall the NSW Corps, also new Letters Patent to replace the Judge Advocate and to reconstitute the Criminal Court. It must be remembered that communication between New South Wales and London took from about five to eight months with a similar period

Conclusion

for a reply. Bligh's family situation did not brook such delays nor did he fancy watching injustices being perpetrated by the monopolists before his eyes without his intervention.

The criticism that he suffered from "the defect of his merits" is probably a fair one. Misrepresentation of the causes of the Mutiny in "Bounty" has coloured views about Bligh's administration in New South Wales. Judge Therry [393] wrote that Bligh "had proved his incapacity to govern a ship's crew, whom he had driven to mutiny..." He did however recognise Bligh was trying to govern well.

How well then did Bligh measure up to the "Bill of Rights" written by free settlers?

The Right of Freedom of trade he promoted by restricting the monopoly of the rum traders, through prohibition of the barter of rum and other spirits. He promoted a fair open market to prevent other monopolies and extortion.

The Right of public and private property he promoted by enforcing public rights in "the domain" within Sydney as established by Governor Phillip and by publicising those lease conditions laid down by other Governors. He did not cancel any Government leases, but offered to swop leases.

The Right of individual liberty he promoted by protecting that with the force of law. Treasonable activity was however subject to the law.

The Right that the Law should take its due course he promoted by holding fast to duly constituted legal procedures as set out in the Letters Patent constituting the Court of Criminal Jurisdiction.

The Right of payment in money value he promoted by establishing value in sterling currency and prohibited promissory notes in kind.

There is no doubt therefore that Governor Bligh made considerable progress in making a reality of those Rights as set out in the "Bill of Rights" of the free settlers.

By his personal sacrifice, he ensured that the lawless British Forces comprising the NSW Corps were withdrawn and that a new Judge Advocate was sent out with Governor Macquarie.

---

[393] "Reminiscences of Thirty Years Residence in NSW" Sir R Therry 1863

Dr Mackaness writes [394] of Governor Bligh's place in Australian History: "When coming years sum up the comparative merits of early Governors, Bligh's name will be bracketed with those of Phillip, Macquarie and Bourke, all men who never turned their backs, but marched straight forward".

It is tragic that folk myths, travesties of the truth, have grown up, promoted by men with perverse interests in degrading the reputation of this man. The list of men with such perverse interests is a long one: Fletcher Christian, Professor Edward Christian, Peter Heywood, James Morrison, John Fryer, Lt John Frazier, Lt Col Johnston, Lt Col Foveaux, Lt Col Paterson and John McArthur among many others, especially novelists and film script writers.

Sir Joseph Banks, the President to the Royal Society, in writing to Mrs Bligh, while Bligh was in Australia, lauded her husband as "honourable, just and equitable", an estimation not easily obtained.

The author, Owen Rutter[395] said Bligh's "courage in battling against adversity was close to the sublime".

The biographer M Darby reminded [396] her readers of the words of a Nazi "the immensity of a lie contributes to its success.... the plainer proof of its falsehood may be forthcoming, but something of the lie will nevertheless stick".

The proof of the falsehood about Bligh in terms of cruelty was already made known by Dr Mackaness and Professor Kennedy, but this book aims to remove "something of the lie" which still sticks.

There is one conclusion which Bligh himself would have rejected out of hand and that is the verdict that he was a victim, deserving of pity.

He faced up to life and coped with adversity. He tried to do his duty even if this meant taking risks which involved personal sacrifice.

William Bligh is undoubtedly a British Naval Epic Hero and may yet be seen as an Australian National Tragic Hero.

---

[394] "The Life of Vice Admiral Bligh" G Mackaness Ch XLVIII 1951
[395] "The Turbulant Journey", O Rutter, p269.
[396] "Who caused the Mutiny on the Bounty" M Darby Ch 15 1965

TOPGRAPHICAL FEATURES NAMED AFTER BLIGH

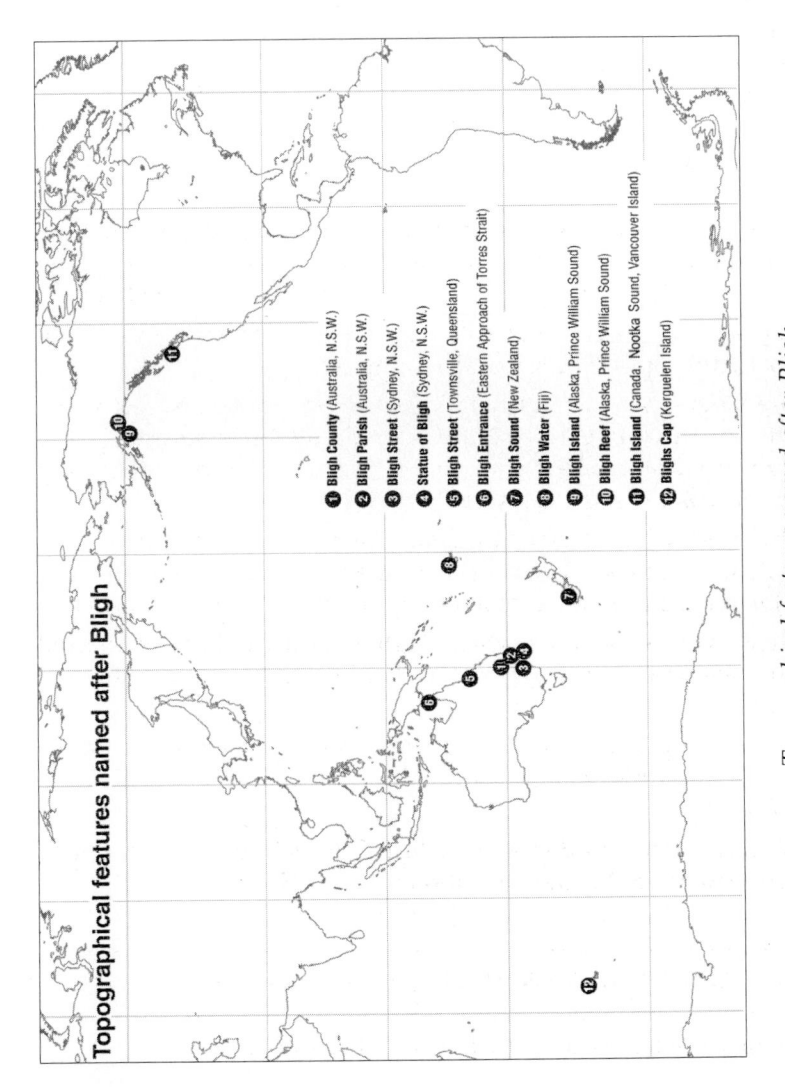

1. Bligh County (Australia, N.S.W.)
2. Bligh Parish (Australia, N.S.W.)
3. Bligh Street (Sydney, N.S.W.)
4. Statue of Bligh (Sydney, N.S.W.)
5. Bligh Street (Townsville, Queensland)
6. Bligh Entrance (Eastern Approach of Torres Strait)
7. Bligh Sound (New Zealand)
8. Bligh Water (Fiji)
9. Bligh Island (Alaska, Prince William Sound)
10. Bligh Reef (Alaska, Prince William Sound)
11. Bligh Island (Canada, Nootka Sound, Vancouver Island)
12. Blighs Cap (Kerguelen Island)

Topographical features named after Bligh
© Bartholemew Ltd. 2000. Reproduced by permission of Harper Collins Publishers

COUNTY OF BLIGH
EASTERN & CENTRAL DIVISIONS
N.S.W

Bligh County, including Bligh Parish, New South Wales, Australia

Bligh Street, Sydney, Australia

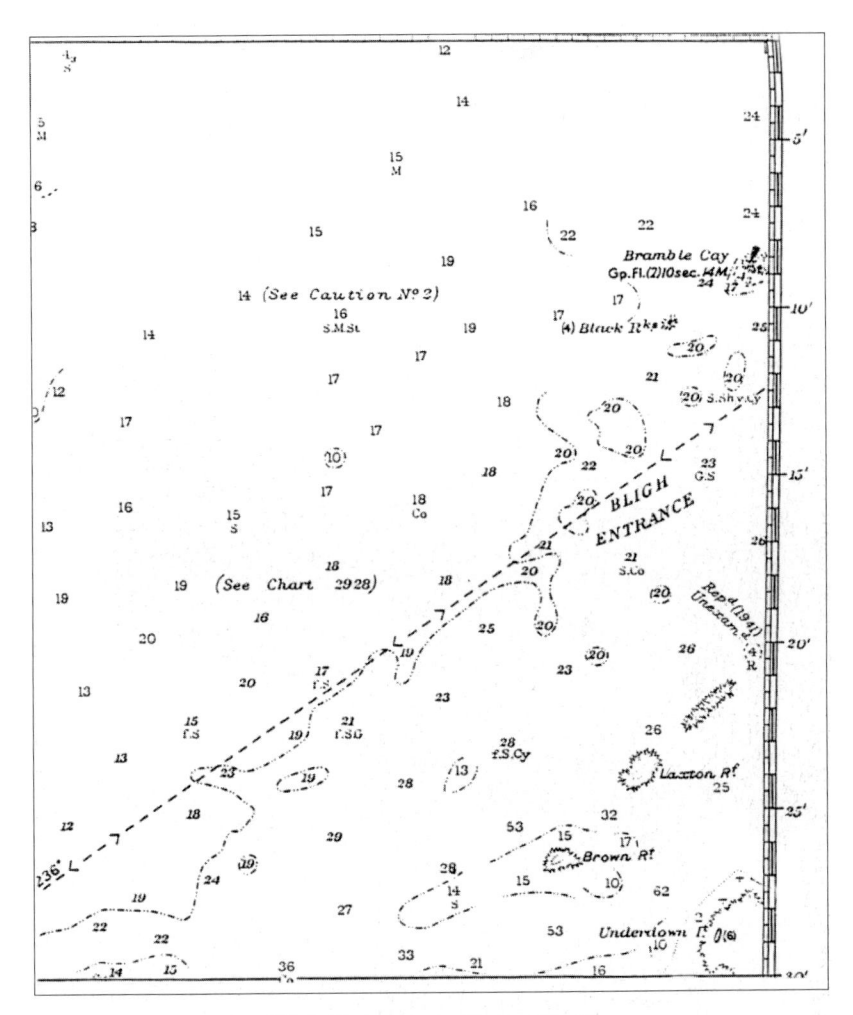

Bligh Entrance to Torres Strait
© Crown Copyright.
Reproduced with permission of the Hydrographer of the Royal Navy

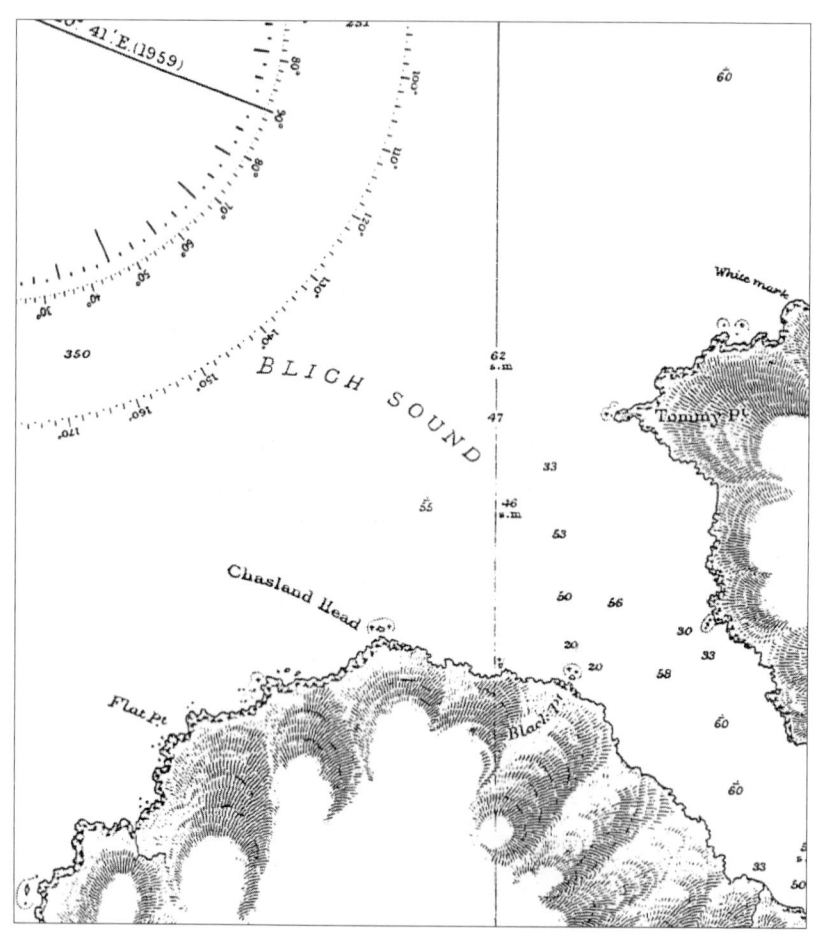

Bligh Sound, South Island, New Zealand
By kind permission of the Hydrographer of the Royal New Zealand Navy

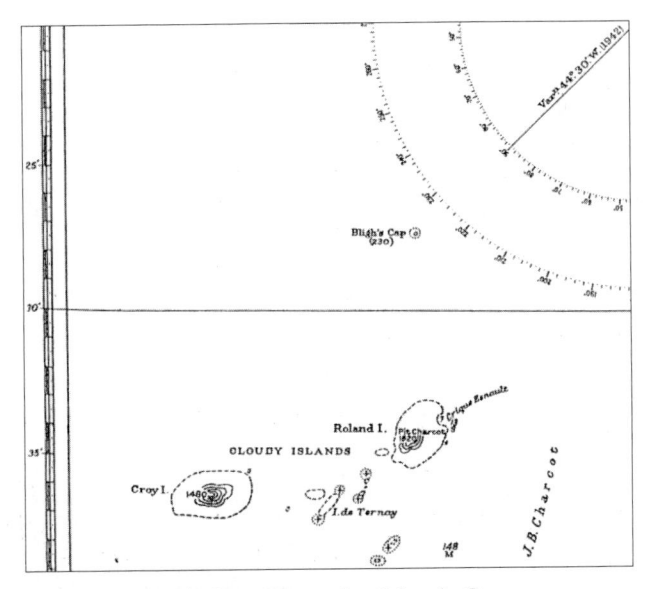

Topographical Features named after Bligh

Bligh's Cap, Kergeulen Islands Group
© Crown Copyright. Reproduced with permission of
the Hydrographer of the Royal Navy

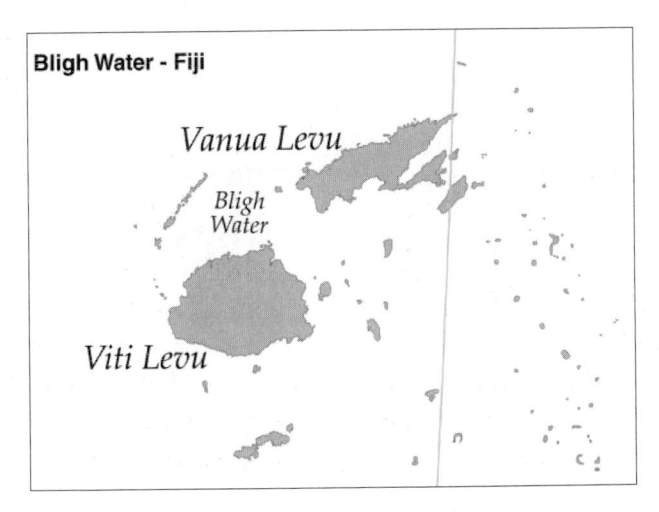

Bligh Water, Fiji Islands
© Bartholemew Ltd. 2000.
Reproduced by permission of Harper Collins Publishers

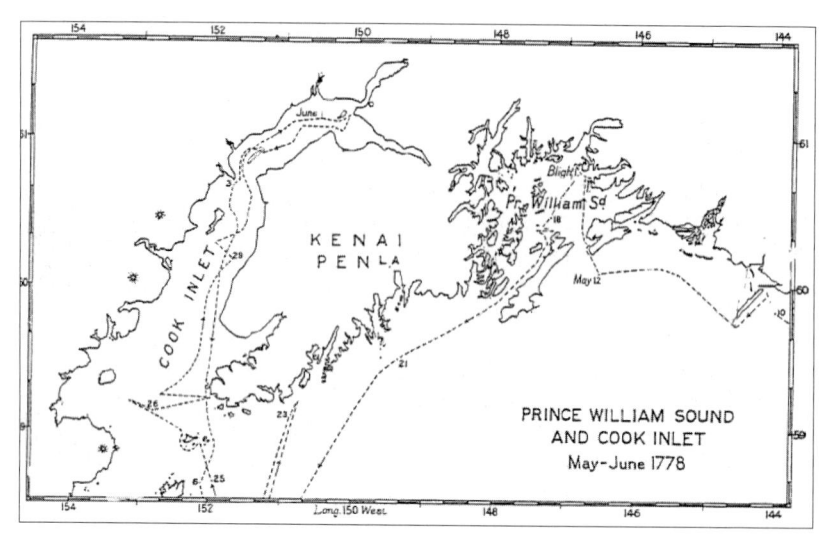

Bligh by Bligh

Bligh Island, Alaska, within Prince William Sound.
In "The Journals of Captain Cook" Vol iii Edited by J.C. Beaglehole
By kind permission of the Hakluyt Society and Cambridge University Press

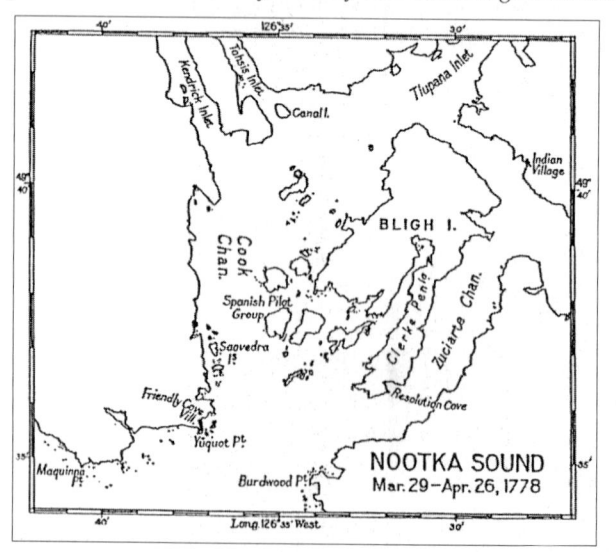

Bligh Island, Nootka Sound, Vancouver Island, Canada.
In "The Journals of Captain Cook" Vol iii Edited by J.C. Beaglehole
By kind permission of the Hakluyt Society and Cambridge University Press

Topographical Features named after Bligh

Bligh Road, Gravesend, Kent

*Bligh Way
and Bounty Inn*

269

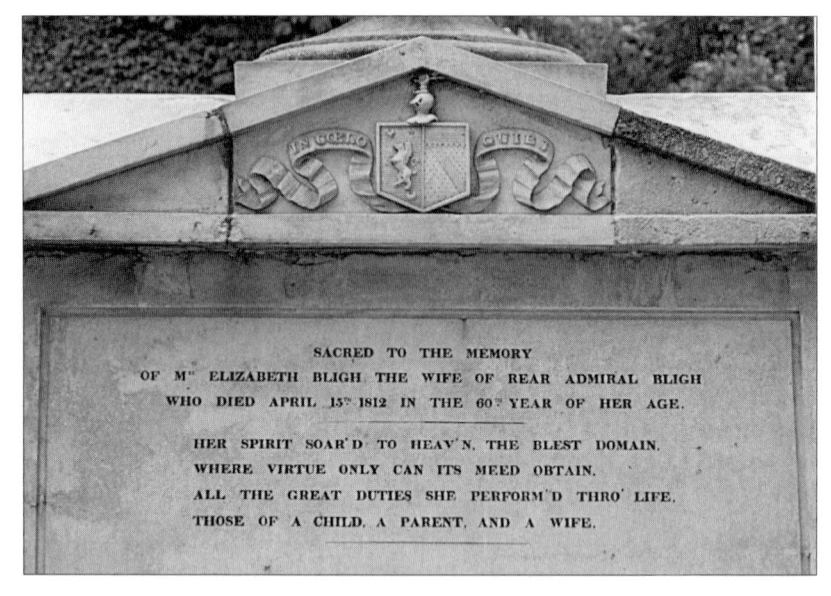

SACRED TO THE MEMORY
OF Mrs ELIZABETH BLIGH THE WIFE OF REAR ADMIRAL BLIGH
WHO DIED APRIL 13TH 1812 IN THE 60th YEAR OF HER AGE.

HER SPIRIT SOAR'D TO HEAV'N, THE BLEST DOMAIN,
WHERE VIRTUE ONLY CAN ITS MEED OBTAIN,
ALL THE GREAT DUTIES SHE PERFORM'D THRO' LIFE,
THOSE OF A CHILD, A PARENT, AND A WIFE.

Betsy's Inscription

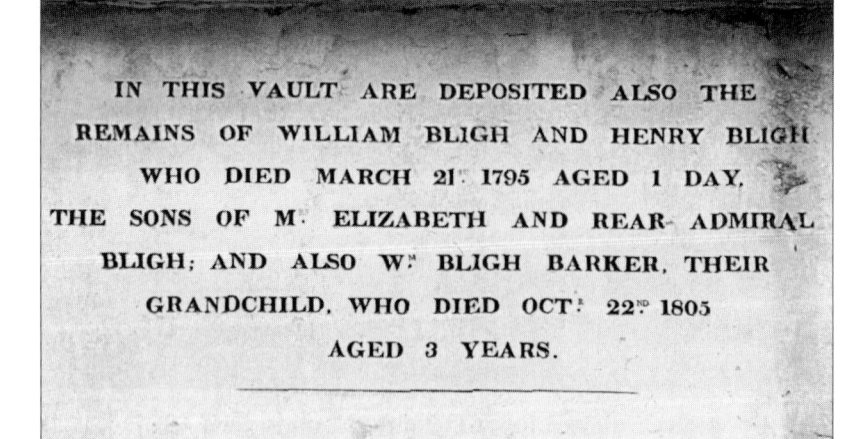

IN THIS VAULT ARE DEPOSITED ALSO THE REMAINS OF WILLIAM BLIGH AND HENRY BLIGH WHO DIED MARCH 21st 1795 AGED 1 DAY, THE SONS OF M. ELIZABETH AND REAR-ADMIRAL BLIGH; AND ALSO Wm BLIGH BARKER, THEIR GRANDCHILD, WHO DIED OCT: 22ND 1805 AGED 3 YEARS.

Boy Twins and Gandchild – Inscription

20th century copy of H.M. armed vessel "Bounty"

Bligh and Tahitian Regent, Tina
Mezzatint engraved by Thomas Gosse 1796
by kind permission of the Dixson Library, State Library of New South Wales

"Bounty's' launch away" Aquatint after the painting by Robert Dodd, Published 1790

by kind permission of Sotheby's, London

The Battle of Camperdown 1797
*The "Director" 64 gun ship of the line under the command of Captain Bligh engaging the "Vrijheid"
flagship of Admiral de Winter off Camperdown, the Netherlands
by kind permission of Jennifer Bligh Innes*

The Battle of Camperdown 1797
The "Director" rakes the "Vrijheid"
by kind permission of Jennifer Bligh Innes

The Battle of Camperdown 1797
*The "Director" at the conclusion of the engagement, behind the "Vrijheid"
by kind permission of Jennifer Bligh Innes*

Portrait of Admiral Bligh FRS wearing a gold medal won at the Battle of Camperdown 1797
by kind permission of the Mitchell Library, State Library of New South Wales

*Statue of
Governor General
Wm Bligh RN FRS
in Sydney,
New South Wales*

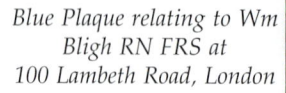

*Blue Plaque relating to Wm
Bligh RN FRS at
100 Lambeth Road, London*

APPENDIX 1

Further information on the Family Names

The forms of the family names must be distinguished from "Blyde" and "Blie", which are likely to be derived from the old English "Blide" meaning "gentle or merry".

An alternative but less convincing explanation [397], as it does not account for the synonymity of Blight with Bleit, is that the family names derive from the Irish O'Blighe meaning "descendants of Blighe", where the derivation is from the old Norse by-name Bligr (from Bligje "to gaze").

---

[397] "A Dictionary of Surnames" P Hanks and F Hodges, Oxford 1988 by permission of the Oxford University Press.

APPENDIX 2

Baptism records of the sons of Vice Admiral Bligh's great grandfather showing the use of the surnames Blight and Bligh.

St Mabyn – Baptism records
John the son of John Blight Gent' by Mary his wife, was baptised the fifth day of July 1680. (P132/1/1 p64)

St Mabyn – Baptism records
Richard, son of John Blight Gent' by Mary his wife was baptised on the thirteenth day of June 1687. (P132/1/1 p70)

St Tudy – Baptism records
Charles, son of Mr John Bligh by Mary his wife, baptised fourteenth day of April 1697. P241/1/1 p67)

Transcripts of entries from the parish records of St Mabyn and St Tudy reproduced by permission of Cornwall County and Diocesan Record Office. Copyright and publication rights reserved.

APPENDIX 3

Genealogy of Vice Admiral William Bligh FRS

Key:

† (ba) baptized at St Mabyn
* (ba) baptized at St Tudy
= Married
d died
b born
— — — — — Married

Appendix 3

GENEALOGY OF VICE ADMIRAL WILLIAM BLIGH FRS – MARKED **WILLIAM**

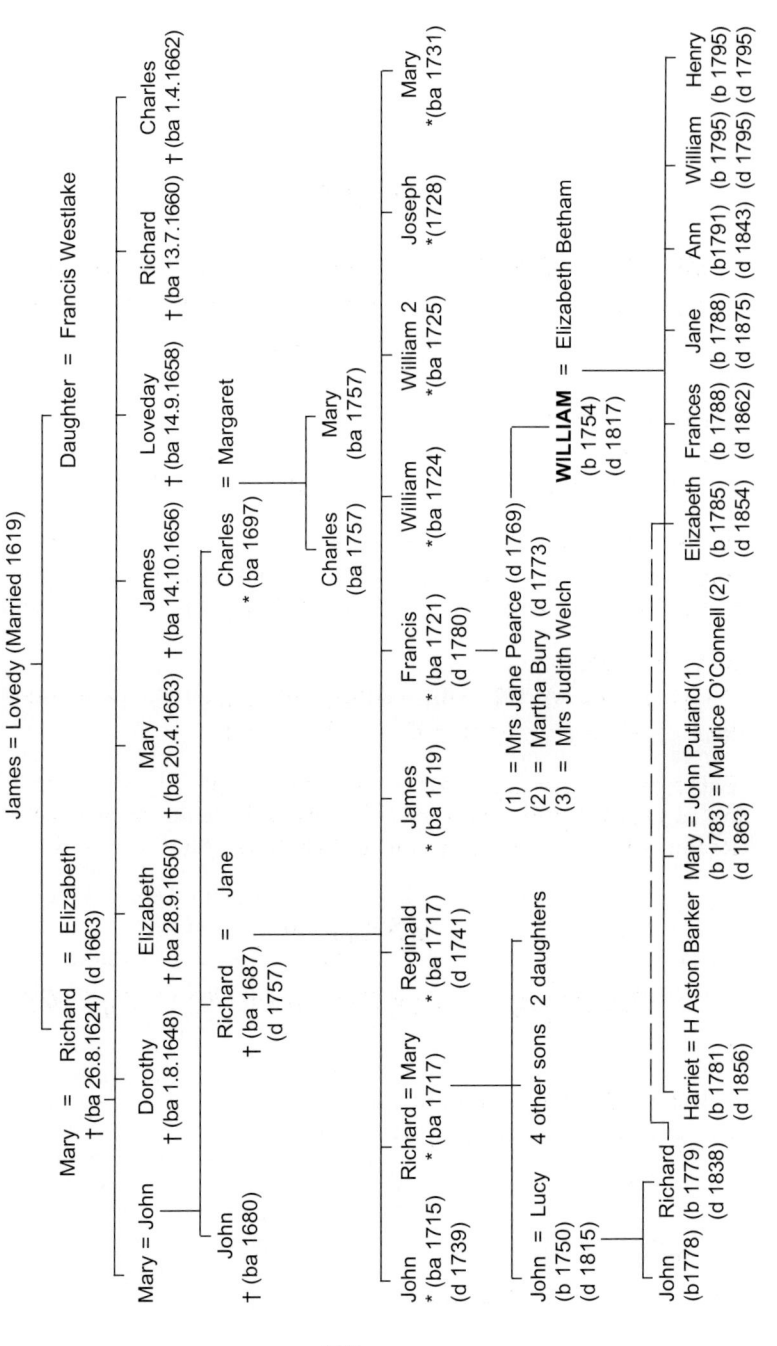

James = Lovedy (Married 1619)

Daughter = Francis Westlake

Mary = Richard = Elizabeth
† (ba 26.8.1624) (d 1663)

Dorothy
† (ba 1.8.1648)

Elizabeth
† (ba 28.9.1650)

Mary
† (ba 20.4.1653)

James
† (ba 14.10.1656)

Loveday
† (ba 14.9.1658)

Richard
† (ba 13.7.1660)

Charles
† (ba 1.4.1662)

Mary = John

Richard = Jane
† (ba 1687)
(d 1757)

Charles = Margaret
*(ba 1697)

William 2
*(ba 1725)

Joseph
*(1728)

Mary
*(ba 1731)

John
† (ba 1680)

Charles
(ba 1757)

Mary
(ba 1757)

William
*(ba 1724)

WILLIAM = Elizabeth Betham
(b 1754)
(d 1817)

Reginald
*(ba 1717)
(d 1741)

James
*(ba 1719)

Francis
*(ba 1721)
(d 1780)

(1) = Mrs Jane Pearce (d 1769)
(2) = Martha Bury (d 1773)
(3) = Mrs Judith Welch

Richard = Mary
*(ba 1717)

Elizabeth
(b 1785)
(d 1854)

Frances
(b 1788)
(d 1862)

Jane
(b 1788)
(d 1875)

Ann
(b1791)
(d 1843)

William
(b 1795)
(d 1795)

Henry
(b 1795)
(d 1795)

John
*(ba 1715)
(d 1739)

John = Lucy   4 other sons   2 daughters
(b 1750)
(d 1815)

Harriet = H Aston Barker
(b 1781)
(d 1856)

Mary = John Putland(1)
(b 1783) = Maurice O'Connell (2)
(d 1863)

John   Richard
(b1778) (b 1779)
         (d 1838)

283

SELECTED BIBLIOGRAPHY

A

ANDERSON C. (1949), "Aspects of Pathological Grief and Mourning" in "International Journal of Psycho-Analysis" 30:48.

ANON (1831) "Obituary Notice for Captain Peter Heywood" in "United Services Journal.." April 1831, Part 1, pp 468-481. London.

ANON (1837) "Review of Brenton's History" Reference to Camperdown in "United Services Journal.." Part 2, pp 147-149. London.

ANSON G. Lord (1748) "A Voyage Round the World.. 1740-1744". London.

AUSTRALIAN ENCYCLOPAEDIA (1926)(ed) Jose A.W. and Carter H.J. Sydney.

B

BACH J. (ed) (1986) "The Bligh Notebook: Rough account – Lieutenant Wm Bligh's voyage in the Bounty's Launch from the ship to Tofoa and from thence to Timor, 28th April to 14th June 1789". Canberra.

BANKS J. Sir. Correspondence. M.L. Sydney.

BARNEY S. (1794) "Minutes of the Proceedings of the Court-Martial held at Portsmouth August 12 on ten persons charged with Mutiny on Board His Majesty's Ship the Bounty with an Appendix containing a Full Account of the real Causes and Circumstances of that unhappy Transaction, the most material of which have hitherto been withheld from the Public". London.

BARROW J. Sir. (1831) "The Eventful History of the Mutiny and Piratical Seizure of HMS Bounty – its Cause and Consequences". London.

Selected Bibliography

BARTRUM (ed) (1811)	"Proceedings of a General Court-Martial held at Chelsea Hospital, which commenced on Tuesday May 7 1811 and continued by Adjournment to Wednesday 5th of June following, for The Trial of Lieut-Col Geo Johnston, Major of the 102 Regiment, late of the New South Wales Corps on A Charge of Mutiny. Exhibited against him by the Crown for deposing On the 26th of January 1808 William Bligh Esq F.R.S. Taken in short hand by Mr Bartrum of Clement's Inn, who attended on behalf of Governor Bligh, by Permission of the Court". London.
BEAGLEHOLE J.C. (1967)	"Captain Cook and Captain Bligh" Collins D.E. Lecture, University of Wellington N.Z.
BEECHEY F.W. Captain (1831)	"Narrative of a Voyage to the Pacific and Beering's Strait to co-operate with the Polar Expeditions: performed in his Majesty's Ship Blossom ... 1825-1828". London.
BELCHER D. Lady. (1870)	"The Mutineers of the Bounty and their Descendants in Pitcairn and Norfolk Islands". London.
BLIGH R. (Richard) K.C.	Rough draft "Defence of Bligh". M.L. Sydney.
BLIGH Wm. (1787-1790)	Log of "Bounty", private copy, 2 vols, M.L. Safe 1/46 and 1/47. Sydney.
"	Log of "Bounty", official copy, P.R.O. Admiralty 55/151.
" (1790)	"A Narrative of the Mutiny on board His Majesty's Ship Bounty; and the subsequent voyage of part of the crew in the ship's boat from Tofoa, one of the Friendly islands, to Timor, a Dutch Settlement in the East Indies" illustrated with charts. London.
" (Burney J.(ed) (1792)	"A Voyage to the South Seas, undertaken by command of his Majesty for the purpose of Conveying the Bread-Fruit Tree to the West Indies,..." with seven charts, diagram and portrait. London.
" (1791-1793)	"Log of "Providence'" P.R.O. Admiralty: Log 51/1507.

" (1794)	"An Answer to Certain Assertions contained in the Appendix to a pamphlet, entitled 'Minutes of the Proceedings on the Court-Martial held at Portsmouth, August 12th, 1792, on Ten Persons charged with Mutiny..'". London.
"	Private Correspondence M.L. Sydney.
"	Book of illustrations. M.L. Sydney.
BONWICK J. (1882)	"First Twenty Years of Australia". London.
BOWLBY J. Dr: (1960)	"Separation Anxiety" in "International Journal of Psycho-Analysis" 41, 89-113.
" (1961)	"Processes of Mourning" in "International Journal of Psycho-Analysis" 44, 317.
" (1973)	"Separation – Anxiety and Anger" in "Attachment and Loss" Vol 2. London.
" (1977)	"The Making and Breaking of Affectional Bonds" in "British Journal of Psychiatry", 130, 201-210.
" (1980)	"Loss – Sadness and Depression" in "Attachment and Loss" Vol 3. London.
BRAIM T.H. Rev: (1846)	"History of New South Wales from its settlement to the close of the year 1844". London.
BRENTON E.P. (1837)	"The Naval History of Great Britain". London.
BREWSTER A.B. (1922)	"The Hill Tribes of Fiji". London.
BRIAN T.H. Rev: (1824)	"The History of New South Wales". London.
BYRON Lord (1823)	"The Island, or Christian and his comrades". London.

C

CALLENDER G. (1936)	"The Portraiture of Bligh" in "Mariner's Mirror" vol xxii, no 2.
CARTERET P. Admiral (1773)	"An Account of a Voyage Round the World.." in HAWKSWORTH J. "Account of the Voyages... by Byron, Wallis, Carteret and Cook" vol i. London.
CASTLEREAGH Viscount (1848-9)(ed by his brother)	"Memoirs and Correspondence". London.

Selected Bibliography

CHAUVEL C. (1933) "In the Wake of the Bounty..". Sydney.
CHRISTIAN E. (1794) "Appendix" in BARNEY S. "Proceedings..". London.
" (1795) "A Short reply to Captain Bligh's Answers". London.
CHRISTIAN F.(?) (1796) "Letters from Mr Fletcher Christian, and a Narrative of the Mutiny on Board His Majesty's Ship Bounty, at Otaheite. With a succinct account of the Proceedings of the Mutineers with a Description of the Manners, Customs and Religious Ceremonies, Diversions, Fashions, Arts, Commerce; Method of Fighting; the Breadfruit and every interesting particular relating to the Society Islands. Also His Shipwreck on the coast of America, and travels in that extensive country; with a history of Gold Mines and general account of the possessions of the Spaniards. In Chili, Peru, Mexico &". London. (Dr Mackaness believes this to be a clever forgery).
" (1798) "Voyages and Travels of Fletcher Christian and a narrative of the mutiny on board HMS Bounty at Otaheite, with a succinct account of the proceedings of the mutineers, with a description of the manners, customs and every interesting particular relating the Society Islands". London. (Dr Mackaness believes this also to be a clever forgery).
CHRISTIAN G. (1982) "Fragile Paradise: the discovery of Fletcher Christian, Bounty Mutineer". London.
" (1989) "Mutineer who made History" in "Mutiny on the Bounty". (Exhibition publication). London.
" (1989) "Film-makers and Bounty" in "Mutiny on the Bounty" (Exhibition publication). London.
CLOWES W.L. Sir (1897-1903) "The Royal Navy: A History" 7 vols. London.

COOK J. and KING J.
Captains (1784) "A Voyage to the Pacific Ocean; Undertaken by Command of his Majesty for making Discoveries in the Northern Hemisphere; performed under the Direction of Captains Cook, Clerke and Gore. In the years 1776-1780. Being a copious, comprehensive and satisfactory Abridgement of the Voyage written by Captain James Cook F.R.S. and Captain James King LL.D. and F.R.S. Illustrated .. in Four Volumes". London.

COOPER K.E. See WING J.K.
COULTER J.L.S. See LLOYD C.
CUNNINGHAM C. (1829) "A Narrative of Occurrences that took place during the Mutiny at the Nore..". Chatham.

D

DANIELSSON B. (1989) "Tahiti: paradise on earth" in "Mutiny on the Bounty" (Exhibition Publication). London.

DARBY M. (1965) "Who caused the Mutiny on the Bounty?". Sydney and London.

" (1966) "The causes of the Bounty mutiny: a short reply to Mr Rolf Du Rietz comments". Studia Bountyana Vol 2. Uppsala, Sweden.

DAVID A.C.F. (1976) "The Surveyors of the Bounty..". Taunton.

" (1977) "The Surveys of William Bligh" in "Mariners Mirror" vol 63, No 1.

" (1989) "The epic open boat voyage" in "Mutiny on the Bounty" (Exhibition publication). London.

DAWSON W.R. (ed)(1958) "The Banks Letters..". London.
DELANO A. (1817) "A Narrative of Voyages and Travels..". Boston, USA.
DICTIONARY OF NATIONAL BIOGRAPHY
DILLON J. Captain (1829) "Narrative of a Voyage in the South Seas..". London.

Selected Bibliography

DRAKE H.H.   See VIVIAN J.L.
DUGAN J. (1966)   "The Great Mutiny". London
DU RIETZ R.E. (1965)   "The Causes of the Bounty Mutiny: some comments on a book by Madge Darby". Studia Bountyana, Vol 1. Uppsala, Sweden.
" (1979)   "Thoughts on the present state of Bligh Scholarship". Banksia 1. Uppsala.
" (1981)   "Fresh Light on John Fryer of the "Bounty"". Banksia 2. Uppsala.
" (1986)   "Peter Heywood's Tahitian vocabulary and the narratives by James Morrison: some notes on their origin and history" Banksia 3. Uppsala.

E

EDGELL J.A. (1937)   "Bligh's navigation" in "Log of the Bounty" RUTTER O. (ed). London.
EDWARDS B. (1819)   "History of the British West Indies". London.
EDWARDS E. and
HAMILTON G. (1915)   "Voyage of HMS Pandora..." THOMSON B. (ed). London.
EKINS C. (1824)   "Naval Battles from 1744 to the peace in 1814". London.
ELDER J.R. (ed)(1932)   "The letters and Journals of Samuel Marsden 1765-1838". Dunedin, N.Z.
ELLIS M.H. (1947)   "Lachlan Macquarie: his Life, Adventures and Times". Sydney.
" (1963)   "The Mutiny on the Bounty – Bligh white washed again" in "The Bulletin". Sydney.
ELLIS W. Rev; (1829)   "Polynesian Researches". London.
EVATT H.V. (1938)   "Rum Rebellion". Sydney.

F

FARINGTON J. (1922)   (GREIG J. (ed)) "The Farington Diary". London.
FERGUSEN J.A. (1951)   "Bibliography of Australia". Sydney.

Bligh by Bligh

FLANAGAN R. (1862)	"History of New South Wales". London.
FLETCHER W. (1876)	"Fletcher Christian and the mutineers of the "Bounty"" in "Transactions of the Cumberland Association for the Advancement of Literature and Science" Part II. Carlisle.
FLINDERS M. (1814)	"A Voyage to Terra Australia..". London.
FOLGER M. (1815)	Letter to Admiralty in "Quarterly Review" April, pp 376/7. London.
" (1819)	Letter to Delano in "Quarterly Review" Vol 1, pp 263-271. London.
FOX U. (1935)	"Bounty's Launch" in "Sailing, Seamanship and Yacht Construction" Book 2, pp 137-9. London.
FREUD S. (1895)	"Project for a Scientific Psychology" S.E.1. London.
FRYER J.	See RUTTER O.
FRYER M.A. (1938)	"John Fryer on the Bounty". London.

G

GENTLEMANS MAGAZINE (1792-1835). London.

GILBERT D. (1938)	"The Parochial History of Cornwall". London.
GILL C (1913)	"Naval Mutinies of 1797". Manchester.
GILL M.M.	See RAPAPORT D.
GLICK I.O., WEISS R.S. and PARKES C.M. (1974)	"The First Year of Bereavement". New York.
GOULD R.T. Lt. Commander (1928)	"Bligh's Notes on Cook's Last Voyage" in "Mariners Mirror" vol xiv, No 4, October. London.

H

HALL J.N. (1935)	"Shipwreck: An Account of a Voyage in the Track of the Bounty from Tahiti to Pitcairn Island". London.
	See also NORDHOFF C.B. (novels).
HAMILTON G. (1793)	"A Voyage Round the World in His Majesty's Frigate Pandora..". Berwick.

Selected Bibliography

HAWKESWORTH J. (1773)   "An Account of the Voyage ... by Commodore Byron, Captain Wallis, Captain Carteret and Captain Cook..". London.

HENDERSON G.C. (1933)   "The Discoveries of the Fiji Islands..". London.

HERBERT D. (1875)   "Great Historical Mutinies". London.

HISTORICAL RECORDS OF AUSTRALIA (HRA). Sydney.

HISTORICAL RECORDS OF NEW SOUTH WALES (H.R.N.S.W.). Sydney.

HOFER M.A.   See WOLFF C.T.

HOLT J. (1838)   (Croker T.C. (ed)) "Memoirs of Joseph Holt" General of the Irish Rebels in 1798. London.

HOLWELL G. (1791-1793)   "Illustrations" by Midshipman in "Providence". M.L. Sydney.

HOUGH R. (1972)   "Captain Bligh and Mr Christian: the men and the mutiny". London.

HOUSE OF COMMONS JOURNAL (1788) vol xliii.

HOUSTON N.B. (1969)   "The Mutiny on the Bounty: An Historical and Literary Bibliography" in "Bulletin of Bibliography and Magazine Notes" vol 26, no 2, Apr-Jun, p 37-41. Westwood, Mass, USA.

HOWELL W. Rev: (1792)   "Sermon" After the execution of the three mutineers. Portsmouth.

I

ILLUSTRATED LONDON NEWS (1937)
    Portrait of Wm Bligh by J Smart. London.

J

JACKSON T.S. (1899)   "Logs of the Great Sea Fights 1794-1805" (Publications of the Navy Records Society). London.

JAMES W. (1837)   "Naval History of Great Britain". London.

JENNY (1819)   Her story in "Sydney Gazette" 17.7.1819. Sydney.

JOHNSTON G. Lt. Colonel
   (1811)   "Proceedings of a General Court-marital...". London. – See BARTRUM.
JOSE A.W. (1929)   "History of Australia". Sydney.

K

KALISH R.A. (1964)   "Death and Bereavement: An Annotated Social Science Bibliography" unpublished.
KENNEDY G. Professor (1978) "Bligh". London.
   " (1989)   "Captain Bligh. The Man and his Mutinies". London.
   " (1989)   "Turning a Mutiny into legend" in "Mutiny on the Bounty" (Exhibition publication). London.
KENT W.G.C. R.N. (1811)   "Court-martial...". Portsmouth.
KING J.   See COOK J.
KLEIN M. (1940)   "Mourning and its Relationship to Manic-depressive States" in "International Journal of Psycho-Analysis" 21:125.
KNIGHT C. (1936)   "H.M. Armed Vessel Bounty" in "Mariner's Mirror" Vol 22, No 2, April, pp 183-199.

L

LANG J.D. Rev: (1875)   "An Historical and Statistical Account of New South Wales". London.
LAUGHTON J.K. (1886)   "Letters and Despatches of Horatio Viscount Nelson". London.
LEDWARD T.D. (1903)   "Letters to his Family" in "Notes and Queries" 9th series, vol xii, pp 501/2.
LEE I. (1920)   "Captain Bligh's Second Voyage to the South Sea". London.
   " (1939)   "The Morrison Myth" in "Mariner's Mirror" vol 25, No 4, pp 433-8.
LEVIS M. (1960)   "A Social History of the Navy, 1793-1815". London.

Selected Bibliography

LINDEMANN E. (1944)	"The Symptomatology and Management of Acute Grief". in "American Journal of Psychiatry" 101. 141.
" (1960)	"Psychosocial Factors as Stress Agents" in Tanner J.M. (ed) "Stress and Psychiatric Disorders".
LINDSAY P. (1931)	"Bligh in New South Wales" in "Ruffians Hall" by the same author.
LLOYD C. and COULTER J.L.S.	
(1957)	"Medicine and the Navy". London.
LLOYD C. (1963)	"St Vincent and Camperdown". London.
" (1968)	"The British Seaman: 1200-1860 – a social survey". London.

M

MACDONALD A.C. (1911)	"Discovery of Pitcairn Island; Mutiny of the Bounty; Life of the Mutineers on Pitcairn and their Removal to Norfolk Island" in the "Report" of the Australasian Association for the Advancement of Science.
MACKANESS G. Dr: (1931)	"The Life of Vice Admiral Bligh R.N. F.R.S.". Sydney.
MACKANESS G. Dr:(1936)	"Sir Joseph Banks: His Relations with Australia". Sydney.
" (ed) (1938)	"A Book of the 'Bounty'..". London.
" (1943)	"Captain William Bligh's Discoveries and Observations in Van Dieman's Land". Sydney.
" (ed) (1949)	"Some Correspondence of Captain William Bligh with John and Francis Godolphin Bond 1776-1811" in "Australian Historical Monograph" No 19. Sydney.
" (1951)	"The Life of Vice Admiral Bligh R.N. F.R.S.". Sydney.
" (1953)	"Fresh Light on Bligh – Being some unpublished Correspondence of Captain William Bligh R.N. and Lt: Francis Godolphin Bond R.N. and Lt: Bond's manuscript Notes made on the Voyage of H.M.S. Providence..." in "Australian Historical Monograph" No 29. Sydney.

293

" (1960) "Extracts from a log-book of H.M.S. Providence kept by Lt: Francis Godolphin Bond" in "Journal and Proceedings of the Royal Australian Historical Society" vol 46, pp 24-66.

MACKENZIE J.M. See SACHER E.J.

MACLEAN J. Sir (1873) "The History of the Deanery of Trigg Minor". London.

MADDISON D.C., VIOLA A and WALKER W.L. (1967) "Factors affecting the Outcome of Conjugal Bereavement" in "British Journal of Psychiatry" 113: 1057.

MAIDEN J.H. (1909) "Sir Joseph Banks, the Father of Australia". Sydney.

MANN D.D. (1811) "The present Picture of New South Wales". London.

MARINERS MIRROR (1936) "Portraits of Bligh" vol xxii. London.

MARSDEN J.B. (1857) "Memoirs of the Life and Labours of Rev: Samuel Marsden". London.

MARSHALL J. (1823-1835) "Royal Naval Biography". London.

MASON J.W. see WOLFF C.T.

MAUDE H.E. (1958) "In search of a Home: From the Mutiny to Pitcairn Island" in "The Journal of the Polynesian Society" vol 67, No 2, pp 115-140.

McFARLAND A. (1884) "Mutiny in the 'Bounty' and Story of the Pitcairn Islanders". Sydney.

McMAHON J. (1913) "Fragments of the Early History of Australia". Melbourne.

MONTGOMERIE H.S. (1937) "William Bligh of 'the Bounty', in Fact and in Fable". London.

(1938) "The Morrison Myth..". London.

MORRISON J. (James) see RUTTER O. and (sources) M.L. Sydney.

MORRISON J. (Jane) (1935) "The Journal of James Morrison...". London.

MORTIMER G. (1791) "Observations ... in the Brig Mercury". London.

MUDIE J. (1837) "The Felonry of New South Wales". London.

Selected Bibliography

MUIR H. (1950) "The Literature of the Bounty". Melbourne.
MURRAY T.B. Rev: (1853) "Pitcairn, the People..". London.

N

NAVAL CHRONICLE. London.
NAVAL COURTS-MARTIAL. London.
NAVAL RECORDS SOCIETY publications. London.
NICOLAS N.H.(ed)(1844) "The Dispatches and Letters of Vice-Admiral Lord Viscount Nelson". London.
NICHOLS G.R. (1904) "Governor Bligh's farm". in "Historical Notes on the Hawkesbury" by the same author. Sydney.
NORDHOFF C.B. and HALL J.N.
   (1933) (novel) "Mutiny". London.
" (1934) (novel) "Men Against the Sea". London.
" (1935) (novel) "Pitcairn Island". London.
NOTES AND QUERIES. London.

O

O'HARA J. (1817) "History of New South Wales". London.
OMAN C. (1947) "Nelson". London.
ONSLOW S.M. (McArthur)
   (ed) (1914) "Some Early Records of the McArthurs of Camden". Sydney.
ORMOND R. (1989) "William Bligh's Royal Navy" in "Mutiny on the Bounty" (Exhibition publication). London.
OWEN J.B. (1976) The Eighteenth Century 1714 – 1815. N.Y. and London.

P

PAGE W. (ed)(1900) "Domesday Survey for Cornwall" translation by Taylor T in "the Victoria History of the Counties of England – A History of the County of Cornwall" vol 2, part 8. London.
(no reference to the Bligh family)

PARKES C.M. (1959) "Morbid Grief Reactions: A Review of the Literature" (Dissertation). London.

" (1964) "Recent Bereavement as a Cause of Mental Illness" in "British Journal of Psychiatry" 110:198.

" (1964) "The Effects of Bereavement on Physical and Mental Health.." in "British Medical Journal" (2): 274.

" (1965) "Bereavement and Mental Illness – Part 1, A – Clinical Study of the Grief of Bereaved Psychiatric Patients. Part 2, A Classification of Bereavement Reactions" in "British Journal of Medical Psychology" 38:1.

" (1969) "Separation Anxiety: An Aspect of a Search for a Lost Object" in LADER M.H. (ed) "Studies of Anxiety" in "British Journal of Psychiatry Special Publication No 3" (Published by authority of the World Psychiatric Association and the Royal Medico-Psychological Association).

" (1970) "The Psychosomatic Effects of Bereavement" in HILL O.W. (ed) "Modern Trends in Psychosomatic Medicine". London.

" (1970) "The First Year of Bereavement" in "Psychiatry" 33:444

" (1970) "'Seeking' and 'Finding' a Lost Object: Evidence from Recent Studies of the Reaction to Bereavement" in "Social Science and Medicine" 4: 187-201.

" (1972) "Bereavement: Studies of Grief in Adult Life" (including statistical Appendix). London.

PARKES C.M., GLICK I.O. and WEISS R.S. (1974) "The First Year of Bereavement". New York.

PHILLIP A. (1789) "The Voyage of Governor Phillip to Botany Bay; with an Account of the Establishment of the Colonies of Port Jackson and Norfolk Island..". London.

PHILLIPS M. (1909) "A Colonial Autocracy in N.S.W. under Governor Macquarie, 1810-1821". London.

Selected Bibliography

PIPON P. (1834) "The Descendants of the Bounty Crew" in "United Services Journal" vol 63. London.
" (undated) "Interesting Report..." M.L. Sydney.
PITCAIRN ISLAND REGISTER BOOK (undated) (ed) LUCAS C. Sir (1929), London.
POLWHELE R. Rev: (1816) "History of Cornwall". London.
" (1826) "Traditions and Recollections". London.
POLWHELE R. Rev: (1831) "Biographical Sketches in Cornwall". Truro.
POOL B. (1966) "Navy Board Contracts 1660-1832". London.
POPPER K.R. (1934) "The Logic of Scientific Discovery". London.
PUBLIC RECORD OFFICE (P.R.O.) – Admiralty Division.

R

RAPAPORT D. and GILL M.M.
(1959) "The Point of View and assumptions of Metapsychology" in "International Journal of Psych-Analysis" 40, 153-162.
RAPHAEL B. (1975) "The Management of Pathological Grief" in "Australian and N.Z. Journal of Psychiatry" 9: 173-180.
RAWSON G. (1930) "Bligh of the 'Bounty'". London.
RICKMAN J. (1951) "Methodology and Research in Psychopathology" in "British Journal of medical Psychology" 24, 1-7.
ROBINSON A.H.W. (1952) "Captain William Bligh R.N., hydrographic surveyor" in "Empire Survey Review" vol xi, no 85, p 301-6.
(1962) "Marine Cartography..". Leicester.
ROYAL AUSTRALIAN HISTORICAL SOCIETY – Journal.
RUTTER O. (1931) (ed) "The Court-Martial of the Bounty Mutineers". London.
" (1933) "Vindication of William Bligh" in "Quarterly Review" (October). London.
" (1934) (ed) "The Voyage of the Bounty's Launch as related in William Bligh's despatch to the Admiralty and the Journal of John Fryer". London.

" (1935) (ed) "The Journal of James Morrison". London.
" (1936) "Turbulent Journey: A Life of William Bligh – Vice Admiral of the Blue". London.
" (1936) "The True Story of the Mutiny in the Bounty". London.
" (1936) "Bligh's Log" in "Mariner's Mirror" vol 22, no 2, April, pp 179-182.
" (1937) (ed) "The log of the Bounty... from the manuscript in Admiralty records". London.
" (1937) (ed) "Bligh's voyage in the Resource". London.
" (1939) (ed) "John Fryer of the Bounty". London.

S

SACHER E.J., MACKENZIE J.M., BINSTOCK W.A. and MACK J.E.
(1967) "Corticosteroid Responses to the Psychotherapy of Reactive Depressions. 1. Elevations during Confrontation of Loss" in "Archives of General Psychiatry" 16: 461-470.
SARTORIUS N. see WING J.K.
SCOTT B.W. (1989) "Pitcairn – what happened" in "Mutiny on the Bounty" (Exhibition Publication). London.
SCOTT E. (1914) "Life of Captain Matthew Flinders R.N.". Sydney.
(1916) "A Short History of Australia". London.
SHILLIBEER J.A. Lt: (1817) "A Narrative of the 'Briton's' Voyage to Pitcairn Island". London.
SIGGINS L.D. (1966) "Mourning – A Critical Survey of Literature" in "International Journal of Psycho-Analysis". 47: 14-25.
SIMCOCK W. (1890) "Principal landowners in Cornwall 1165-1220" in "Journal of the Royal Institution of Cornwall" vol x. Truro. (No reference to the Bligh family)
SLOCUM V. (1911) "Voyage of the Bounty's Launch" in "Yachting" vol 40, p 37-40.

Selected Bibliography

SMITH E. (1911) — "Life of Sir Joseph Banks". London.

SPENCE S.A. (1970) — "Captain William Bligh R.N. and where to Find Him: Being a Catalogue of works wherein reference is contained to this remarkable seaman". London.

SPHERE the (1936) — "The Bounty – contemporary documents – Exhibition at P.R.O." (facsimiles). London.

STAINES T Sir and PIPON P. (undated) — "Interesting Report of the only remaining mutineers of His Majesty's ship 'Bounty'". M.L. Sydney.

SYDNEY GAZETTE (1819) — "Jenny's Story" 17.7.1819. Sydney.

T

TAGART E. (1832) — "A Memoir of the Late Captain Peter Heywood R.N.". London.

TANNER J.M. (ed)(1960) — "Stress and Psychiatric Disorder". Oxford.

TAYLOR A.H. (1937) — "William Bligh at Camperdown" in "Mariner's Mirror" vol 23, No 4, October, pp 417-434.

TENCH W. (1793) — "A Complete Account of the Settlement at Port Jackson". London.

THERRY R. Sir (1863) — "Reminiscences of Thirty Years Residence in New South Wales". London.

THOMSON B. (ed)(1915) — ".. Voyage of H.M.S. Pandora.. being the narratives of Captain Edward R.N. and George Hamilton, Surgeon". London.

TOBIN G. Lt: — "Private Journal ('Providence') 1791-3". M.L. Sydney.

"   — Book of Illustrations. M.L. Sydney.

TRANSPORTATION (1812) — "Report of the Committee on Transportation". London.

U

UNITED SERVICES JOURNAL. London.

V

VIDA A.   see MADDISON

VIVIAN J.L. and
DRAKE H.H. (1874)   "Visitation of the County of Cornwall in 1620". Harleian Society Publication, vol 9.

VIVIAN J.L. (1887)   "The Visitations of Cornwall". Exeter.

VOLKAN V. (1970)   "Typical Findings in Pathological Grief" in "Psychiatry Quarterly" 44: 231-250.

VOLKART E.H.   "Bereavement and Mental Health..." in LEIGHTON A.H., CLAUSEN J.A. and WILSON R.N. (eds). "Explorations in Social Psychiatry". New York.

W

WALKER W.L.   see MADDISON

WALTERS S. (1976)   "The Literature of Bligh" in "Sea Breezes". (magazine) vol 50, no 370, p 608-611.

" (1989)   "Bligh and the Mutiny" in "Mutiny on the Bounty" (Exhibition Publication). London.

WATERS D.W. R.N. (1966)   "Navigational Instruments and Timekeepers" in Gervis Frere-Cook (ed) "The Decorative Arts of the Mariner" p 165-192.

WEISS R.S.   see GLICK I.O.

WENTWORTH W.C. (1819)   "A Statistical, Historical and Political Description of the Colony of New South Wales". London.

WESTERN ANTIQUARY. Plymouth.

WILKINSON C.S. (1953)   "The Wake of the Bounty". London.

WILSON E. (1958)   "Adams of the Bounty". Sydney.

WING J.K., COOPER K.E. and SARTORIUS N. (1974)   "The Measurement and Classification of Psychiatric Symptoms...". London.

WOLFF C.T., HOFER M.A. and MASON J.W. (1964)   "Relationship between Psychological Defences and Mean Urinary 17 – Hydroxy – corticosteroid Excretion Rates. Methodologic and Theoretical Considerations" in "Psychosomatic Medicine". 26: 592-609

Selected Bibliography

WRETMARK G. (1959) "A study in Grief Reaction" in "Acta Psychiatrica et Neurologica Scandinavica" Supplement 136:292.

Y

YEXLEY L. (1911) "Our Fighting Sea Men". London.
YONGE C.D. (1863) "The History of the British Navy". London.
YOUNG G. Sir (1928) "HMS Bounty" in "Young of Formosa". London.
YOUNG R.A. (1894) "Mutiny of the Bounty and Story of Pitcairn Island...". California.

ALPHABETICAL INDEX

A

ABBOTT	Captain	Senior officer at Parramatta	191
		Plan to replace Kemp	203
		Re Conspiracy	214
		Protest at McArthur's trial	216
		Irish rebellion?	238
		At Johnston's trial	239
ACCUSATIONS		Re Separation and loss	64
ADAMS	John	Background. See also SMITH Alexander	37
ADMIRALTY	Re "Bounty"		30
AGGRESSION		Separation and loss	64
		" " "	
		" " " (Fletcher Christian)	79
AMBIVALENCE		" " "	64
		" " " (Fletcher Christian)	80
AMERICA – NW coast			23
AMIENS		Peace with France	171
ANGER		Re Separation and loss	64
		" " " (Fletcher Christian)	79
ANNA MOOKA			68
ARNDELL	Thomas	Letter to Bligh	216
		Letter at Johnston's Trial	239/240
ARREOYS			54
ARTICLES OF WAR		Mutiny or its concealment	73
ASSISTANT HMS		Tonnage etc	119
ATKINS	Richard	Acting Judge Advocate	186
		Dispute with McArthur	186
		Address to Bligh	190
		Assessment by Bligh	201
		Request ignored	202
		Issues warrant	202
		Re debt payment	204
		To McArthur – no communication	204

Index

		Adjourns court	218
		Memorial to Bligh	210
		Rebel land grant	225
		At Johnston's trial	236/7
ASSISTANT	HMS	Tonnage	119
AUCKLAND	Lord	Authorises second Breadfruit voyage	118
AUSTRIA			157

B

BADGERY		Re McArthur's petition	211
BANKS	Joseph Sir	Background	22
		Re breadfruit	29
		Breadfruit proposal	29
		Voyage preparations	30
		Appointment - Cook's voyage	30
		Offer of breadfruit voyage	31
		Employed Phillips	116
		Offer to Bligh	179 ff
		Rebuffed by McArthur	187
		Reduced offer to McArthur	187
		Message from Bligh	199
		Assessment on Bligh	262
BARBARISM		Re Cook and Edwards	150
BARNEY	Stephen	Muspratt's attorney	116
		Minutes of Court Martial	116
		Indemnified	117
BARROW	John Sir		19
		Re mutiny	143
BARTER			37
BATAVIA			100
BAYSEN		Spanish defeat French	219
BAYLY	Nicholas	Re McArthur's petition	211
		Conspiracy	226
		Eve of insurrection	237
BEECHEY	Captain		71
		Report	106/7
		Evidence	109
		Narrative	141/2
		Discrepancy re Heywood	144
BEEF		Appears light	44

BELCHER	Lady		144
BELLE POULE HMS			26
BERTIE	Captain	Relative of Heywood	114
BERWICK	HMS		27
BETHAM	Elizabeth	William's wife	20
	Richard Dr	Father-in-law	20
		Assessment of enterprise	38
BETHIA		Listed as "Bounty"	30
BETRAYAL		By Fletcher	80
BILL OF RIGHTS			261
BLAXCELL	Garnham	Re McArthur's Petition	211
		Conspiracy	226
		Eve of Insurrection	237
BLAXLANDS		Letter against Blight	200
		A 'firm' offer	201
		At law	217
		Conspiracy	226
		Accusations	252
BLEIT		"Old Cornish" for "Wolf"	17
BLIGH	William	Portrait 1791	7
	Richard	Grandfather of William	18
	Francis	Father of William	18
	William	Birth	18
		Midshipman	20
		Lieutenant Certificate	22
		Master of "Resolution"	22
		At Karakakooa	23/4
		Marginal notes to Cook's Voyages	24/5
		Cartography	26
		Marriage	26
	Harriet	William and Betsy's daughter	27
	Mary	"	28
	Elizabeth	"	28
	Frances	"	28
	Jane	"	28
	Ann	"	28
WILLIAM		Agent for Campbell	28
		Profit on Cook's Voyages	30
		Selects Fletcher Christian	30
		Breadfruit voyage offered	31

304

Index

		Promise from Lord Howe	34
		Re "Bounty's" launch	34
		Initial appointments	34
BLIGH	William	Seeks promotion 10/1787	34/5
		Lieutenant of "Bounty"	35
		Ready to leave Spithead 8.11.1787	38
		On his pursing	40
		Introduction of 3 watches	40
		Reduction of bread (biscuit)	41
		Answer to missing cheese	43
		Response to pumpkin complaint	43
		Re Beef and pork	44
		Crew appreciation	44
		No punishment for about two months	44
		First punishment	45
		Re sheep's death	45
		At Cape Horn	46
		Gave up cabin	46
		Thanks crew at Cape Horn	47
		Heywood's obituary re William	47
		Health Management	47
		On Slavery	48
		Purcell's trouble	49
		Dance refusals – grog stopped	50
		Library – books on scurvy	51
		Rules of conduct – Tahiti	54
		Purcell refuses to cut stones	55
		Trading constraints	56
		On petty officers – Tahiti	58
		Re taboo	58
		Re mildewed sails	58
		Tracked down deserters	59
		Accusation of collapsed authority	61
		Gifts to Tinah	61
		Lost his head?	68
		Coconut incident	69
		Hough says Bligh is paranoid	69
		Seized	75
		Offer to Fletcher	76
		I'll do you justice	77

	Threatened with death	80
	Log, reaction to disaster	82
	Special prayer	85
	Beats Lamb	89
	Human in adversity	90
	A prayer	91
	Altercation with Fryer	96
	Master reprimanded	97
	Tribute to Nelson	97
	To Betsy from Coupang	97/8
	Fryer's charges rebutted	99
	Purcell's charges rebutted	99
	Fryer apologises	100
	Fever at Batavia	100
	Returns to Portsmouth	101
	Finishes "Narrative"	101
	Court Martial re "Bounty"	101
	No compliants by crew	101
	Complaint against Purcell	101
	Bligh acquitted	102
	Promoted Commander	102
	Promoted Post Captain	102
	Affidavits exonorating	114
	No charge of ill treatment	114
Ann	Born and baptised	119
William	On Peckover	120
	Refuses Fryer a reference	120
	Post traumatic stress disorder?	120/1
	Trees, plants, herbs at Tasmania	121
	Discoveries – West Fiji	123
	Letter to Betsy (2nd Voyage)	123
	By Francis G Bond	125/6
	No favouritism	126
	Floggings - very moderate	126
	Second voyage – high estimation by crew	126
	Out of pocket pursing	127
	Claims Society gold medal	127
	Answer to Appendix	130
	Representation by Charles Laughton	132
	Representation by Trevor Howard	133

Index

Representation by Anthony Hopkins	133
Treatment of Fletcher Christian	137
Charges by Morrison	139
Justified by Dutch authorities	139
Assessment by Alexander Smith	141
McFarland rebutted	145
The Don	146
Tobin assessment	147
Hough's paranoia	147
Kennedy's hypothesis	148
Walter's hypothesis	148/9
Preliminary assessment	150 ff
Re Purcell's treatment	151
Progressive and versatile	152
Not repacious or mean	152
Conceit	155
Navigator	155
Offers Bond a post	158
Loss of twin boys	158
Re flogging – lenient	159
Response to petition	159/160
Nore mutiny	162
To report on mutiny	162
Gold medal – at Camperdown	165
Compliment by Duncan	165
Inventor – navigation	166
Nelson's thanks after battle of Copenhagen	169
Surveying 1803	171
Court Martial of Frazier	173-179
William Bligh's Court Martial	175-179
Offer by Banks	179 ff
Governor General NSW	181

Mary Leaves for New South Wales with her father 189
William Plotted against 190

Land grants from Governor General King	190
Meeting with McArthur	191
Supplies to van Diemen's land	192
New Port Regulations	192
Address by Hawkesbury settlers	192
Meat for Hawkesbury settlers	192

307

Bligh by Bligh

Forward price guarantees	192
Assessment by Rev Marsden	193
Government Order – banning barter of spirits	193
Promissory notes only in sterling	193
Land purchases and grants	194
Bailiff – Andrew Thompson	195
Wentworth affair	196
Captain General NSW Corps	196
To Sir Joseph Banks	199
Letters against	200
Dangerous militia	201
Assessment of Atkins – Judge Advocate	201
McArthur agent against Bligh	201
Promoted Commodore	201
Questions McArthur's objection	203
Instructions to Thompson	203
Letter from Thompson	203
Provoked by McArthur	209
Summons Johnston	209
Given emergency powers	210
Resignation demanded	212
Secures papers	212
Hiding to a good purpose	213
Deposed	215
Correspondence with Betsy	216
To Castlereagh re Foveaux	218
Removed from Government House	220
Agreement with Paterson	221
Letter – 6 civil officers	222
Proclamation – mutiny	222
Recall – no loss of King's confidence	223
To Castlereagh – Collins mutinous	225
Returns to New South Wales	227
Mildness	228
Macquarie's estimate	228
Reaction to Macquarie	228
Macquarie to Castlereagh	228
Final address presented	229
To Betsy	229
Prosecutor – trial of Johnston	233 ff

Index

		Witnesses re prosecution	233 ff
		Trial of Bligh?	244
		Rear Admiral of the Blue	244
		Judge Advocate General assessment	246
		Assessment by Robert Campbell	247
		No tyranny	248
		No oppression	248
		Legally suspended Wentworth	249
		Six officers' investigation	250
		Humour – successes	253
		Matthew Flinders	254
		Evidence to the Select Committee	254
		Rear Admiral of the White	255
		Rear Admiral of the Red	255
		Move from Lambeth	255
		Vice Admiral of the Blue	255
		Died	256
		Family crest and motto	256
		Physical description	258
		Versatility	258
		Sir Joseph Banks estimate	262
		Owen Rutter's assessment	262
		A hero	262
BLIGH'S CAP			25
BLOODY BAY		Tubuai	92
BOAT	Open	see LAUNCH	
BOOBY	bird		85
BOND	Jane	Mother of William	18
	John		18
	FG	Son of William's half sister	19
(Francis Godolphin)			
	"	First Lieutenant "Providence"	120/1
	"	To HMS Assistant	121
	"	Letter to his brother	125/6
	"	Grievances – not much	126
		About Bligh	126
	"	Not purgatory	146
	"	Request denied	158
BORROW	George	Re gentility	144

309

BOUNTY	HMS	Previously Bethia	30
		Complement, tonnage	30
		Deck plans	32/3
		Establishment	34
		Armament	34
		Boats	34
		Provisions	37
		Attempts to sail	38
		Provisions – gale damage	40
		Reaches Matavai Bay	52/3/4
		Aground at Oparre	56
		Damage to cable	60
		Leaves Tahiti	62
		Film '84	133
BOWLBY	John Dr	Separation and Loss	64
BRANDO	Marlon	As Christian	133
BREADFRUIT		Background	29
		1st voyage	39
		1015 loaded	56
			61
		2nd voyage	123
		Unpalatable	126
		Assessment	126/7
BREWSTER	A B	About Fiji	83
BRITANNIA		Vessel	28
		Breadfruit offer	31
BRITISH GOVERNMENT		NSW Corps	182
		Responsibility for the disaster	184
BRITON	HMS	See Staines	105
BROOKE	Rupert	'Tiare Tahiti'	53
BROWN	William	Botanist's assistant	36
		Refuses to dance	50
		To Pitcairn	103
		Killed	107
BROWN	A	Left by "Mercury"	110
		Lived in South Tahiti	111
		Signed on "Pandora"	111
BRUCKNER	Vice Admiral	Mutiny	162
BRYTHONIC language			16/17

Index

BURKITT	Thomas	AB	36
		Called up	75
		Hanged	115
BYRNE	Michael	AB	36
		Origin	37
		Held in "Bounty"	78
		Exonerated by Bligh	114
		Spoke well of Bligh	123
BYRON	Lord	The island – poem	109

C

CALCUTTA	HMS		130
CALVERT	Harry	Adjutant General	243
CAMBRIAN		Vessel	28
CAMBRIDGE	HMS		27
CAMDEN	Lord	Offer to McArthur	187
CAMPBELL	Duncan		21
		Merchantman offer	27
	John	Son of Duncan	28
	Duncan	Bligh as agent	28
		Employed Bligh	30
	Robert	Naval offer NSW	197
		Loses court case	198
		Sued for loss of Parramatta	203
		Bligh's plan	211
		Re Bligh	247
CAMPERDOWN		Battle	64/5
		William's role	260
CANNIBALISM		Rejcted	89
CAPE HORN		Orders	38
		Storms after month	47
CAPE ST VINCENT			160
CARIB			20
CARNOT			157
CARTERET	Captain		104
CARTOGRAPHY			21
			156
CAUSE(S) of the mutiny			135-149
CARTEL		NSW Corps	186

CASTLEREAGH Lord	Compliments Williams	92
	Re Wentworth	204
	Approval re Monopoly	204
	Johnston's letter	216
	Memorial from Settlers	221/2
	Macquarie's orders	223
	Legal advice	225
CELT	Re William Bligh	16 and 258
CHANNEL FLEET		161
CHATHAM Lord	Would not meet Bligh	117 and 127
CHEESE	Missing	41
CHRISTIAN Charles	Fletcher as Lieutenant	40
Edward	Coconut incident	68-9
	Falls out with Heywood	116
	Appendix	116
	Court of Enquiry!	116
	Appendix	128
	Appendix floor	129
	Short reply to Bligh's answer	130
	Criticism by Chief Justice	130
	Cause – pressure	142
	Perpetual infamy	143
Fletcher	AB on Britannia	30
	Master's mate	35
	Age	36
	Background	37
	Promoted Acting Lieutenant	44
	Venereal disease	51
	In charge – Point Venus	55
	Titriano	61
	Personal details	62
	Potentially long term relationship	63-4
	Quintal's attachment	65
	Watering party	66
	Bligh's criticism	66
	Morrison's version	66
	Fryer sent to help	67
	Coconut incident	68
	Gives away mementos	70
	Talk with Purcell	70

Index

	Declined dinner invitation	70
	Desertion plan	70
	To seize ship	73
CHRISTIAN Fletcher	With cutlass	75
	Original plan	75
	With bayonet	75
	Bligh... villain	76
	In hell after 14 days	76
	Used like a dog	77
	I am in hell	78
	Gift of Sextant	78
	Return to Tahiti	92
	Steward second-in-command	92
	Lies about Bligh	92
	Forestalls plot	93
	Disapproved on lottery idea	94
	Professed intentions	94
	Celebration at Tahiti	95
	Gave away jacket	104
	Shot	107
	Earlier remorse	109
	Burial	109
	Captain Lamb's view	130
	Clark Gable	132
	Background	135
	Treatment by Bligh	137
	Secret	153-4
'CHRISTIAN (Fletcher)		
and his companions'	Byron's poem	109
CHURCHILL Charles	Corporal/Master at Arms	36
	Missing	57-59
	Called up	74
	Arms chest and key	92
	Tahiti return	111
	Sovereignty	111
	Killed by Thompson	111
CLARENCE Duke of	Visit	126
CLERKE Captain		24
	death	26

313

Bligh by Bligh

COCONUT INCIDENT			68 and 138
COFFIN	Isaac		
	Sir Admiral		190
COLE	William	Bo'sun	35
		Sails mildewed	58
		Told of Fletcher's plan	70
		Begged for launch	76
		Collected materials	76
		Tried to pacify Fletcher	76
		In launch	78
		Sauce from Tinkler	96
COLEMAN	Joseph	Armourer	36
		Re Fletcher's girl	61
		Keys	74
		Hold in "Bounty"	78
		Exonerated by Bligh	114
		Spoke well of Bligh	123
COLLINGWOOD			
	Vice Admiral		174
COLLINS			
	David Lt Governor	Dilemma	224
		Mutinous	225
COMPLAINTS		Threat of flogging	43
		To blight	139
CONVICTS			182
COOK	James	Captain – background	21-2
		Third voyage to the South Seas	23
		At Karakakooa	24
		Author	24
		Re Breadfruit	29
COPENHAGEN		Battle	168-9
			260
CORNER	John		20
CORNISH LANGUAGE			17
CORNWALL			16-18
COUPANG		Arrival	90
		West Timor	96
		Bligh leaves	98
		"Pandora"	113

314

Index

COURT MARTIAL	Of Mutineers	39 and 114
COURT	Illegal	203 ff
	Of appeal	241
COWARDICE	Charge rebutted	252
COX Captain		110
CRESCENT HMS		20
CREST		256
CROSSLEY George	Pardoned by Governor King	187
	Papers lost; given to McArthur	206
	Advice	252
CRUELTY	No charge of cruelty	141
	Denial	150
CURACAO HMS		62
CUTLASS	Four thrown in launch	78

D

DAMPIER William		29
DANCE	Heiva	55
DANCING		47
DANNEBROG	Danish Flagship	168
DARBY Madge	Freudian theory	63
	Cause of Mutiny	146
DARLING Gov General	On McArthur	255
DART	Vessel	195
DEATH approaching	Open boat voyage	89-90
DEATH SENTENCES		163
DELANO Captain		106
DENING		
Greg Professor	Re flogging	151
DENMARK	Northern Alliance	167
	Crown Prince	167
DEPRESSION		64
DEPTFORD		23 and 38
DERWENT	Bligh sails to river	223
	Settlers to Bligh	224
DESERTION		37
		57-59
DESPAIR		64, 72 and 79
DILLON Captain		103
DIOMEDE HMS	Irish plot	166

315

Bligh by Bligh

DIRECTOR HMS		158
	At Campendown	164-5
	Master convicted	166
DISCOVERY HMS		23-4 and 26
DISORGANISATION		64
DIVINE Nicholas	At Johnston's trial	235
DOGGER BANK		27
DOMAIN		183
	Private property and leases	241
DOUGLAS	Isle of Man	20
DRUGS		149
DU RIETZ		146
DUNCAN Admiral		159
	Re Camperdown	164-5
	Re Bligh	165
DUTCH FLEET	Off Dogger Bank	27
DUTCH AUTHORITIES	Justified Bligh	139

E

EAST HINTON	Re Breadfruit	29
EDWARDS		
Edward Captain	Appointment	101
	HMS Pandora	110
	Reaches Tahiti	111
	Not with Bligh	133
ELEPHANT HMS	Nelson's Flagship	168
ELLISON Thomas	AB Seaman	36
	Recommended by D Campbell	37
	Armed	75
	Hanged	115
	Spoke well of Bligh	123
ELPHINSTONE William	Master's mate	35
	Buoy loss	66
	Water party	66
	In launch	78
	Drunk at Sourabaya	98
	Died of fever	100
ERRE RA HIGH	Boy King (Tahiti)	122
ETUAH	God (Tahiti)	122
EVATT Mr Justice	Source of letters	200
	Bligh exonerated – charge of cowardice	213

Index

F

FACTION		132
FALSIFICATION	Denial by Bligh	152
FARNINGHAM	To Manor House	255
FIJI	Open boat journey	82-3
	Discoverers	124
FINANCE	1797	160
FIRST FLEET		182
FISCHER	Admiral (Danish)	168
FITZ		
Deputy Commissary	Letters against Bligh	200
FLINDERS Matthew	Midshipman "Providence"	120
	On Bligh at Torres Strait	124
	Re Bligh	254
FLOGGING		20
	First flogging on "Bounty"	45
	John Williams	47
	Alexander Smith	55
	Matthew Thompson	55
	William Muspratt	56
	Robert Lamb	56
	Churchill, Muspratt, Millward	59
	Isaac Martin	59
	Native thrieves	60
	John Sumner	66
	Second Breadfruit voyage	126
	Dead seaman	133
	By Bligh – few and mild	150
	Comparisons	151 and 159
	To death	161
	Round the fleet (Nore)	163
FLYING FISH	Bligh's painting	87
FOLGER Captain		105
FORT GEORGE	Tubuai	93
FOVEAUX Joseph	Lt Governor, Norfolk Island	187
	Lt Col back in Sydney	218
	Liable to Court Martial	226
FRANCE		157-8
FRAZIER	John Lieutenant	173-179

FRYER	John	Appointed by Bligh	34
		Master "Bounty"	35
		Relative of Tinkler	37
		Complaint re Quintal	45
		Purcell's trouble	48
		Certificate demand	50
		Grounding of "Bounty"	56
		Sails mildewed	58
		Restoration of mat	61
		Sent to help Christian	67
		On coconut incident	69
		Armed in his cabin	75
		Forced to leave	75
		In launch	78
		Sunday Island incident	88
		Fire danger	89
		Altercations with Bligh	96
		Dangerous advice to Tinkler	96
		Reprimanded by Bligh	97
		Given written orders	97
		Charges against Bligh	99
		Charges rebutted	99
		Yam shortage – cause of mutiny	99
		Apologies – not accepted	100
		Apologies required in writing	100
		Advice to loyalists	114
		Refused reference	120
		"Could have done as well"	156
FULTON			
	Henry Reverend	Re NSW	191
		To Castlereagh re Paterson	224
		At Johnston's trial	234

G

GABLE	Clark	As Fletcher Christian '35	132
GARDENER	George		62
GATTY	Dr		19
GEORGE III	King	Presents to Tinah	54-5
GIBBS	V	Legal advice to Lord Liverpool	226
GIBRALTAR		Relief	27

Index

GIBSON	Mel	As Fletcher Christian '84	133
GLATTON	HMS		167
GORE	William	Provost Marshal charged and acquitted	198
		To Secretary of State complimenting Bligh	201
		Re rebels	225
		Chairman of Sydney meeting	228
		At Johnston's trial	233
GRAND SABLE ISLAND			20
GRIEVANCES		Naval	161
GRIEVING			65
GRIFFIN	Edmund	At Johnston's trial	234
GRIMES	Charles	To McArthur re Lot 77	205
		Signed McArthur's petition	212
		Appointed Judge Advocate	215
		Resigns as Judge Advocate	217
		Signed after Bligh's arrest	238
GROSE	Colonel	Recruited NSW Corps	182
		Acting Lieutenant Governor	183
		Leaves NSW	185

H

HALL	J N	Novelist	132
		Cause of the mutiny	146
	Thomas	Cook	36
		In launch	78
		Died of fever	100
HAMILTON	Sir William and Lady		170
HALLET	John	Midshipman	35
		Sister – friend of Betsy	36
		Asleep on arms chest	74
		In launch	78
		Drunk at Sourabaya	99
		Complaint at Sourabaya	99
HARRIS	John Dr	Stills decision	195
		Dismissed as Naval Officer	197
		Letter against Bligh	200
		Dismissed as magistrate	217
		Johnston's trial	239
		No legal interference	249

319

T G	Legal advice to Castlereagh	225
	Legal advice	232
	No tyranny by Bligh	248
	Bligh's threats	252
HARWOOD Dr	In support of Bligh	129
HASSELL		
Roland Reverend	Re rebellion	247
HAWKESBURY RIVER	Flood	190-1
HAWKESWORTH	Author	104
HAYWARD Thomas	Midshipman (acting)	35
	Loss of prisoner	57
	In irons	59
	Told of Fletcher's plan	70
	Asleep on arms chest	73
	In launch	78
	Lieutenant in "Pandora"	111
HECTOR HMS	Court Martial of Mutineers	113
HEIVA	Dance (Tahiti)	35
HELL	Fletcher's distress	79
	Definition for human	80
	Life on Pitcairn	108
	Re Richard Hough	133
	Cause of Fletcher's hell	137
HENSHAW John Commander		20
HEYWOOD Peter	Midshipman	35
	Recommended by Richard Betham	36
	Background	36
	Obituary	47
	Venereal Disease	51
	One of the ringleaders	75
	Plot with Stewart	93
	Evidence against	101
	Peter's family – letters by Bligh	101
	Re Pasley	113
	Wrote to Bligh	113
	Defence	114
	Purcell said Peter armed	114
	Reprieved	114
	Letter to Edward Christian	115
	Falls out with Edward Christian	116

Index

		Pasley uses Flinders	120
		Bligh's patronage	258
HILLBRANDT	Henry	Cooper	36
		Origin	37
		Missing cheeses	41
		Drowned	112
		Spoke well of Bligh	123
HOBART	Lord	Dalrymple settlement	187
HOLLAND			157-8
HOLLYWOOD			13-14
HOLT	George	Midshipman and artist	121
HOLYHEAD			107
HOOD			
Lord Vice-Admiral		President of Court Martial	114 and 157
HOOK		Publicises Bligh's proclamation	223
HOPKINS	Anthony	As William Bligh ('84)	14 and 133
HOSTAGES		Chiefs at Annamooka	167
HOUGH	Richard		14,58,69,147 and 151
HOWARD	Trevor	As William Bligh ('62)	13
			133
HOWE	Lord Admiral		27
		Promise to William	34
HOWELL	Reverend	Re Morrison	116
HUGGAN	Thomas	Surgeon Appointment	34-5
		Drunken sot	42
		Death of Valentine	50
		Dines apart	50
		Sick	50
		Died	56
HUMANE		William Bligh	150
HUMBLE	Richard	Re flogging	159
HUMOUR		Mutineers' refusal	78
HUNTER	HMS		20
	Governor General		
		Arrives	185
		Rebuke to Paterson	185
		Dispute with McArthur	185
		Complains about McArthur	186
		Changes Government order	186
		Recalled	186
HYDE PARKER	Admiral		36

I

IDDEAH	Tinah's wife	54
INDICTMENT	Alternative for McArthur	206-7
INFAMY	Novels and films	132
INTERFERENCE	In the law. Not by Bligh	240
INTERNATIONAL EXHIBITION		
	Mutiny	148
IRELAND	French abortive expedition	160
	Plot re HMS Diomede	166
IRISH STATE PRISONERS	Revolt 1804	188
IRISH PRISONERS TRIAL		195
IRRESISTIBLE HMS		171
ISABELLA	See Mauatua	62
ISLAND the	Byron's poem	109

J

JAMAICA	House of Representatives – canvass for Bligh	119
	" " – 500 guineas gratuity	119
	" " – 1000 guineas to Bligh	126
	" " – 500 guineas to Portlock	126
JAMISON Thomas	Chief Surgeon	196
	Loses magistracy	197
	Letter against Bligh	200
	Conspiracy	226
JENNY	Consort of Martin	103
JERVIS Admiral	Naval encounter	160
JOHNSTON George	NSW Corps	182
	Quarrels with Paterson	186
	Sent to England under arrest	186
	Put down revolt	188
	Address to Bligh	190
	Complaint	197
	Complaint to the Duke of York	199
	NSW Corps dinner – not attending	207
	Too ill to respond to summons!	209
	Returns to Sydney	211
	Petition from McArthur	211
	Marches on Government House	212
	Proclaims Martial Law	213
	Revoked Martial Law	215

Index

	Government and General Orders	215
	Letter to Lord Castlereagh	216
	Statement by McArthur	217
	Hands over to Foveaux	218
	Sails for UK	223
	Rheumatic and old	225
	To be court martialled	226
	Conspiracy	226
	Court martial	232 ff
	Address with threats	235
	Defence	235 ff
	Verdict	243
	Causes of rebellion	245
	Ridiculous claim	250
	Accusations - no evidence	250
	Motive	252-3
	Returns to NSW	255
JUDGE ADVOCATE	see Atkins, GRIMES	
	Replaced	261

K

KARAKAKOOA BAY (now KEALAKEKOA)			123
KEEL HAULING			132-3
KEITH			
Admiral Lord		Re Nore	163
KEMP			
Fenn Lieutenant		Planned to be replaced by Abbott	205
		Threat to arrest Judge Advocate	208
		Illegal court	208-9
		Deputed to obtain Bligh's resignation	212
	Captain	At Johnston's trial	237
		Illegal court	250
KENNEDY			
Gavin Professor		Bligh versus Purcell	49
		Cause of mutiny	64
		Criticism of Bligh	68
		Cause of mutiny	148
KENT	Lieutenant	Plot against Bligh	190
		Arrested by Porteous	219
		Land grant by rebels	224
		Acquitted on technicality	232

KEPPEL
       Lieutenant General   President of Court Martial   244
KING   George III   President to Tinah   54-5
                  James Lieutenant
                               Cook's third voyage to the South Seas   24-5
                  Governor General
                               On McArthur   183
                               Appointment   186
                               Criticism on McArthur   186
                               Offers conditional recall   187
                               Pardons Crossley   187
                               Port regulations   188
                               Leases in the Domain   188
                               Succeeded by Bligh   188
                               Land grants to Bligh   190
                  Mrs   Land grant   194
KRONSTADT   167

                                                                    L
LAMB   Robert   Butcher   36
                          Flogged   56
                          In launch   78
                          Beaten by Bligh   89
                          Died on journey   101
              Captain   Re Bligh and Fletcher   129, 139
LAMBETH   14 Moor Place   28
                          3 Durham Place (now 100 Lambeth Road)   119
LAMB GRANTS   Early Governors   188
                          Bligh and the rebels   224
LAUGHTON Charles   13
                          As William Bligh   132
LAUNCH   82
                          Sold   100
LEASES   In Sydney   195
LEBOGUE   Lawrence   Sailmaker   35
                          Background   37
                          Re Fletcher's girl   61
                          In launch   78
                          Giving way   89
                          Mistake   129
                          Accused of perjury   130

324

LEDWARD	Thomas	Surgeon's mate	35
		On Bligh at Cape Horn	48
		Signs sick list	50
		In launch	78
		Giving way	89
		Complaint at Sourabaya	99
		Security for money	100
LEITH		Mutiny	158
LINKLETTER Peter		Quartermaster	35
		In launch	78
		Died of fever	100
LISBON		Siege raised	219
LIVERPOOL Earl		Legal advice	226
		Letter from McArthur	231
LOG		Bligh's	82
LOSS		Psychiatric effects	63 ff
LUCEA	Jamaica	Bligh as agent	28
LUXBOROUGH Galley		Cannibalism	260
LYE	Daniel	Acting master	194
LYNX	vessel	Jamaica run	28

M

MACARTHUR			
	Edward	To John	218
	James	No corruption proved	250
MACKANESS			
	Dr	Bligh versus Purcell	49
		Re open boat voyage	90
		Bligh's treatment of Fletcher	137
		Cause of mutiny	145
		Re Bligh on Purcell	151
MACMILLAN			
	Surgeon		224
MACQUARIE Lachlan Col			223
		Secretary of State's instructions	223
		Arrives in New South Wales	226
		Government and General orders and proclamations	227
		Friend of Foveaux	227
		To Castlereagh re Bligh	228
		To the O'Connell's a farm	230

MAINMAST	See MAUATUA	62
MANALE or MANARII	See MENALEE	
MANN D D	Re domain leasehold	240
MARINES		24/5 & 182
MARLBOROUGH		
Lance Corporal	Arrests Bligh	212
MARRO OORAH	Feather Belt	122
MARSDEN		
Samuel Reverend	Assessment of Situation	192
MARTIN Isaac		36
	American	37
	Told of Fletcher's Seizure	73
	Joined in?	74
	Converse with Bligh	74
	To Pitcairn	103
	Killed	107
MARY	McIntosh's consort	123
MASON Martin Dr		234-237
R Sergeant		240
MATAVAI Bay	Bounty arrives	52
MAUATUA		62
	Reunited with Fletcher	92
	Third child Mary Ann	108
	Children by 'Young'	108
	Fletcher's girl	129
	To Tubuai	129
	To Pitcairn	129
	'84 Film	133
	Cause of the mutiny	
	Fletcher's pathological grieving	258
McARTHUR John	Background	183
	View by Gov King	183
	Dispute with Hunter	185
	Criticised by Gov King	186
	Dual with Paterson	186
	Sent to England under arrest	186
	Took wool samples	187
	Approached Sir Joseph Banks	187
	Riches	187
	Sir Joseph Banks rebuffed	187

Index

Returns to NSW 1805	188
Address to Bligh	191
Meeting with Bligh	191
Part owned vessel 'Dart'	195
Part owned vessel 'Parramatta'	195
Charges Thompson	195
Lost case against Thompson	195
Discontinued visits to Bligh	195
Wins Campbell case	198
Common source of anti-Bligh letters	200
Letter to Captain Piper	200
Anti Bligh subscription	201
Forfeited bond	202
Abandons 'Parramatta'	202
Refuses to pay	202
Declines to attend	202
Deflects first warrant	202
Arrested on second warrant	203
Committed for trial	203
Re Atkin's debt	203
Memorial re Judge Advocate	203
Re Lot 77	
Charge	206/7
Interrupts Court	208
Provocation to Governor	209
Petition to Johnson	211
Acquitted by illegal court	215
Address of thanks	216
Appointed Colonial Secretary NSW	216
Monopoly and extortion	217
Scourge of the Colony	217
Principal agitator	217
On Johnston	217
Starts for UK	223
Conspiracy	226
On NSW Corps	230
To sue Bligh for £20,000	231
Letter to Earl Liverpool	231
Five year embargo	244
Cause of rebellion	245

		Requisition – a fraud	246
		Principal agitator	247
		Motive	253
		Trial threat lifted	255
		Darling's estimate	255
McCOY	William	Able bodied seaman	36
		Not paying attention	67
		Called up	74
		To Pitcairn	103
		Cruelty	107
		Over-indulged	108
McFARLAND		Judge	114
		Attack on Bligh	144/5
McINTOSH	Thomas	Carpenter's crew	35
		Held in 'Bounty'	78
		Exonerated by Bligh	114
		Spoke well of Bligh	123
McKOY		see McCOY	
McTAGGART Lt		Extended Nore list	163
MENALEE		to Pitcairn	103
		Killed Temua	107
		Killed by Quintal and McKoy	107
MENDANA DE NEYRA			29
MERCURY	Brig		110
MEREDITH	George		80
MGM	(Metro Goldwyn Mayo)		
		1935 film	132
		'62 film	133
		Cause of mutiny	196
MILLS	John	Gunner's mate	35
		Refuses to dance	50
		Called up	75
		Mutineer's gunner	92
		To Pitcairn	103
		Killed	107
MILLWARD	John	AB	36
		Missing	57-59
		Hanged	115

Index

MI'MITTI	See MAUATUA	
MINCHIN Lt	Re double jeopardy	195
	To ex Governor King	199
	Elevating screws taken	208
	Conspirator	234
	Charges double jeopardy	237
	Charge rebuffed	238
	Misrepresentation	249
MOBILISATION 9/1789		34
MONARCH HMS		170
MONMOUTH	HMS	18
MONTAGU Captain	Friend of Pasley	114
MONTGOMERY HS	Bligh exonerated	213
MORRIS Valentine		29
MORAI	Temple	122
MORRISON James	Bo'sun's mate	35
	Journal and Memo	39
	Re sheep's death	45
	Trading problems	56
	Mutineer's bo'sun	92
	Boat plan	110
	Reprieve	114/5
	Memorandum	115
	Re 'Journal' ready	116
	Charges re Bligh	139/140
MOTTOS	Bligh family	256
MUSPRATT William	Steward	36
	Flogged	56
	Missing	57-59
	Reprieve on technicality	115
MUSTER		194
MUTINEERS		92 ff
MUTINIES	Leith, Spithead and Nore	157 ff
	"Bounty" – causes	135-149
	Leith	158
	Spithead	162
	Nore	162 and 260

329

			N
NAPOLEON			160
		In Egypt	166
		Coup d'Etat	166
		Re Louisiana	171
NATIONAL MARITIME MUSEUM			148
NAVY	British	Size	160
NEHOW or NEHOU		To Pitcairn	103
		Killed by Young	107
NELSON	David	Botanist	36
		Forecast re breadfruit	60
		In launch	78
		Sunstroke	88
		Died at Coupang	97
		Bligh's tribute	97
NELSON	Horatio	Nile Victory	166
		Copenhagen	167
		Plan of attack	168
NEW SOUTH WALES (NSW) Corps			182
		Develops monopolies	183
		Assessment after two dcades	184
		Assesment by free settlers	184
		Bligh's assessment	201
		To 102nd Regiment	225
NIAU	see NEHOW		
NIGHTINGALL Brigadier General			223
NILE	Battle of the		166
NODDY	Bird		85
		Illustration	87
NOMUKA			66
NORDHOFF C B		Novelist	132
		Cause of mutiny	146
NORE	Mutiny		260
NORFOLK	Island	Directive	197
NORMAN	Charles	Carpenter's mate	35
		Held in "Bounty"	78
		Exonerated by Bligh	114
		Spoke well of Bligh	123
NORTH	Sea Fleet		161

Index

NORTHERN	Alliance		166/7
NORTON	John	Quartermaster	35
		In launch	78
		Death	82
NUMBING			64
NUMBNESS			79

O

OAKES	Francis	Chief Constable, Parramatta	196
		Takes warrant for arrest	202
		Returns with letter	202
		At Johnston's trial	234
O'CONNELL			
	Lieutenant Colonel	73rd Regiment	227
		Proposal	229
O'DWYER		No double jeopardy	237/8
OHER		See OHOO	
OHOO		To Pitcairn	103
		Killed by natives	107
OHUHU		See OHOO	
OOPEE		See OHOO	
OPARRE		Move from Point Venus	55
		"Bounty" grounded	56
OPEN	boat voyage		82 ff
		Summing up	90
OPPRESSION		None by Bligh	248
ORO		God	122/3
OTAHEITE		TAHITI	
OTOO		Tinah's father	123
OXLEY	Lieutenant		224

P

PALMER		Publicises Bligh's proclamation	223
		Returns with Bligh, not charged	231
		At Johnston's trial	233
PANDORA	HMS		110
		Box	112
		Loses jolly boat and resolution	112
		Holed	112

?KER	Hyde Admiral		26
			167
PARKES	C M	Separation and loss	64
PARRAMATTA		Vessel	195
PASLEY	Captain (Admiral)		113
		Flinders as correspondent	120
PATERSON		Acting Lieutenant Governor	185
		Rebuked by Governor Hunter	185
		Quarrels with Johnston	186
		Duel with McArthur	186
		Senior officer	214
		Declines to return	217
		Takes over from Foveaux	220
		Agreement with Bligh	221
		Agreement broken by Paterson	221
		To Castlereagh re concubines	222
		Commendation of NSW Corps	223
		Land grant to Atkins	225
		Death (Lieutenant Colonel)	230
		Cause of rebellion	245
		Charges rebutted	251
PATHOLOGY		Christian's psychology	135/6
PAY		Naval	160/1
		Increase	161
PEARCE	Jane	William's mother	18
	Catherine	William's half sister	18
	Lieutenant	Marines	120
PECKOVER	William	Gunner	35
		Assaulted	61
		In launch	78
		Remonstrated with Fryer	89
		Bligh's appraisal	120
		Sole trader	141
PETTY OFFICERS		"Bounty" worthless	58
PHILLIP		Governor General	182
PHILLIPS		Lieutenant Marines	24
	Captain	Working for Banks	116
PILFERING			67
PINING			64

Index

PIPER	Captain	Norfolk Island	197
		Letter from McArthur	200
PIPON	Captain	Report	105/6
		HMS Tagus	143
PITCAIRN		Mutineers	103
		Reached by Christian	104
	Island Register		105
PLANTS		Second breadfruit voyage	123
PLUMER		Legal adviser to Liverpool	226
PLYMOUTH		William's birthplace	18
		Mutiny spread	161
POINT VENUS		"Bounty" camp	55
POLYNESIAN		Language	80
PORK		Appears light	43
PORPOISE	HMS	Leaves for NSW	184
PORT REGULATIONS		Bligh	192
PORTEOUS	Captain	Arrests Kent	219
		Land grant from rebels	224
PORTLAND	Duke of	Secretary of State	185
PORTLOCK	Nathaniel	Selected	119/120
		To "Providence"	121
		Bligh well pleased	123
POST TRAUMATIC STRESS DISORDER (PTSD)			
		Re Bligh	121
POTATOES		Incident	143
PRENTICE	Rina Dr		149
PRINCE REGENT			243
PRINCESS AMELIA HMS			27
PRODIGAL SON			109
PROSSER	Thomas		237/8
PROVIDENCE HMS		Tonnage	119
PRUSSIA			157
PSYCHOLOGY		Separation and loss	63/4
			133 and 135
PUMPKINS		Incident	42
PURCELL	William	Carpenter	35
		At Adventure Bay	48
		Refusal to cut stones	55
		Talk to Fletcher	70

		In launch	78
		Sunday Isle incident	88
		Chalk incident	96
		Story fabrication	98
		'Stoping provisions' cause of mutiny	99
		Reprimanded at court martial	102
		Evidence that Heywood was armed	114
		Resentment against Bligh	128
PUTLAND	Lieutenant	Married to Mary	189
	Mr & Mrs	Land grant	194
	Lieutenant	Death	205

				Q
QUIBERON	Bay, Brittany			158
QUINTAL	Matthew	AB		36
		Insolence to Master		45
		Serious attachment?		65
		Told of Fletcher's seizure		73
		Refused joining in?		74
		Called up		75
		Mutineer AWOL		93
		To Pitcairn		103
		Cruel		107
		Made 'still'		108
		Consort died		108
		Death by Young and Adams		108

				R
RAFT				71
RAMSEY		Master of "Director" convicted		166
RANGER	HMS			20
RAWSON	Geoffrey	Lieutenant Commander		213
REBELS		Sleaze		225
RECAULKING		"Bounty"		48
REGENT		Of Otaheite region		54
RELATIONSHIP		Potentially long term		63 ff
RESOLUTION		HMS		21,23,26
	Vessel	Mutineer's Boat		110
		Lost by "Pandora"		111
		Reunited with Survivors		113

Index

RESOURCE		Schooner purchased	96
		Sold	100
RESTORATION Island			88
REVAL		Russian naval station	167
RICHMAN	Lieutenant		24
RICHMOND Admiral Sir Herbert			163
RIOU	Captain	Died	169
ROBERTS	Henry Lieutenant		26
RODNEY			27
ROYAL SOCIETY			171
RUM	rebellion	Causes	245 ff
RUSSELL	Captain	Vessel "Brothers" at Law	217
	John	Painting of William 1791	258
RUSSIA			158
		Northern Alliance	167
		Convention with Britain	169
RUTTER	Owen	On floggings	126
		Not cowardice	213
		Re Bligh	262

S

SADISM		Denied	150
SAILS		Mildewed	58
ST (SAINT) HELENA		Visit	126
ST	TUDY		18
	VINCENT	Visit	126
	Earl	Nelson re Bligh	170
SAMUEL	John	Clerk	36
		Re cheese loss	41
		Bread, compass and quadrant	76
		In launch	78
		Re provisions	139
SANDWICH Islands			23
	Lord		25,30
SCHELDT		Estuary	157
SCOTT	Professor	Re naval language	143
SCURVY		A disgrace	47
		Biassed diagnoses	50/1
		Damage and prevention	51
		Bligh's library	51

SEARCHING			64, 72 and 79
SECOND FLEET			183
SELKIRK	Lord	Re "Bounty" establishment	34
SEPARATION			63, 64
SETTLERS	Free	Assessment of NSW Corps	184
		Bill of Rights	192
		Address to Castlereagh	219 and 221
		Derwent to Bligh	224
		Final address to Bligh	228
		To Castlereagh – cause of rebellion	245/6
		Addresses	246
		Baulkham Hill – cause of rebellion	247
		Re Bligh and locusts	277/8
SHORT	Joseph	Position only	189
		Apology	190
		Court Martial	194
SIMPSON	George	Quartermaster's mate	35 and 78
SINCLAIR	Madeline Lady		189 ff
SKINNER	Richard	AB	36
		Drowned	112
SLAVERY		Bligh's remarks	48
SMITH	John	Commander's cook	36 and 78
	Alexander	AB. see also ADAMS John	36
		Flogged	55
		Re Christian's girl	
		Fletcher's plan	71
		Called up	74
		To Pitcairn	103
		Background	104/5
		Organised Quintal's death	108
		Re Bligh	141-2
		Moment of excitation	142
SOCIETY	for the encouragement of the Arts		29
SOCIETY	Islands	Cook's visit	23
SOLANDER	Dr	Re Breadfruit	29
SOURABAYA			92
SPAIN			157
		Alliance with France	160
SPIKERMAN	Captain		97

336

Index

SPITHEAD		Ready to leave	38
		Attempts to leave	38
STAINES	Captain Sir	Report	105
STANHOPE	Lord		255
STEPHENS			30
STEWART	Keith Captain		18
	George	Midshipman (Acting)	35
		Loss of hostage	60
		Told of Fletcher's plan	70
		Wakes Fletcher	73
		Advises Fletcher	73
		Supports Fletcher	75
		Plot to leave Tubuai	93
		Died at loss of "Pandora"	112
		Mutiny suggested	142
SUBVERSION of the Law		No!	248
SUMNER	John	AB	36
		Flogged	66
		Called up	75
		Absence without leave (AWOL)	93
		Died on "Pandora" loss	112
SUNDAY Island			88
SURVEY		Humber to Harwich	160
		Dublin harbour	166-7
SURVEYING		1803	171
		1804	173
SWEDEN			158
		Northern Alliance	167
SUTHERLAND	Sergeant	Arrest of Bligh	212 and 241
SUTTON			
	Charles Manners	Judge Advocate General	204
		Prosecutor	233
		To Lord Liverpool	244
		Re Bligh	246
SUTTOR	George	Declined muster	219
		At Johnston's trial	234
SYDNEY	Lord	Re vessel	30
	(NSW)	Address re McArthur	191
	Gazette		238

337

SYMONS	James	Dismissed as Magistrate	217
		Carried dispatches	220
SYMPTOMS			
of approaching death		Open boat voyage	90

T

TAAROAMIVE		See Talaloo	103
TAGUS	HMS		105
TAHITI		Matavai Bay reached	52
		Tiare Tahiti	53
		Fletcher returns	92
		Re mutineers	92-3
		Revisted a second time	94
		Providence reached	122
TALALOO		To Pitcairn	103
		Killed by natives	107
TARARO		See Talaloo	
TASMANIA		Then 'van Diemen's land'	121 and 148
TATOO		Polynesian initiation	62
TEEHUTEATUAONOA		See Jenny	
TEIMUA		See Temua	
TEMUA		To Pitcairn	103
TEERREEOBOO		King (Hawaii)	24
TETAHEITE		To Pitcairn	103
		Killed by Young's consort	107
TETAHITE		See Tetaheite	
TETLEY		HMS Porpoise	194
THERRY	Judge	Re "Bounty"	261
THOMPSON	Charles		20
	Matthew	AB	36
		Flogged	55
		Called up	74
		Rape on Tahiti	111
		Lived in South Tahiti	111
		Killed for killing Churchill	111
	Andrew	Charged by McArthur	195
		Letter to Bligh	203
		Organises address	205
		Johnston's address	235
		Perculations	250-1

Index

TIMOA	See Temua	
TIMOR		83
	Arrival	90
	Coupang	96
	Re "Pandora's" crew	113
TINAH	Regent	54
	Also called Matte, Tynah	54
	Present to King George III	55
	Comparable punishments	56
	Intercedes for Martin	59
	Gifts for King George	61
	Gifts for Bligh	61
	Upset at being misled	110
	Renewed friendships with Bligh	122
TINKLER Robert		35
	Bag in hammock	71
	In launch	78
	Saucy to bo'sun	96
TINTEN (Cornwall)		18
TOBIN George	Third Lieutenant "Providence"	120
	Brushes with authority	121
	To Bond re Bligh	147
TOFOA		82
TOOTAHA	High Priest	122
TORRES STRAIT	Examination	109
	Second Breadfruit voyage	124
TORRES VEDRAS	Fortified	219
TOULON		157
TOWNSON Dr	Conspiracy	226
TREASON	Charges	206
TREKRONER FORT		168
TUBUAI ISLAND		92 ff
	Revisit	93 ff
TYRANNY	Denial	150
	No!	248

U

UNITED STATES OF AMERICA (USA)	Independence	27
USURPATION		211

V

VALENTINE James	AB	36
	Death	50
VANCOUVER George		100
VAN DIEMEN'S LAND	See Tasmania	
VAN ESTE William	Coupang	96
VANSITTART Nicholas		167
VENEREAL DISEASE	Before and at Tahiti	51
VENUS POINT	Camp	55
VIMIERO	Wellesley victory	219
VLYDTE	Vessel: William embarks	100
VOYAGE to the Pacific Ocean		24
VRIJHEID	Dutch Flagship	164

W

WALKER	Commander Johnston's trial	235
	Assessment of Bligh	247
WALTERS Stephen		148-9
WANJON T		96
WAPPING	Bligh lived there	101
WARLEY HMS		130
WARRIOR HMS		173
WEBBER John	Painting of William 1776	258
WELLESLEY Arthur	To Portugal	219
	Victory at Vimiero	219
	Talavera	219
WENTWORTH D'Arcy	Assistant Surgeon	196
	Letter against Bligh	200
	Legally suspended	240
WEST INDIES		20
	Re Breadfruit	29
	Disease losses	158
WILLIAMS John	AB	36
	Flogged	47
	Called up	74
	To Pitcairn	103
	Loses consort	107
	Shot	107

Index

WILLIAMSON			
John Captain		Court Martial	165
WYETOOA		Tinah's brother	59-60

X

Nil

Y

YEARNING			64
			79
YOUNG	Edward	Midshipman (Acting)	35
		To Pitcairn	103
		Kills Nehow	107
		Organises Quintal's death	108
		Dies of asthma	108
	Consort	Kills Tetaheite	107

Z

ZEALAND	Isle	167
ZOUTMAN	Rear Admiral	27